# From a Welfare State to a Welfare Society

## The Changing Context of Social Policy in a Postmodern Era

John J. Rodger

Consultant Editor: Jo Campling

First published in Great Britain 2000 by
**MACMILLAN PRESS LTD**
Houndmills, Basingstoke, Hampshire RG21 6XS
and London
Companies and representatives throughout the world

A catalogue record for this book is available from the British Library.

ISBN 0–333–73037–2 hardcover
ISBN 0–333–73038–0 paperback

First published in the United States of America 2000 by
**ST. MARTIN'S PRESS, INC.,**
Scholarly and Reference Division,
175 Fifth Avenue, New York, N.Y. 10010

ISBN 0–312–23122–9

Library of Congress Cataloging-in-Publication Data

Rodger, John J.
From a welfare state to a welfare society : the changing context of social policy in
a postmodern era / John J. Rodger
p. cm.
Includes bibliographical references and index.
ISBN 0–312–23122–9 (cloth)
1. Social policy. 2. Welfare state. I. Title.

HN18 .R575 2000
361.6'1—dc21                                                        99–054953

This book is printed on paper suitable for recycling and made from fully managed and
sustained forest sources.

10  9   8   7   6  5   4   3   2   1
09  08  07  06  05  04  03  02  01  00

Printed in Hong Kong

*To Alexis and Patrick*

# Contents

# Acknowledgements

My main debt is to Pamela Rodger who provided her usual inestimable advice and critical observations about some of the ideas and the style of their presentation. Jo Campling has spurred the project along and her part in bringing the book to fruition is appreciated. I have not burdened friends and colleagues directly with the task of reading drafts but I am grateful to David Judge, Chik Collins and Gerry Mooney for their assistance by lending me material at crucial times in the production of the book. Finally, I am grateful to the anonymous referee who offered helpful and encouraging comments on the first draft.

JOHN J. RODGER

# Introduction

This book is about the changing social, political, economic and cultural context within which social policy will be formed as we enter the new millennium. The welfare 'contract' between governments and the people fashioned in Western Europe at the end of the Second World War has been in a process of renegotiation since the 1970s and will continue to be a focus of bargaining as the 21st century progresses. The interesting feature of this bargaining process is that the participants in it have changed in the last thirty years: what started as a political contest between organised labour and capital over the social wage in the 1950s and 60s has become a far more fragmented political tussle involving claimant groups organised around ethnicity, gender, sexuality, age, disability and, increasingly, postmaterialist values. It also involves interests and opinions hostile to a society which organises its welfare services from the heart of the state instead of mobilising human resources in the community. It has both conservative and radical dynamics operating simultaneously. Indeed, the ways and means of pursuing welfare claims on the state today are far less likely to be channelled through a trade union, although the trade union movement remains active in welfare struggles, than through a welfare lobby or social movement. The reasons for these changes are many:

- The key assumption of the Beveridge welfare state regarding the existence of a 'standard worker family' based on a male breadwinner income no longer holds – lone parenthood, the increase in divorce, the emergence of the reordered or multiple family and the uncoupling of fertility from marriage appear to reinforce this change.
- Membership of trade unions and political parties has in general declined as the industrial and occupational structure has been transformed by the demise of primary manufacturing industries and the creation of non-unionised working environments in new high technology, leisure and service industries – issues of welfare and employment security are more likely to be pursued by means other than a mass trade union movement.

1

- The position of women in society has changed as their labour market participation has risen and their earning capacity in relation to men continues to improve – their dependence on men is an assumption which no longer holds.
- The deference of social groups which in the past were marginalised, such as ethnic minorities, gays, the elderly and the disabled, can no longer be assumed by policy makers. Increasingly, they are organising their own alliances and political claims for welfare and social citizenship.
- The effectiveness of the state as a provider of universal welfare services has been subjected to continual questioning since the 1970s from both the right and the left – the perceived failure of the welfare state to eliminate poverty and meet social need has led to the widespread acceptance of the inevitability of a mixed economy of welfare involving commercial, voluntary and informal sources of provision in addition to the state.
- The economic foundations of social policy have become less secure because of the intensity of global competition and the pooling of nation state sovereignty in supranational political and economic blocs such as the European Union (EU) and North Atlantic Free Trade Area (NAFTA). Participation in international trading and business agreements such as the General Agreement on Tariffs and Trade (GATT) entered into at a global level has raised questions about the autonomy of the nation state in policy formation.
- As the growth of welfare states has slowed there is evidence that social polarisation has, in some countries, increased due to long-term unemployment and the shift of poverty from old and large households to small and young households (Simpson and Walker, 1993). Welfare systems continue to enshrine the principle of the work ethic as the foundation for their social policies in spite of the fragility of secure long-term employment throughout the rich Organization for Economic Co-operation and Development (OECD) countries.

In order to set the scene for the analysis being offered here, I want to suggest that a new 'moral' framework for social policy in the 21st century is being worked out in the rich OECD countries in response to the social changes listed above. It is possible to identify a distinctive vocabulary emerging from policy documents and academic debate which suggests that the social principles upon which future welfare strategies are to be built will differ markedly from those which have underpinned the Beveridge model of welfare. These changes have taken a particularly

British form in the social policies of New Labour but they are also detectable in other European countries, including those with a strong welfare tradition such as Sweden and Denmark.

## The new moral economy of welfare

The axial principle around which the new moral economy of welfare will revolve is the 'privatisation of responsibility': in its broadest sense this means that it will be individuals rather than society who will carry the primary obligation to meet their own welfare needs in the future. The relationship between the welfare state and what I shall choose to call a 'welfare society' is, therefore, changing. However, if a welfare system based on collectivist and universalist principles of solidarity, and underwritten by the state, has to give way to a welfare system founded on individualist assumptions rooted in markets, family and community, can contemporary Western societies rely on there being an infrastructure of caring networks to replace the state's overarching responsibilities for welfare which is passed back to civil society? The significance of this question arises because there are those who would argue that in the context of welfare provision within the rich OECD countries the 'move from socialised to a privatised mode of consumption is now firmly entrenched and is probably irreversible' (see Saunders, 1993: 59). Indeed that 'privatisation', and we could add 'individualism' and 'self-reliance', are structural features of mature capitalism (see Saunders, 1993). Such principles, it is argued, are best supported by family and community rather than by the state and they do not merely, or mainly, relate to market relationships but, importantly, they should also underpin caring and welfare relationships. The new moral economy would have us acknowledge that there is a relationship between the complex institutional provision of health and welfare in contemporary society and the nature of social consciousness. Indeed, this has been one of the central themes in recent attempts to re-examine the democratic socialist approach to welfare reform throughout Western Europe, and manifest in the New Labour government's efforts to express a critical judgement on past Labour approaches to welfare policy through their succession of Green Papers and legislative initiatives (New Ambition for Our Country; Supporting Families; The Crime and Disorder Act and the revisions to the Family Law Act). These policy initiatives announce a new left of centre position on welfare which appears to acknowledge that there may have been a negative influence of social policy on social behaviour in the period since 1945. The result of this neglect has been to reinforce social attitudes which are too accepting of welfare dependency. Indeed, writing in the *Sunday Times* following his decision to resign as the Minister for Welfare Reform in the Labour government, Frank Field commented:

> I took into government a set of beliefs about human nature and welfare's pivotal role in society. The greatest driving force in practically everyone is self-interest... Yet self-interest is clearly a different motive from selfishness, and selfishness is once again a different quality from greed. The task of the politicians is to harness self-interest in a way that promotes the public good. (the *Sunday Times*, 2 August 1998)

Field's primary concern was, and remains, the way in which welfare distorts people's conception of what their self-interest is to such an extent that they lose the incentive to work and their sense of responsibility to their families. A recent example of an issue which crystallises the 'new' debate about welfare principle in the Labour government is the proposal to means test incapacity benefit. Originally intended as a benefit to compensate those who were forced to give up work because of long-term illness or sickness, in the 1980s and 90s it became a mechanism for removing people from the unemployment register by securing their early retirement when they remained capable of work. The issue of principle surrounding this controversy is that the social insurance principle upon which the benefit was based is undermined by means testing: discretionary payment converts the citizen with entitlements to payment in to a problem claimant. A new conception of the relationship between welfare and society has, therefore, to be constructed. And, most importantly, a new conception of social citizenship is required to underpin a new welfare morality.

Evidence of this new moral vocabulary is to be found in the Labour government's consultation document *New Ambition for Our Country: a new contract for welfare* (Stationery Office, 1998). Commenting on the document, Heron and Dwyer (1999) encapsulate the 'moral' tone of the New Labour strategy when they observe that its objective is that of

> refocusing public welfare towards policies that emphasise reciprocity rather than monadic individualism; that is to say, a politics based on a 'bounded individualism' and 'moral community'... welfare organised along these lines looks likely to endorse a specific moral agenda and a concern that individual recipi-

ents of social welfare 'do the right thing' by conforming to a particular welfare system that emphasises the values of both individual and moral responsibility (Heron and Dwyer, 1999: 92).

The talk is of a 'new contract between citizen and the state' and the matching of 'rights by responsibilities'. There is also a strong restatement at the outset that the welfare state must be built around the 'work ethic': work for those who can, security for those who cannot. The duties of the individual are to:

- seek training or work where able to do so
- take up the opportunity to be independent if able to do so
- give support, financial or otherwise, to one's children and other family members
- save for retirement where possible
- refrain from defrauding the taxpayer.

The document continues by distributing responsibilities to all areas of social life. The duties of society, conceptualised as the social networks embedded in family, neighbourhood and community, are to work with government to assist family life, promote economic independence through work by relieving poverty where it cannot be prevented and contribute to the building of a strong and cohesive society where rights are matched by responsibilities. In the British context this welfare project was originally to be organised around the themes of 'communitarianism' and 'stakeholding'. These themes remain a part of political rhetoric providing guidance to social policy design but their sonorous power may appear to have weakened as the New Labour government deals with the routines of political business rather than the electoral battles of the hustings.

The changing moral economy of welfare which has become apparent in Britain can also be identified in other countries. In the different context of the Scandinavian welfare states, Sorensen (1998) identifies a problem which he calls rent-seeking in modern welfare systems. What is meant here is that welfare benefits share with the notion of property the quality of being a right to payment for possession of something: while ownership of land gives rights to the payment of rent, ownership of welfare rights yields payment of benefit (rent). The fundamental point being made in the context of the Danish welfare state is that the discipline and order characteristic of Scandinavian societies, which Sorensen claims was grounded historically in a 'Pietist culture' which ensured obedience to the state and the king, are being replaced by an 'individualist culture of rent-seeking': *gratitude* for welfare support has been replaced by *greed* as the modern citizen breaks the rules and changes his or her behaviour in order to obtain welfare benefits to supplement income rather than to meet a genuine social need (rent-seeking). This view of welfare states is shared by both Zijderveld (1986) and Offe (1996). In the context of the Dutch welfare system, Zijderveld talks of the absence of 'moral energy' in welfare systems because of their abstract nature: unlike charitable giving where resources are passed on personally, modern welfare states have an 'in-built lack of moral principles'. Offe talks about their 'self-augmenting dynamic of demands' which stimulates rising expectations and inevitably transforms minimal standards into maximum standards. The abstract and mediated nature of complex modern welfare systems means that the display of accountability, loyalty and gratitude by beneficiaries is not required, and could not be expressed in any case: with no moral obligations the potential for 'moral hazard' and 'free riding' remains an issue. The general point is that contemporary welfare politics in *all* European countries is centred on redefining citizenship, changing social behaviour and generating a 'new moral economy' for social policy. What the content of that 'new moral economy' should be is the substance of contemporary social policy debate.

The OECD has been leading opinion throughout the affluent countries by translating the moral agenda on welfare into one which stresses *activeness* in social policy design rather than the *passiveness* associated with systems inclined to compensate citizens for loss of earnings: it is the *duty* to work and to contribute to society which now appears to be the key axiom (see OECD, 1999a, 1999b). The reason behind this fundamental change in social policy formation is that globally there is a heightened awareness of the economic and political pressures to adjust welfare obligations on the state downwards in the face of fierce international competition for jobs and prosperity. However, the continuing ineffectiveness of state welfare in tackling the problems of inequality, poverty and social exclusion has meant that the political contest to provide a new vision of a welfare society has been joined by a variety of interests: by those who are committed to persisting with the project of reforming the welfare state; by those committed to rediscovering the virtues of the pre-welfare state days as a basis for fashioning an alternative concept of welfare; and by those who want to transcend the worker-centric Beveridge model characteristic of the period since 1945 in order to build a welfare system more in keeping with the rapidly changing economic, political and cultural context of contemporary life. These three general orientations to political and social meaning represent broad *ways of seeing* the role of state welfare in Western societies. They encapsulate the ideological dimension of political and economic debate surrounding welfare certainly but more widely they direct us to what has become known as the 'modernity debate': the political and intellectual battle to secure a particular trajectory of social change for contemporary societies at a point in history when the certainties of science and rationality yielded to us by the Enlightenment are being questioned (see O'Brien *et al.*, 1999). I will discuss this issue in relation to welfare in Chapter 1.

What is clear today is that either by chance or by design the state in the 21st century is redrawing the boundaries of its responsibilities for the welfare of its citizens (see Millar and Warman, 1996). We are moving away from a concept of the welfare state which provided, for most of its citizens, something which we called a *social wage*: a package of benefits which supplemented income from employment, pooled risks against unforeseen hardship through state-sponsored and managed insurance and provided a range of services underwritten by the state which were accessible to all, either through local government or by fiscal incentives, and moving towards a society in which family and community relationships are being required to take on a more explicit responsibility for sustaining the well-being of their members, based less on a commitment to a collective sense of social solidarity than on a sense of kindred obligation and charitable civic virtue. Millar and Warman (1996) make it clear that the changing boundaries between family and state in the sphere of welfare support is a phenomenon which is manifest in all European countries. Their research indicates that in the Scandinavian countries there is 'more willingness to suggest that families have moral, if not legal, obligations' (p. 49). In Austria they talk about the need to 'reinvent the family as a means of saving public expenditure' (p. 49). And, of course, in the Mediterranean rim countries the role of the extended family in welfare provision continues to be assumed. The development of community care policies throughout the European Union has underlined the trends identified by Millar and Warman (see Tester, 1996). Further, this movement is one in which collective responsibilities seated in the state are being replaced by responsibilities which lie with the individual to purchase and manage their own welfare capital. Three areas in particular are likely to become widely discussed as the new century progresses: first, the social insurance principle could be reinterpreted in terms of private insurance coverage for unemployment, sickness and injury backed by a government guarantee; second, all working people below a certain age may be required to take out insurance against the risk of needing residential care in old age so obviating the need to sell the family home to pay for costly care; and third, private pensions may replace the basic state pension as the main source for augmenting occupational pensions in old age. This trend in social policy has been called the 'individualisation of the social' by some observers of social policy (see Ferge, 1997) and appears to symbolise a departure from past principles. It will be civil society rather than the state which is likely to be the foundation for this new concept of welfare: a welfare society rather than a *welfare state* may be a more accurate description.

## The concept of welfare society

The conceptual distinction between a welfare state and a welfare society requires a clear explanation. In a useful article examining the conceptual distinction between welfare state and welfare society, Robertson (1988) starts by offering a concise definition of both. Following Schottland (1967), he observes that 'a welfare state is a *legal state* in which entitlement to a range of goods is guaranteed by statutory rights'. This conception of a welfare state treats it as performing an administrative function within the general apparatus of the state charged fundamentally with ensuring the defence of statutory rights while also delineating the limits of legal obligations on individuals and social agents to meet welfare responsibilities within society. By contrast a welfare society is 'a social system in which welfare assumptions are an organic part of everyday life'. It is probably germane to observe that the notion of a welfare society constituting 'an organic part of everyday life' is grounded in the assumption that social consciousness is effected by the creation of a welfare state. Matters relating to caring, social solidarity, the recognition of citizenship and social justice are inevitably fostered by welfare state activities. This is, of course, only one perspective on the idea of a welfare society. Alternative perspectives drawing on *anti-modern* themes in politics and philosophy might view a welfare society as the antithesis of state welfare rather than as an integral part of its evolution, a view articulated quite explicitly by Marsland (1996). Nevertheless, whichever perspective is taken, it appears that the concept of a welfare society encapsulates this undertheorised relationship between state-sponsored welfare programmes and their reception by and impact on society, both at the level of individual behaviour and of social or community relations.

In the preface to his book *Welfare State and Welfare Society* William Robson argues forcefully that the welfare state should not be 'mainly or exclusively concerned with providing social services of various kinds to the needy and underprivileged members of the community. It is my firm conviction that a welfare state worthy of the name must be concerned with the well-being of the entire nation' (Robson, 1976:7). In fact Robson's extension of the concept of welfare to embrace environmental concerns, the needs of minorities, obligations as well as rights and the abuse of centralised power in the state and other large commercial and political organisations in what should be a pluralist society, anticipated a great deal of the contemporary political debate about the future of welfare provision. His distinction between the welfare state and welfare society conceptualises an issue which remains submerged in the welfare debate:

> The welfare state is what Parliament has decreed and the Government does. The welfare society is what people do, feel and think about matters which bear on the general welfare. Failure to understand the difference is the cause of much conflict, friction and frustration, for there is often a yawning gulf between public policy and social attitudes. Unless people generally reflect the policies and assumptions of the welfare state in their attitudes and actions, it is impossible to fulfil the objectives of the welfare state. (Robson, 1976: 7)

The conflict between what I am calling *modernist* and *anti-modernist* traditions in the contemporary social policy debate about the future of welfare is at a very fundamental level about the nature of a welfare society and its relationship to the state.

The *modernists* can be understood in terms of a strategy which requires the instrument of the state to bring about changes in social consciousness and to encourage what Richard Titmuss (1970) saw as the core of the welfare state, *altruism*. The anti-modernist tradition appears to believe that the essence of a welfare society lies in human relationships which are unencumbered by the state and indeed a welfare state can only destroy social cohesion by taking to itself social and welfare responsibilities which should properly be shouldered by the family. How, then, is social integration to be accomplished and social solidarity sustained? The prescriptions vary enormously and so the future outcome of the conflict must, at this stage, remain uncertain. These themes will be discussed more fully in Chapters 2 and 3.

Walters (1997) highlights a very interesting distinction, not between welfare state and welfare society, because he appears to define the one by the other, but between welfare society and the concept of 'the active society' being sponsored by the OECD (see Gass, 1988; Walters, 1997). A welfare society within this perspective is one which defines a welfare state based on social citizenship rather than on the Poor Law tradition which treated the poor as *dangerous* outsiders who required to be coercively supervised. The creation of what Donzelot (1980) called the 'social sphere' and the growth of the concept of social citizenship brought about a change of focus from the 'dangerous classes' to society as a whole. Walters (1997) suggests that 'welfare societies are integral societies' and as such they are *inclusive*, at least as far as they can be compared with the *exclusive* treatment of the socially disadvantaged in the 19th century. However, modern welfare societies are also worker-centric societies in which the sphere of welfare develops to deal with people exempted from paid labour, or as Walters observes, 'this exemption, as it were, from the duty to perform paid labour is rationalised on a specifically *social* basis' (p. 223). The concept of *the active society* is one that is being promoted as a design for social policy which would tackle the obvious division between those engaged in productive activity and those consigned to a marginal social status passively cared for by the welfare society. Western welfare systems are, of course, based on the adult, male full-time worker to the obvious diminution of status for women, the unemployed, the retired and part-time workers dependent on the welfare society. The OECD would characterise the problem in terms of the tendency for welfare systems to 'define away' their unemployment problems by assigning people to new forms of welfare status, whereas the *active strategy* appears to be a rediscovery of the principles of active labour market policies pioneered by the Swedish welfare state in the 30 years between 1960 and 1990.

These observations are interesting but too narrow for my purposes; tying the concepts of welfare society and welfare state together and focusing exclusively on how the workforce is defined fails to pick up the very significant changes affecting attitudes to caring and welfare and the conflicts over what a welfare society ought to be like. More importantly if the welfare state and welfare society are conflated, there is little scope for analysing the impact of the state, particularly its diminishing role in welfare provision, on civil society and the network of family and community relationships which may have to supplant state liabilities.

However, the concept of welfare society used by van Doorn (1978) to describe the Dutch welfare system relies on there being both a conceptual and institutional distinction between the state and the sphere of welfare provision: the notion of welfare society is used as a description for the informal, private initiatives and charitable welfare institutions based on the confessional pillars (Catholic and Protestant) of Dutch society which used to control and administer the state welfare system despite political efforts to assert central governmental direction. The process of depillarisation, or the decreasing influence of the confessional interests, which has characterised the Netherlands since the 1960s (see Cox, 1993) is easier to analyse if the distinction between welfare state and welfare society is retained. Kraemer (1966) has conceptualised the same phenomenon by referring to the Dutch case as a 'societal state'. He subtitles his book 'the modern osmosis of state and society'. His intention of studying what he calls 'a general trend' towards *osmosis* is assisted by retaining a distinction between developments within the state welfare administration and how welfare responsibilities and obligations are perceived in civil society, or between welfare state and welfare society.

A declining role for an interventionist state in welfare provision appears to be prescribed for the future in Western societies: this means that the modernist conception of the welfare state as a progressive instrument of social change and redistribution of power and wealth is now being questioned. Few now believe that the welfare state can fulfil such an heroic task. Solutions to poverty and social exclusion must be sought elsewhere.

## Outline of the book

The argument of Chapter 1 suggests that the subject of welfare can be understood as part of what contemporary sociology is presenting as the 'modernity debate'. The analysis is, therefore, situated in the contest between competing perspectives on *modernity*. The chapter describes what I consider to be the key aspects of the three competing visions of welfare and a welfare society: *modernism*, *postmodernism* and *anti-modernism*. The themes introduced here run through the analysis offered in the book.

In Chapter 2 the analysis begins by examining the issues of social integration and social citizenship which lie at the heart of the welfare debate.

Following a discussion of the sociological distinction between 'system integration' and 'social integration' it is clear that the contemporary problem facing all Western welfare systems is how to reconcile the *system* demands of the economy with the *social* demands being made by the most vulnerable in society for protection from the vagaries of an increasingly competitive global economy. The principle of citizenship has historically enshrined rights and duties regarding protection from unpredictable events and so the chapter concludes by examining the competing visions of social citizenship emanating from the anti-modernist, modernist and postmodernist perspective.

The declining role for the state in future welfare systems is the main theme of Chapter 3. In order to assess whether the welfare state is in decline we must first understand the determinants of welfare state growth. In social policy analysis debate on the determinants of welfare development has tended to turn on whether structural features of welfare systems are given explanatory priority, such as indices of industrialism and demographic change, or whether political variables should carry the burden of explanation. The 'industrialism' versus 'politics counts' debate has been very productive in advancing comparative knowledge about welfare systems in the world. While I am inclined towards the 'politics counts' school because it better describes the variations found in the richer OECD countries, there are signs in contemporary society that the forces which once sustained welfare state development may be weakening in the face of global economic movements, a theme which the book returns to in Chapter 8.

Chapter 4 reviews a number of ideas which I would describe as anti-modern because they stem from the right's argument that the social fabric of society has been undermined by collectivist welfare. The interest in Victorian social virtues combined with a theory of social capital has shaped this emerging perspective. In posing the question of whether society is in decline the anti-modernist perspective answers affirmatively because incivility and criminality are held to be rife today compared with the mid- to late 19th century. The chapter concludes by pointing up some of the contradictions in the right's political perspective.

The growing interest in *communitarianism* and the attempt to reconcile it with a concept of 'stakeholding' is investigated in Chapter 5. Through a discussion of the philosophical debate between liberals and communitarians about what makes social cohesion possible and of the sociological tradition's concern about the loss of community, the analysis leads back to the theme of a possible welfare future by discussing the concept of associational democracy as a model of how a solidaristic welfare system could be fashioned in a postmodern era.

The question asked in the last section of Chapter 5 effectively introduces the main theme of Chapter 6: urban change, social exclusion and criminality are contemporary problems which have resulted from the breakdown of 'community' in the inner cities and the peripheral housing estates. The notion of the *post-Fordist* city is introduced in an attempt to make sense of the complex changes taking place in our urban centres. A reconstructed welfare system must be able to address the problems posed by the modern city if it is to claim any degree of success in stabilising increasingly unstable communities.

Chapter 7 introduces the novel concepts of 'postemotionalism' and 'amoral familism' in order to better understand the much neglected subject of attachment to welfare in postmodern society. These themes must be acknowledged as fundamental in any discussion of a future welfare society but the chapter raises for future discussion the possibility that we live in a world of selfish individualism and insincerity, even concerning the most horrific events in the contemporary world.

Chapter 8 ends the analysis by examining critically the two major forces likely to shape our welfare society of the future: *globalisation* and the European Union. While the strong globalisation thesis is not supported by the available evidence there are grounds for expecting global economic forces to be influential in shaping welfare options. The EU is unlikely to facilitate the development of a European level of social policy. The nation state will remain significant in shaping future welfare choices but those choices may well be constrained by the disciplines of policing a common currency and increasingly interdependent economic system.

# 1

# The modernity debate and welfare society

In introducing his book *European Modernity and Beyond* Goran Therborn (1995a) poses the questions why modernity? And what is it? I will try to address the second question later but first the concept of modernity needs to be clarified together with its two adversaries, anti-modernity and postmodernity. Primarily, we need to grasp the social and political significance of what the concept uniquely points to. Modern societies have been regarded as the progressive and highest stage of social and historical development: modernisation is conceived of as a process of becoming 'better', or more enlightened, or of having achieved 'the good society' in comparison with earlier less developed stages in social evolution. However, as Claus Offe remarks, in contrast to the optimism of modernisation theory, modernity signals a sceptical 'atmosphere of a preoccupation of "modern" societies with *themselves*' (Offe, 1996: 4). The realisation today that modernity is not the endpoint of progress and development but possibly 'the precarious point of departure for the further development of Western societies' towards something that may be postmodernity has caused both alarm and debate in the social sciences.

At the current juncture of Western societies there is a debate about the direction that should be taken by the state in its dealings with its citizenry and in its relationships with other nations. Welfare strategies are no longer accepted unquestioningly as 'technical' and 'administrative' mechanisms to redistribute resources from the rich to the poor; they are seldom conceived of as panaceas for solving intractable social problems; and they are now believed to be influential in shaping behaviour negatively in ways previously ignored. There is a sense of epochal change regarding the role and functions of state welfare. And, crucially, politics and economics are no longer the pre-eminent forces shaping our thinking about social policy, because it is now acknowledged that culture, particularly its effects on lifestyle and emotional choices about caring and the welfare of others, frames the way societies organise their welfare provision and the meaning they attach to it. In all Western countries there is a wrestle between ideas from the *present* and the *past* about the *future* in the search for principles upon which to base a new welfare settlement for the 21st century. A vocabulary is required to grasp the sense of this significant change. Ideological concepts common in the lexicon of social policy analysis such as *neo-liberalism, democratic socialism, welfare pluralism* and *collectivism* all lack a referent to the wider social and cultural influences which are at work in determining the shape of a future welfare society. While students of social policy have become accustomed to making sense of the welfare state debate through the clash between neo-liberal and socialist politics, they have been slow to recognise that the debate has moved on from a polarised choice between state or markets: ideas from sociological and cultural theory can aid our understanding of what is problematic about contemporary welfare systems. John Carter (1998b) has suggested that social policy is just about the last social science subject to take up the postmodern challenge. He is correct when he suggests that it is now timely for the discipline to engage with the burgeoning postmodern literature (and we could add poststructuralist, post-Fordist and postindustrialist literature too) because it provides a sociological vocabulary with which to describe contemporary social change while sensitising us to the social, political, economic and, significantly, the cultural context within which social policies are being designed for the new century. The nature of society and politics is changing and we may be moving into what has been described either as the era of *late modernity* or postmodernity. Whatever term is chosen to describe contemporary social conditions, we need to engage with ideas and concepts which until now have been unfamiliar to students of social policy.

Modernity has historically been defined by contrasting it with traditionalism: it is said to stem from the Renaissance and to be inextricably bound to the birth of the 18th-century Enlightenment critique of the ancient social order but for the purposes of contemporary analysis it 'implies the progressive economic and administrative rationalisation and differentiation of the social world' (Featherstone, 1988: 197). I will argue that modernism characterises an approach to social change which is rooted in a linear notion of progress: it implies the collection of empirically grounded knowledge and the systematic application of rational scientific principles to the improvement of the human condition. The very concept of a welfare state is modernist *par excellence* because its purpose has been to harness social and scientific knowledge to collective resources with the purpose of eradicating human misery. Indeed the creation of a set of institutions which are collectively named the welfare state is, for many, a wonderful expression of social altruism and a stage on the road to a genuinely just if not socialist society, a view held especially in Scandinavia (see Titmuss, 1970; Korpi, 1978). However, modernity is also associated with failures and subject to criticism from both the anti-modernist and the postmodernist theoretical traditions. The anti-modernists believe that the rationalist approach to enlightenment tends to ignore the tested nature of traditional knowledge and its foundations in the instinctual aspects of human nature. The welfare state since its inception, whether that be located in Bismarckian Germany, the liberal reforms after 1906 or the Beveridge model of the post-Second World War years, has had to contend with anti-modern views which have looked backwards to a pre-welfare age when self-reliance, charity and public virtue were supposedly dominant (see Whelan, 1996). However, the innumerable changes and adaptations which have been made to welfare provision in the rich OECD countries since the 1970s are regarded by some as cumulatively signalling what is being called the era of 'postmodern welfare' (see Leonard, 1997). The concept of *postmodern welfare* will be clarified later but a brief explanation of its meaning in this context is required at this point. It is being suggested that the era of grand theoretical perspectives is over. The key 19th- and 20th-century political ideologies such as Marxism, Socialism, Communism, Liberalism, and even Feminism, are no longer regarded as offering convincing understandings of social and political life in the 21st century. Steven Pinch provides a concise and useful definition of postmodernism which will clarify its general meaning at this point in the analysis. He suggests that postmodernism is: 'A broad trend in social thinking that rejects the idea that there is one superior way of understanding the world... [it] may also be regarded as a style characterised by eclecticism, irony and pastiche' (Pinch, 1997: 146). Political philosophers have referred to this process as the abandonment of what are known as *metalanguages* or *totalising narratives*: the idea that a particular political theory of society and the state can provide superior insights into how people ought to relate to each other or what might constitute fundamental human rights and needs is now being subjected to a critical scepticism which was not characteristic of the period of modernism which gave birth to the great political, economic and sociological theories of the 19th and 20th centuries. In the field of welfare the postmodernist view looks beyond markets and the work ethic in its search for an alternative basis for social citizenship (see Turner, 1994; Bauman, 1998). Its guiding social principle is *particularism* rather than *universalism*: a welfare system which recognises difference and cultural plurality. Perhaps a cautionary note should be made at this point. This book will situate its analysis of change in social policy in the midst of what I will argue is the conflict between modernism, anti-modernism and postmodernism over what ought to constitute the nature of a welfare society. I want to convey the sense of ongoing conflict about our welfare future. It is not my intention, therefore, to assume that we are now living in a postmodern society, despite the frequency with which this concept is used in current social science writing. Theoretical debate in the social sciences around the concept of postmodernism has turned on whether contemporary society can be described more appropriately as late modern rather than postmodern: do the changes being observed in economic, social and cultural life represent a maturing of modernity or, alternatively, mark a significant break with movements and ideas of the past which is so pronounced that they demand to be designated as something novel, namely, postmodern. My preference is to view current rhythms of change in the economy, culture and society as part of a maturing of modernity in a context where there are conflicting tendencies. I am taken with the idea that society in its current stage of development is constituted by what Paul Bagguley (1994) has called 'an imbrication of layers': the metaphor used here is of a slated roof where new slates are inserted alongside old ones, often hastening the decline of the old while the roof is perpetually subjected to running repairs until eventually a new roof either evolves as the cumulative effect of the many small repairs or has to be constructed anew in order to secure the building. The economic and occupational structures of society, its cultural movements and ideas and its social institutions do not progress, or indeed regress, at a uniform rate and at any given moment the old, the established and the novel in social and economic life vie with each other for ascendancy. The Victorian legacy of liberal market thinking about welfare extended well into the 20th century, vying with socialist and collectivist perspectives on the causes and remedies of poverty and indolence. *Modern* theories of society which are founded on the positivist method of gathering social evidence and applying *rational* analysis to arrive at *truth* compete with those anti-modern theories which are founded on what can best be described as 'essentialism': reason, if it is to be used at all in preference to faith in tradition and superior transcendent guidance, must seek out the instinctual and the natural state of human affairs, in short, must acknowledge the *essence* of the human condition and build theories of social order which go with what is often referred to as 'the grain of human nature'. And the perceived conservatism of both anti-modern and modern approaches will continue to be subjected to criticism by those who wish to redefine welfare and social citizenship radically without reference to markets, human nature or the social insurance principle. The iconoclasm of post-modern thinking about welfare may be in its early stages but is nevertheless important and a feature of the contemporary debate. A particular sense of this approach may be gleaned in the notion of associational democracy discussed in Chapter 5.

In the remainder of this chapter I will spell out in slightly more detail the central features and key issues associated with the three ways of seeing the place of the welfare state in contemporary society.

## Modernism and the welfare state

The two central themes which lie at the heart of the debate about the future of the welfare state are family and community. This is unsurprising because the concept of a welfare state was constructed around the issue of the appropriate balance between the state, family and community in the provision of social assistance and support in times of need. The welfare state as a modern social and political institution has, throughout the period since the late 1940s, assumed the main responsibility for providing not only basic safety net protection for citizens but also an extensive range of universal services meeting needs in health, housing and education. The role of the family and community in the provision of these services was, consequently, peripheral in policy terms, as was that of the commercial and charitable sectors, during the years of postwar welfare expansion. The architects of the modern welfare state were part of a wider intellectual movement which had its origins in the 18th-century Enlightenment, where the application of reason, scientific enquiry and humanistic understanding had as their objective the improvement of the human condition: to bring about the eradication of what Beveridge called the five great giants of idleness, want, disease, ignorance and squalor. Writing about social policy at the beginning of the 20th century and, in particular, the intellectual and philosophical foundations of the Charity Organisation Society and its integration within the

London School of Economics just prior to the First World War, Harris (1989) comments:

> [It] was at its core a highly intellectual movement, influenced by and expressing ideas derived from Malthusianism, Benthamism, Ruskinian hierarchic medievalism, and the political philosophies of Aristotle, Plato, Kant and Hegel. (Harris, 1989: 32)

The roles of science and medicine in this grandiose project were readily accepted but gradually the state too came to be acknowledged as a significant instrument of modernity charged with the task of providing political direction to social welfare activities from the centre. Along with Beveridge in Britain, other Western countries joined in a similar project, shaping their welfare systems in accordance with their particular political, cultural and ideological characteristics. Meidner and Rehn in Sweden, Laroque in France and van Rhijn in the Netherlands were a few of the many political elites imbued with a humanitarian zest and a desire to join in the modern quest to build a welfare state (see George, 1996). In most European countries there was an acceptance that the welfare state was a necessary and good thing which could accommodate the demands of growing economies by lowering what Marxists have described as the reproductive costs of labour power. The provision of schools, hospitals and social housing was considered essential to ensure an educated, healthy and adaptable workforce. The welfare state became the embodiment of humanitarianism brought about by the application of scientific reason and administration to the task of abolishing human misery. I think an additional feature of this modern approach to tackling social problems was the recognition in the latter part of the 19th century that a collectivist response to the complexities of poverty was required. Indeed, Midwinter (1994) points to the creeping or piecemeal collectivism which can be detected in such diverse forms of social thinking as 'civic Benthamism' and the 'humanitarian form of *noblesse oblige*' found in Tory philanthropy. The differentiation between strands of conservative social thought, which are today too often conflated, can be seen with the modernist strand convinced of the necessity for society as a whole to bear some of the responsibility for managing and alleviating poverty, while the liberal market strand rooted in a harsh poor law tradition eschews all forms of collectivism as harmful to social character by undermining self-reliance.

The period roughly from 1945 to 1973 was considered to be the height of the welfare age. It was characterised by the accommodation between the interests of capital and the labour movement by their mutual acceptance of the mixed economy in which capitalism and the welfare state constituted a functional unity. The conservative right and the social democratic left in politics in most OECD countries were considered to share a sufficient number of principles to warrant many writers referring to 'the end of ideology' (see Bell, 1960; Lipset, 1960).

The post-Second World War welfare state has now been reinterpreted as the Fordist welfare state because it secured the interests of both capital and labour by lowering the costs of labour while also providing the social security necessary to ensure that a contented population partici- pated fully in making the era of mass consumption and mass production a distinctive feature of post-Second World War economic growth. I will discuss the question of the crisis of Fordism later in the context of the postmodern analysis of welfare. The mass production methods of the Ford motor plants which gave this particular model of welfare its name were, therefore, augmented by the Keynesian welfare state which ensured full employment and a social wage aimed at bolstering the traditional nuclear, patriarchal family. The appropriation of responsi- bility for welfare from family and community by the state as part of the Fordist stage of welfare development was accepted as *reasonable*. Only the state could ensure that there would be equality and justice in the distribution of life chances. Social planning was an integral part of this strategy, used to assess problems by reference to a systematic calculus of how best to distribute public goods effectively while adhering to the principle of universalism. The competence of the state in the field of rational planning has, of course, always been subject to question and the application of humanitarian principles in social policies flawed in their execution. Nevertheless, employing the instrument of the welfare state as a mechanism for tackling social injustice can be understood as part of the modernist impulse to improve the human condition: by using not only bureaucratic expertise and rationality in the service of humankind, but also the collective resources of the nation, the expectation has been that a modern welfare society would be one based on solidarity. The aim was to marginalise intolerance, tradition, religiosity and preju- dice as bases for distributing welfare by privileging the principles of reason, equality and justice as markers of social progress. It is precisely the appeal which the principles emanating from the *philosophes* of 18th-century France and Scotland have for supporters of the welfare state which has led to the notion that the welfare state is an institution par excellence of modernism: it directs society to acknowledge altruism, solidarity and collectivism as the founding principles of a modern society.

## Anti-modernism and the welfare state

If the distinguishing feature of the modernist conception of the welfare state is the pursuit of equality in the distribution of life chances by linking a humanist interest in alleviating poverty and social disadvantage to the instrument of the state to bring about social progress and a civilised society, the distinguishing feature of the anti-modernist view is to regard *social progress*, and in particular the destruction of tradition by *modernisation*, as a major social and political problem. I have already hinted at what I consider to be a distinctive feature of contemporary anti-modernism: the building of sociological theory and social policies around the idea that there is an essential human nature which is antithetical to collectivism in social and community life and which leads people 'naturally' to pursue self-interest. It is argued by many of the conservative writers I discuss in Chapter 4 that the market rather than the state is the most rational means for distributing life chances.

F.A. Hayek is perhaps one of the most acknowledged intellectual forces articulating what I am calling an anti-modernist perspective on welfare. Writing in the 1930s he began a sustained critique of the Enlightenment concept of reason and the collectivist principles underpinning the modern welfare state (see O'Brien and Penna, 1998: Ch. 3). In particular he rejected the notion of reason in positive science in favour of 'tacit knowledge' spontaneously developed in evolutionary adaptation: self-regulating rules embodied in cultural traditions are what guide behaviour. The idea of 'deliberate design' in social and economic affairs is cast out because it is the spontaneous actions of people adapting to contingency and evolution which shape society. However, the defining feature of anti-modernism does not lie with the economic theories of Hayek or Milton Friedman, who in any case articulate a neo-liberal perspective which for many 'neo-conservatives' appears to celebrate the unfettered economic and market forces which some have argued actually destroy tradition (see Oakeshott, 1962; Gray, 1993). Anti-modernism appeals to the past rather than to the future to shape its vision of society: it is faith in religion, traditional and conservative ways of doing things because they have been proved to work in 'practice' (see Oakeshott, 1962) and a preference for stability rather than social change which mark it out.

The family rather than the market is the main focus of the anti-modern critique of the welfare state (see Abbott and Wallace, 1992). The loss of the family's functions over its members to the burgeoning welfare state is a primary concern to writers such as Popenoe (1988). It is the family which is considered to be the basic building block of the social order and without it an atomised and asocial society will inevitably result. Cheal (1991) adds the idea of 'decline' to the anti-modernist discourse. The 'decline' of family life in contemporary society evidenced by divorce, illegitimacy, abortion and the retreat from marriage has stimulated conservative social movements throughout the Western world whose main objective appears to be to resist the expansion of the welfare state because it is uniquely blamed as the *modernising* stimulus for such 'social problems'. The anti-modernist discourse contains at its core a vision of a society free from state welfare in which strong family values and community life based on a sense of civic virtue and charitable works prevail.

It is the designation of the patriarchal family as 'natural' within conservative discourse on welfare which singles it out as the centre of the anti-modern tradition. The welfare state has been accused of undermining what is a 'natural' institution of human society. The removal of nurturing and socialisation functions from the family to the welfare state, and in particular to the growing numbers of health and welfare counsellors and services which have accompanied the development of the state in the past one hundred and fifty years, has led to a modern society which has endangered family life by tolerating what are considered to be deviant social and behavioural practices (see Rodger, 1996). Sexual deviance, the rising divorce rate and welfare dependency are, of course, the main indices of this 'decline' for those inclined towards the anti-modern discourse.

Scruton (1986) argues for this 'essentialist' position while also providing a defence of the heterosexual bourgeois family. By linking sexual desire to a view of the person as a moral entity he criticises the crassness of promiscuous sexual relations in modern society which create a divide between sexual desire and the perception of the sexual partner as a person with a particular moral being: it is the reduction of people to objects or thing-like qualities by pursuing sex as a purely physiological phenomenon divorced from the 'moral personhood' which makes sex obscene. Sexual relations, he argues, are grounded in the 'natural', or *essential*, differences between male and female and the bourgeois heterosexual family provides a 'natural' framework for the expression of this fundamental feature of human reality where the two dimensions of sexual desire and moral personhood become joined. Marriage institutionalises this 'natural' coupling (see Abbott and Wallace, 1992: 53–74). George Gilder (1973, 1974) connects the biologically reductionist theme found in the anti-modernist discourse to welfare and family life. In his analysis, men's 'natural' aggressiveness and women's 'natural' childbearing role which have evolved over millions of years become the building blocks for a critical perspective on American welfare policy. Women are required to civilise men and a welfare system which enables women to live independently from men will challenge the male identity, make them immature and, ironically, so dependent on women that the basis of society will be undermined.

There are echoes of this line of argument to be found in the work of a host of other writers often included in the New Right or anti-modern tradition, such as Charles Murray, Martin Anderson and Lawrence Mead (see Abbott and Wallace, 1992). Conservative family policy in the USA and Britain throughout the 1980s also attempted to build on these very fundamentalist notions, although, it has been acknowledged, without really altering the welfare landscape very much. The role of motherhood has always been a yardstick for measuring policy intentions: if Patrick Jenkins, a minister in the early Thatcher administration, is known for little else it is for his articulation of the view that 'if the good Lord had intended us to have equal rights to go out to work he would not have created men and women. These are biological facts' (speech to the Conservative Party conference, 1977). Again the anti-modernist tone of this view is often contradicted by the extreme libertarians who frequently express the right of women and mothers to work, indeed, in the case of lone mothers positively demand that they do work. I will return to these themes in Chapter 4.

Before leaving this section of the discussion, a point of clarification is necessary regarding the relationship between the project which students of social policy have come to know as Thatcherism and my characterisation of anti-modernism. I have already indicated that the economic theories of F.A. Hayek upon which the contemporary neo-liberal foundations of Thatcherism were built contain a critique of the Enlightenment. The trust in markets and market rationalities which Hayek and neo-liberalism describe as a 'spontaneous order' is juxtaposed to state-organised and directed activities described as a 'constructivist order'. This naturalistic view underlies Thatcherism. In spite of the scientific training acquired by the former Prime Minister, her *instincts* were anti-modern, combining a trust in market processes and strong discipline in civil and family affairs with a zeal for looking backwards to find answers for the future. The corruption of the term 'modernisation' for her project was only accomplished by ignoring her essentially reactionary gaze. Having cast Thatcherism as anti-modern it must be conceded that all political projects and ideologies contain internal contradictions and inconsistencies. British Conservatism, even under the Thatcher leadership, displayed many modernist tendencies but they were often characterised as failures rather than virtues: the lack of success in cutting welfare expenditure in real terms, with the exception of the social housing budgets, because of social policies regarded as too 'wet' is a good example of Thatcher's accidental modernism. I will return to this theme in Chapter 4.

## Postmodernism and the welfare state

In a very perceptive piece of sociological writing C. Wright Mills (1959) identified at the end of the 1950s what many contemporary sociologists are only now recognising as postmodernism:

> We are at the ending of what is called the Modern Age. Just as Antiquity was followed by several centuries of Oriental ascendancy, which Westerners provincially call the Dark Ages, so now The Modern Age is being succeeded by a postmodern period. Perhaps we may call it: The Fourth Epoch. (Wright Mills, 1959: 184)

Mills goes on to talk about the disorienting effect of this transition. The key ideologies of the Enlightenment, liberalism and socialism, were in the 1950s already beginning to reveal their inadequacies because the assumption that there was 'an inherent relation between *reason* and *freedom* was everywhere visibly questionable'. Marxism in the guise of East European communism 'has so often become a dreary rhetoric of bureaucratic defence and abuse' and liberalism for Mills was revealing itself to be a 'trivial and irrelevant way of masking reality' (p. 185). These movements in thought and perception referred to by Mills are grand in scale and perhaps the main problem with 20th-century theorists of postmodernism is their failure to see its origins in earlier stages of 20th-century development.

The problem of applying *postmodern theory* to the analysis of what essentially remain institutions which define modernity, such as the welfare state, is that we risk causing confusion. With this in mind, I believe the role of postmodern theory is as a critique of modernity rather than as a fully fashioned and coherent theoretical perspective. Its pre-eminent method of analysis is *analytical deconstruction*: it analytically dismantles institutions, ideas and processes in order to reassemble and 'rethink the present and future of welfare' (Leonard, 1997). Postmodernism as a critique of modernity does not mean it is the same as anti-modernism. It does not seek answers in traditions and past values. The postmodern condition is described as a 'hyper' manifestation of the modern or 'modernity turned back on itself'. As O'Brien and Penna (1998) observe it is characterised by the 'inversion of social life' including the 'hyper-differentiation' of scientific/technical knowledges and cultural values, the hyper-rationalisation of political economic authority and the hyper-commodification of lifestyles.

Perhaps one of the most subversive notions within the postmodern perspective is the suggestion that culture, and social reality more generally, can be conceptualised as a set of myths: meanings are not incontrovertible but rather, as Denzin (1986) observes, require to be 'deconstructed, taken apart and traced back to the productional activities of readers, audiences and authors' (p. 195). Structural theories of social causation which mark traditional sociological reasoning are questioned as the human subject is displaced as the centre where meanings are constructed and, instead, is viewed as a product of discursive practices, replaced by the analysis of the complex inter-flow of discourses and narratives which create a plethora of 'truths' and supplant grand theories and meanings with *local* narratives and meanings. The failure of science, including social science, to explain macrosystems and *total realities*, and the realisation that the promise of the Enlightenment to bring about social progress, consensus and well-being has not been fulfilled, focus attention on the conflicts and uncertainties of postmodern existence. If the project of modernity cannot deliver the goods then what is to stop people, social organisations and cultures returning to tradition and anti-modern ways of making sense of reality? Denzin (1986) commenting on Lyotard sees a 'conflictual, agnostic model of the social order' emerging. Indeed, the pursuit of consensus and certainty in modern society is viewed as fundamentally flawed (Habermas, in particular, as the defender of the Enlightenment project is criticised for his pursuit, both intellectually and politically, of an authentically democratic communicative society in which consensus can be discovered). Consensus for Lyotard is merely a stage in communication and not an end: there can be no finalised and completed process of understanding meaning.

If the central feature of postmodernism is to debunk the metalanguages and totalising narratives which constitute the main ideologies of the Enlightenment, then a postmodern critique of welfare will seek to unmask the humanitarian pretensions which have fed the myth of welfare state activity for the past century. Where heroic figures are cast as designers of a vast humanitarian project which seeks only to eradicate want, squalor, poverty, idleness and ignorance, postmodern analysis of the welfare state finds motives of social control, bureaucratic inflexibility and the maintenance of social discipline as the main driving forces behind welfare state development and reform. There have been at least three strands to the emerging postmodern critique of welfare: the political economy of post-Fordism, the application of poststructuralism to the analysis of welfare practice and the emergence of a postmodern politics of welfare. I will examine each of these in turn.

## The post-Fordist welfare state

A cautionary note about the emerging *post-Fordist* critique and analysis of the welfare state needs to be made before proceeding. Theories of *Fordism* and *post-Fordism* have been developed from within political economy and, on the whole, appear to be rather economically and technologically determinist when applied to the welfare state. In particular, theoretical constructs which reduce movements in society to changing modes of production and consumption or technological innovations which impact on the occupational structure tend to have difficulty in dealing with the substance of social policy and social relations: the tendency to define all social policy questions in relation to the state and political economy means that those issues beyond the state/individual relationship are neglected. Williams (1994), in particular, has difficulty accepting the application of post-Fordist analysis of welfare to issues such as community care and the evolution of what has become known as welfare pluralism. The relevance of post-Fordism must be demonstrated rather than assumed.

As already indicated briefly, Fordism is a name used to describe a particular period in capitalist development, roughly from the inter-war period until the 1970s when a 'crisis of Fordism' began to become visible. There are a number of different theoretical themes in post-Fordism. First, there is a focus on the ways in which capital is accumulated and, importantly, the mechanisms which are adopted to ensure that the social, political and economic conflicts and contradictions inherent in capitalism are *regulated* in the interests of the accumulation process (variously referred to as the regime of accumulation or the mode of regulation). The emergence of mass production, mass consumption and mass trade unions which characterised long periods of the post-Second World War era crystallises the era of Fordism. The Keynesian welfare state geared to providing universal social security is interpreted as being functional for the accumulation needs of capital at the height of the Fordist period: the maintenance of the social wage in return for prices and incomes policies, corporatist wage bargaining and the pursuit of full employment policies and industrial peace typify the Fordist regime of accumulation. However, the inflexibilities which result from this configuration of structures and interests generate problems: powerful trade unions able to defend over-manning, an inflexible work force, wages rising faster than productivity and the emergence of stagnating growth coupled with high inflation (stagflation) cumulatively give rise to a 'crisis of Fordism'. Post-Fordism by contrast is characterised by flexible working patterns, new management techniques, many imported from the tiger economies of the Far East, and limited trade union power which usher in a new system of accumulation aimed at overcoming the problems of Fordism. Second, there is particular interest in the shift from mass markets (Fordism) to fragmented or niche markets (post-Fordism). Technological innovations fundamentally alter both the way business is conducted and the nature of the labour force. The rapid expansion of internet commerce is a contemporary reminder of this development. Third, there is a managerialist analysis of what economists call the *flexible firm* and new techniques for organising production and the labour force. Dual labour market theory is one particular way of describing new and emerging work patterns which have evolved. Within this context, the occupational structure is divided into core workers, with technically marketable skills, careers and benefits and some measure of security, and peripheral workers who are unskilled or semi-skilled and so lack security and benefits, are often employed on part-time or fixed-term contracts and on the whole lack union representation. The post-Fordist analysis of the welfare state is read off from this underlying economic analysis. For example, it is argued that the restructuring of the welfare state since the 1980s in all OECD countries represents an attempt to adjust Keynesian welfare systems to the changing economic conditions of post-Fordism. Two developments indicative of this accommodation to post-Fordism are the marketisation of welfare services and the evolution of a contract culture governing the relationship between the voluntary sector of care and the state. Post-Fordism is, therefore, the economic theory of post-modern welfare but, as I have already indicated, the complexities of social relations and human need cannot be neatly reduced to this approach. I will return to the concept of post-Fordism in Chapter 6 in the context of urban processes and the conditions leading to the weakening of community and again in Chapter 8 in the context of discussing the impact of globalisation on social policy.

## Poststructuralism and welfare

The weaknesses identified with the theory of post-Fordism, specifically its tendency to reduce all issues to the state/individual relationship, are addressed by *poststructuralism*. The clearest example of the application of poststructuralism to the analysis of welfare is contained in the analysis of social work of Rojek *et al.* (1988) . They take the idea of the decentred subject, that is to say the notion that human beings do not generate meaning from scratch, to argue for something called 'subjectless social work'. It is the language and professional discourses of health and welfare practitioners which construct the identities of the client, the claimant, the victim, the deserving and the undeserving poor. This argument raises for our consideration the possibility that the work of the welfare services consists of the manipulation of a 'reality' which the welfare services have themselves created rather than responding to problems and human issues formed 'out there' (see Rodger, 1996).

The concept of 'soft policing', which is often used to describe the work of community health practitioners and social workers, is a further example of the application of poststructuralist theory to welfare analysis, this time to the measurement of deviance within the client groups of the welfare state in terms of their conformity to a 'reality' constructed by the welfare services. The subtle forms of discipline which Foucault has described in terms of the *panoptic gaze* are the clearest indication of this process (see Rodger, 1996 for a discussion).

The critical uses of postmodern theory in the analysis of the welfare state serve to undermine the humanitarian pretensions of welfare state development and reform. Squires (1990) questions the purpose of the welfare state: is it to alleviate poverty and integrate the socially excluded into society? Poststructuralism suggests that welfare has always been about managing incentives to work and applying mechanisms of classification to order and sort deviants from 'normal' members of the community. In an interesting application of this insight, Dean (1989) draws on Foucault's observations about 'disciplinary partitioning' and the segregation of lepers to illuminate developments in the management of social security claimants. From the 'badging' of different types of pauper under the Elizabethan poor law to the classification and targeting of contemporary welfare claimants, the welfare state has been more about managing indolence by *partitioning* than about helping the excluded poor:

> Thus, the social security system affords quite different and distinctive treatment to the various categories of claimant which it creates – to retirement pensioners, to single parents, to the sick and disabled, to the unemployed and so on – and all these categories may be partitioned and sub-partitioned with reference to criteria pertaining to age, gender, dependency, health, aptitude and so forth. (Dean, 1989: 77)

These various statuses are, of course, applied to claimants in terms of their usefulness as participants in the economically productive community. Moral censure will express itself in the way the social security system treats those considered to be less deserving of welfare because of their indolence or unwillingness to submit to assessment processes which are even harsher today than in the times of Thatcherism when Dean originally fashioned his analysis.

## Postmodern politics of welfare

The politics of modern welfare systems is, fundamentally, about how to restructure the provision of welfare services in accordance with modern conditions where the occupational possibilities for the sub-educated, unskilled and inarticulate are few in an increasingly high technology, information-based society. As the post-Second World War welfare settlement breaks down those who remain outside what Galbraith (1992) has called 'the contented society' must find a voice: social movements based on race, gender, age and the environment are now challenging the premises of the bureaucratic welfare systems found in all Western societies. More importantly, those groups who feel excluded from postmodern society are seeking a redefinition of *citizenship* consistent with post-modern conditions (the conflict over differing conceptions of postmodern citizenship will provide the main theme for the following chapter). The visions of the founding fathers of the Beveridge welfare state no longer make sense when the new patterns of poverty affect young households rather than old ones; single parent families rather than large families; and when the concept of the social wage appears to have disappeared along with Fordist ways of organising production and consumption. The vocabularies of humanitarianism, of the emancipation of the poor, of the eradication of want, idleness, disease, ignorance and squalor, no longer command the same respect that they did.

Postmodernism signals a social order characterised by conflicting and competing 'truths' and in the place of the large-scale certainties which were a feature of the ideologies of modernity, of which welfarism and the welfare state are the clearest expression, there is fragmentation, relativism and the need to acknowledge *communitarian* and *local narratives*. It is the movement from the notion that the state should be responsible for welfare to the idea that individuals, communities and families should be responsible for their own and others' welfare which colours the contemporary debate about the shape of welfare in the 21st century.

Leonard (1997) articulates the political project of postmodern welfare explicitly. He subtitles his book *Postmodern Welfare*, 'reconstructing an emancipatory project'. His starting point is to recognise what he terms the dual nature of modernity: on the one hand, its interest in bureaucracy and *technicist* control of social life described in the work of the Frankfurt School (see Marcuse, 1969; Adorno and Horkheimer, 1972) and conceptualised by Habermas (1986, 1987) as the 'colonisation of the lifeworld' by a rationality grounded in scientific and managerialist domination of society (see Layder, 1994: Ch. 11 for an accessible account of lifeworld and system in Habermas' work); and, on the other, the pre-eminence given to enlightenment and the pursuit of equality, liberty and social justice. The objective is to recover only those aspects of modernity which have an interest in emancipation and liberation. The critique of modernist welfare from Leonard's standpoint is founded on the rejection of centralised planning because it is clumsy and divisive. The mobilisation of state mechanisms to drive large-scale social services have been based historically on distinctions between deserving and undeserving claimants which are often crude. He talks of the need to supplant 'programmes' with a concept of 'social process', presumably because he wants community participation in dialogue about welfare goals and the determination of needs and priorities. Consistent with postmodernism's fascination for diversity and plurality, Leonard wishes to see a strategy adopted which acknowledges the plurality of ways that welfare can be met. His dilemma is, of course, an awkward question: from what moral position can matters of human need, priorities and welfare be decided when the postmodern condition undermines the validity of grand totalising narratives and rejects large universal social theories and philosophies? The dilemma is deepened by the problem of how to support 'an ethics of diversity' while also seeking to promote a sense of solidarity and interdependence in a society beleaguered by global and impersonal forces which appear to privilege individualism and atomised, asocial behaviour. The tension created by the struggle to reconcile *universal needs* with *particularist needs* lies at the heart of the postmodern politics of welfare.

The solution to these difficult issues is increasingly being sought through theories of communitarianism and the analysis of and support for new social movements, especially those which appear not to be based on traditional conceptions of social class. The market is being challenged by the idea that there is, after all, an alternative to impersonal economic and cultural forces. Welfare is to be built upwards from the community but there remains a role for the state: its classical role of co-ordinating and guaranteeing citizenship and fairness remains a vital part of this post-modern vision of a welfare future. New types of participant political party are envisaged, such as the Green Party, which would seek to release what Etzioni (1993) has called 'the spirit of community'. The twin movements of postmodernism, of increasing globalisation on the one hand and devo-lution of political power to regions and communities on the other hand, would nevertheless create problems of immense complexity which have not so far been addressed adequately by those inclined towards post-modern political theory. I will return to these themes in Chapter 5 in the context of a discussion of communitarianism and associational democ-racy and welfare.

## Competing visions of welfare society

The analytic theme running throughout the book will revolve around the competing visions of a welfare society which are emerging in the contem-porary politics of welfare. The modernists reject the intolerance of the anti-modern vision which eschews all attempts to use collective resources to meet social and human need and reject the nihilism which they perceive in the extreme relativism of postmodernism. Both the anti-modern and postmodern perspectives have been accused of sharing conservative traits (see Habermas, 1981). However, as indicated in this chapter there are some contemporary theorists of the welfare state such as Leonard (1997) who attempt to reconcile Marxism with postmodernism and who envisage a continuing role for the state in a postmodern welfare future. The anti-modernists will tend to view the problem of social integration and welfare dependency as antithetical notions and seek to reduce to an absolute minimum the role of the state in the provision of welfare: it is self-reliance coupled with a renewed emphasis on family and community responsibility which above all else the anti-modernists see as rescuing modern society from its malaise of incivility, indolence and welfare dependency. The analysis will examine these themes in more depth as it progresses. The following chapter will address the issues of social integration and social citizenship which lie at the heart of a welfare society.

# 2

# Social integration and social citizenship

The central concern of this chapter is to examine the notions of social integration and social citizenship which lie at the heart of the welfare debate. Central to this debate is a dispute about the purpose of state welfare: whether its main objective is that of redistributing wealth and life chances; of increasing a sense of social solidarity; of marking the limits of a civilised society's tolerance of human misery and impoverishment; or, alternatively, whether its primary aim is the management of deviance in its various guises; of managing incentives to work; of instilling a sense of discipline, self-reliance and mutual obligation between people through the services and benefits it does not provide as much as through that it does provide. The modernist architects of the welfare state probably had few doubts about the efficacy of state welfare to bring about a sense of social solidarity and social integration by the development of the welfare benefits and services which are now a feature of most welfare systems within the OECD. The anti-modernist critics of the system of state welfare (Marsland, 1996; Murray, 1996) take the opposite view and see state welfare as a force which destroys social integration by undermining the fabric of social relations and obligations which have 'traditionally' resided in family and community. If the possibility of a welfare society is to be realised, whether that be based on collective and communitarian principles or instead on principles of self-reliance and charitable aid, there has to be an interest in what makes society cohere. And in contemporary Western societies social integration has become inextricably bound up with how social citizenship is defined because it enshrines rights of access and eligibility for support.

## Social inequality and the strategy for equality

In reference to a 1952 article in *The Times* reviewing the performance of the welfare state, Vincent (1991) observes the references made to notions such as the 'strengthening of civic solidarity' and the provision of services which would underpin 'common citizenship' in a piece which clearly thought the aims of the original plan were visible and moving towards attainment. The assumption, then as now, was that social inequality, especially if it was particularly visible and extreme, would undermine the social fabric of postwar Britain and contribute to a lack of social integration. The themes of social integration and social citizenship will be explored more fully below, but the general success of governments throughout Western Europe in tackling the problem of social inequality through the mechanism of the welfare state should be examined as a prelude to that more conceptual analysis. Whether the growth and complexity of the European Union will lead to uniform effects on European welfare systems is a matter I will deal with substantively in Chapter 8. The focus of my analysis at this point is the comparative failure of British social policy, in the context of the European Union, to tackle the problem of social inequality and so prepare the ground for a radical movement away from state provision.

The welfare state by its very nature as a universal protector against hardship destroyed the network of mutual support systems which existed prior to the modernist impulse of the 19th-century philanthropists and the 20th-century social reformers. The infrastructure of caring and supporting networks needed to augment and possibly replace state involvement in welfare provision, irrespective of the crucial issues of female labour market participation and the ageing of the population, is difficult to conceive of in a context of growing social inequality and visible disparities in wealth and well-being.

A division emerged throughout Europe in the postwar era regarding the purpose of welfare: the European countries which have developed strong and expansive welfare systems in the post-1945 period, such as Belgium, the Netherlands, France and Germany appear to have laid stress upon restoring economic efficiency to their war-torn countries whereas Britain drew on its humanist heritage which gave rise to earlier pre-war reforms and framed the welfare issue as a matter of morality. Theorists of the British welfare system such as Tawney (1931) and, of course, Marshall (1950), saw the main issues as moral: the strategy for equality through the instrument of the welfare state was to be supported because it was virtuous and would reduce social divisions. However, the main feature of the Beveridge model of welfare, which established Britain as one of the leading welfare systems in postwar Europe, was its grounding in the social insurance principle. That tradition, as Vincent observes, was founded on the model of empowering bureaucrats and system managers rather than citizens or claimants. In other words it was in reality a rather elitist, top-down approach to welfare. Ignatieff refers to the phenomenon as 'passive equality of entitlement' rather than 'active equality of participation' (Ignatieff, 1989). By contrast the forces which drove continental European systems, particularly Catholicism, appear to have institutionalised the principle of collective obligation to a far greater extent than the Beveridge tradition which has characterised the British experience since 1945. Van Kersbergen and Becker (1988) draw our attention to the Dutch word for their welfare state, *verzorgingsstaat* or caring state. Contained within that concept is a model of welfare predicated on the strong taking responsibility for the weak in society. The Catholic principle of *subsidiarity* which institutionalised the concept of devolved responsibility for welfare to its lowest possible level, whether that be family, community or local government, also encouraged an attitude to welfare in the Netherlands rooted in local responsibilities which seems to have resulted in a faster rate of growth and generosity when compared with the Beveridge model in Britain. In the Dutch case, the synergetic links between welfare principles derived from the Christian Democratic tradition and the secular influences to be found elsewhere in Europe, including the influence of Beveridge during the period of war exile for the Dutch government (see Cox, 1993), created a welfare system in which the state funded welfare services were managed by the private and charitable interests forming the *pillars* of Dutch society: the layer of insulation between government and civil society in the Netherlands has led a number of Dutch sociologists to apply the label of welfare society rather than welfare state to the Netherlands (see Kraemer, 1966; van Doorn, 1978), a point made in the introduction but worth emphasising again.

The assumption, therefore, that Britain rather than continental Europe provides the leading model of an advanced welfare state has over time had to be questioned, leaving aside the incredible postwar expansion of the Swedish welfare state which has surpassed the best that can be found anywhere in Europe. It is to Scandinavia and the Netherlands that we must look for examples of complex and expansive welfare systems, and it is in France that we find the most developed range of family policies (see Hantrais and Letablier, 1996). It is in these European countries that the process of retrenchment of welfare state activities which characterised the years immediately following the oil crisis of the 1970s is least visible, especially when compared with the welfare systems of the English-speaking countries of Britain, the USA, Australia and New Zealand (see Castles, 1990). This phenomenon can be explained.

Rosenberry (1982) observes that those welfare systems which manage their redistributive commitments by making a clear and visible distinction between providers and recipients of benefits are also most vulnerable to the phenomenon of *welfare backlash:* a social and political reaction which can lead to a withdrawal of legitimacy from the whole welfare enterprise. Her research focuses on the empirical reality that welfare states within the OECD group of countries have varied in the way they have reconciled the competing demands made by dependent and productive sectors of their society. So if a welfare system has institutionalised a wide range of universal benefits and services, most notably as the Scandinavian welfare systems have, and as the Netherlands, France, Germany and Britain had before the 1980s, then the division between who pays for welfare and who receives it is unclear, or irrelevant if everyone regardless of income is receiving a universal benefit or service. By contrast, countries which seek to reconcile these competing demands by means testing and using social assistance rather than social insurance-type benefits and services will create a more visible line between providers and receivers of welfare so increasing the system's vulnerability to welfare backlash. A social context is constructed in which the tax contributors to welfare budgets may become politically organised to resist further welfare state expansion, as was the case in Britain and the USA, especially during the 1980s. The strategy for equality which marked the immediate postwar period was brought to an end abruptly in what Castles (1990) calls 'the English-speaking welfare systems' of Britain, Australia, New Zealand and Canada. In the English-speaking countries the movement towards targeting and welfare state retrenchment has been more marked than in the continental European countries. And, of course, social inequality has tended to rise at a faster rate in countries without welfare systems which might afford protection to the poor against the most severe effects of global economic fluctuations. Castles (1990) offers us, in addition, an historical analysis which explains the popularity for welfare retrenchment in the English-speaking countries in terms of their early development of welfare provision and past global economic dominance: their economic decline, which became comparatively more evident in the

1970s and 80s because of their weakening global economic advantage, prompted welfare backlash.

Recent enquiries into trends in social inequality (see the Rowntree Foundation inquiry into income and wealth in Hills, 1995) indicate that there is international divergence among the affluent Western countries in their rates of social inequality (measurable by comparing the income gap between the poorest and the richest households in a country, invariably excluding the super rich). The first notable feature of the data on international income inequality trends discovered by the Rowntree evidence (see Hills, 1995) is that the drift towards increasing inequality is not a universal movement throughout the main Western countries: Spain, Portugal, Ireland, Canada, Denmark, Finland and Italy have all been experiencing falling inequality, ranging from a falling rate of approximately -10 per cent per year for Spain (between 1984–89) to nearly -0.70 per cent for Italy (1987–91). In Britain the long-term trend towards greater equality came to an end in the latter part of the 1970s, as it did for many other European countries as well as Australia, New Zealand and the USA (the speed with which inequality increased in the UK between 1977 and 1990 was, according to Hills (1995), 0.75 per cent per year). The factors which have caused the increasing gap between the wealthier and poorest members of society can be identified: a growing income gap between those in work and those not; growing numbers of those wholly dependent on state benefits which are means tested and not linked to average earnings; income premiums for the better educated and credentialled compared with those without qualifications coupled with the ending of mechanisms protecting the lowest paid workers; the rise of two earner households but the accompanying increase in no earner households. The crucial variable which marks out the two countries with the largest annual increase in inequality rates, Britain (0.75 per cent) and New Zealand (a full 1 per cent increase in the inequality trend between 1983 and 1989), has been the extent to which welfare policies in the 1980s and early 1990s, under the Thatcher governments in Britain and the Bolger government in New Zealand, have stimulated the progression of these trends rather than having been designed explicitly to undermine them or alleviate their worst impact. Both countries have seen governments seeking to replace a system of state welfare with a system based on a welfare pluralist strategy involving policies geared to marketisation, privatisation and the utilisation of community, voluntary and family resources. The movement towards what is often described as a 'mixed economy of welfare' is evident in all of the OECD countries but is more marked in those countries with the highest rates of social inequality. The virtues and vices of welfare pluralism are not what is immediately at issue. It is the resulting social inequality and what we might describe as 'the welfare gap' between state provision and non-state provision which is significant. One consequence of increasing inequality is social polarisation. This has generated a growing concern about social order and social stability: the formation of an 'underclass' and rising crime and civil disorder are only some of the factors which have become an accepted but very worrying part of the contemporary social condition of modern societies. The relationship between the state and civil society is one we must examine if we are to understand how late modern and postmodern societies are to provide a stable framework of social welfare.

## Welfare state and welfare society: system integration and social integration

It is to a classic sociological distinction that we should turn in order to understand the unstable social context within which contemporary social policy must be formed. In seeking to accommodate the insights and transcend the limits of functionalist sociological analysis in the 1960s and 70s, a conceptual distinction between *social integration* (referring to the social interaction and relationships between social actors) and *system integration* (referring to the relationships between institutions and systems such as the welfare system and the economic system) was made, mostly notably by Lockwood (1976). The purpose of this important sociological distinction is to differentiate between social changes brought about by conflicts and contradictions occurring within a society's institutional systems, including the complex relationships between the state, economy and welfare systems, from those brought about by conflicts between social actors at the level of interpersonal interaction. At the time of its original formulation, the social/system distinction was attempting to address the problems created by the unwarranted stress in functionalist sociology on the notion of 'normative integration': that the social order largely depended on people supporting core social values for its stability. By acknowledging that contradictions between a society's system parts can generate conflicts which may lead to social instability, theorists such as Lockwood (1976) provided a useful corrective to the one-sided analysis of *normative integration*. The thrust of this critique of functionalism, in particular the Parsonian version of it, was to restate a classic

Marxist insight that the economic infrastructure shaped and conditioned the ideological superstructure. Lockwood (1976) was especially interested in establishing the importance of material interests, or economic and class interests generated at the level of economic relationships, for influencing the ideological and normative integration of societies. This important conceptual distinction is relevant for our understanding of the relationship between a welfare state and a welfare society.

The task of examining the interplay between system and social levels of analysis in the context of the welfare state has been started by Habermas (1976). It is his analysis of the legitimation problems of advanced capitalism which awakened sociological interest in the relationship between a welfare state and a welfare society (see Offe, 1984). Despite its location in the analysis of the economic and political conditions prevailing in the 1970s, its weakness as a contemporary analysis of economy and society can be overlooked because it provides a helpful conceptual analysis of the different levels at which social malintegration can be exhibited. The basic thesis underlying the analysis of welfare state crisis and legitimation problems can be restated very briefly. Underlying Habermas' analysis of the legitimation problems of late capitalism is an analysis of the fiscal crisis of the capitalist state (see O'Connor, 1973). It is premised on there being a fundamental contradiction between the capitalist state's need to secure the best conditions for capital accumulation, and therefore to ensure a healthy and profitable economic system, and the ability of the capitalist state to secure the loyalty of the population for a system in which profits are appropriated privately. The growth in welfare expenditure and, in particular, the growing fiscal gap between the income that the state can generate through taxation to pay for welfare and the increasing demands for ever more welfare benefits and services give rise to the *fiscal crisis of the state* with all that that entails for *legitimation problems*. The dilemma is formulated as that of a *steering problem* of the state. The growth in welfare state expenditure is sanctioned because it is assumed to be instrumental in securing the loyalty of the population to the system: it legitimises the gross inequities which become visible by trading social security for tolerance of disparities in income and wealth. Social inequalities and gross public injustices would, if left unattended, lead to major steering problems for planners, administrators and political leaders. Offe (1984) and Gough (1975) provide very similar analyses of the contradictions of the welfare state. The particular insights which Habermas' analysis adds to this work are the distinctions, first, between system and lifeworld, and second, between four levels of crisis tendencies.

## System and lifeworld

The distinction between system and lifeworld can be understood for our purposes as similar to that between system integration and social integration but Habermas develops the distinction by arguing that what characterises late capitalist societies is the *colonisation of the lifeworld* by the system: matters relating to intersubjective understanding and the creation of values and normative structures based on the imperatives of consensual living, for want of a better form of expression, are subordinated increasingly to the logic of bureaucratic systems and what Habermas has called *instrumental reason* with its logic embedded in the scientific and technological control of society and its institutions. It is clear that this aspect of modernity has found expression in the way modern welfare systems have developed in the affluent capitalist societies, particularly through their subordination of social needs to the fiscal and monetary needs generated at the level of the economic system.

## Crisis tendencies

Habermas' thesis is founded on the conceptualising of different crisis tendencies expressing themselves variously as economic, rationality, legitimation and motivational crisis. The point of origin of a crisis tendency, therefore, can be at the economic level, the political or governmental level or the socio-cultural level where meanings are constructed and ratified. At the heart of the analysis offered in *Legitimation Crisis* (1976) is the relationship between objective and subjective components of crisis tendencies. He enquires into how problems generated at the level of the economic system relate to the ways people might make sense of the so-called crisis at the level of inter-personal relationships. As a result contradictions that manifest themselves as an *economic crisis* (currency devaluation; a decline in the balance of payments; rising inflation combined with low economic growth and increasing unemployment) can be *displaced* on to the level of the policy management of the state giving rise to tendencies leading to a *rationality crisis*. This particular type of crisis tendency was characteristic of Western economies in the 1970s with large sectors of socialised industry which were subject both to the operating disciplines of the market and political direction simultaneously. Today it may manifest itself in different ways: community care policies which have as their main purpose the 'restructuring' of welfare provision to save public money by shifting the economic burden from the state to families and communities may conceal those blunt economic imperatives by the enactment of contradictory legislation such as the Carers (Recognition and Services) Act 1996 which imposes a legal duty on the state to assess the needs of carers. A welfare system which attempts to deny its responsibilities for meeting caring needs while concurrently legislating to enshrine 'rights' to have those same needs professionally assessed by agents of the state may provide a contemporary welfare example of *rationality* crisis. Pressure for increased public funding is encouraged by the contradictory community care legislation which causes public anxiety and discontent when it is not forthcoming.

Tendencies towards legitimation crisis in the welfare context will arise, therefore, when the decisions of bureaucratic rationality are found wanting by those experiencing actual rationing. It becomes unclear which principle is *steering* the welfare system: humanitarian concern for the unproductive, disabled and disadvantaged or saving public money to reduce the tax burden for the productive members of society? In such circumstances the gap between a political and economic system and its cultural and social underpinnings becomes visible. Habermas talks about the system's inability to 'generate generalised motivations' supportive of the system, in our example the community care system. Tendencies to *motivational crisis* may arise at the level of inter-subjective meaning: the welfare system is perceived as either intrinsically unjust, profligate, uncivilised or whatever. There have been a number of competing public attitudes to welfare provision finding expression over the past two decades.

The contemporary problem affecting all welfare systems within the OECD is, therefore, how to reconcile the system imperatives of modern welfare systems, which are driven by policy assumptions that they drain scarce economic resources away from productive purposes, with the necessity of maintaining social integration, and social security, for those who are increasingly finding the evolution of the postindustrial and post-Fordist economy aggressive and unforgiving to their poverty, lack of educational qualifications, old age or disabilities. The problem of social integration, as I have posed it here, is inextricably connected to the management of social and civil disorder in periods of welfare restructuring and to those mechanisms which can be constructed to ensure the participation of all in society. At a time when the economic and occupational structures are leading to growing social inequality and social polarisation, the levels of tolerance for state-funded welfare provision appear to be waning. The inclusivist concept of social citizenship, which traditionally has institutionalised welfare rights by guaranteeing access to a minimum level of material well-being for all, is being subjected to critical attack and reappraisal, especially as the forces of modernity clash with those of anti-modernity and postmodernity in the contemporary politics of welfare.

## Social integration and social citizenship

The issue of citizenship arose originally in the working-class struggle for admission to the main institutions of society during the 18th and 19th centuries. The fight then was to overcome social exclusion by securing political rights (free association) to augment the purely formal civil rights granted to the labouring classes in the 18th century. At a fundamental level the struggle for citizenship was a social class-based movement to win substantive use powers for what Marxist economists would call 'formally free labourers' in the early stages of capitalist development. Today the axes of division in welfare societies have multiplied as part of the broad social struggle involving gender, ethnicity, age, disability and sexuality to secure and extend what Marshall (1950) called social rights (access to free health, welfare and educational services). Our understanding of what constitutes social integration in a welfare society necessarily has to take account of this contemporary reality.

Classic Marxist analyses of social inequality and class relationships start from an analysis of the social and class structure of capitalist society and attempt to identify the socio-economic conditions which will generate the *appropriate* social consciousness among the disadvantaged and excluded to bring about a transformation of the system: asking effectively when does *social mal-integration* become so intolerable that it leads to a fundamental change in the *social system* as a whole. The standard analyses of class structure and social inequality in sociology, while not necessarily adopting Marx's political agenda, have largely relied upon his method of analysis. The glaring problem for both Marxism and the orthodox sociological analysis of class structure is that social class is decreasingly the form through which discontent about welfare and citizenship rights is expressed in late modern or postmodern societies. The concept of status incongruity derived from the Weberian distinction between class, status and power may be a better way of understanding social divisions in postmodern societies: race, gender, age, disability and social class, for example, can often vary independently and so provide different bases upon which people can mobilise politically and make sense of their social reality.

David Lockwood (1996) has recognised the need to move beyond the orthodox approach in the sociological analysis of class formation, and incidentally to develop his original social/system distinction, by posing a different set of questions which are organised around the concept of *civic integration*:

> Instead of starting with class structure and asking how class formation affects social integration, might it not be more advantageous to reverse the question and ask how the institutional structure central to social integration affects class formation, and is perhaps even conducive to class deformation? (Lockwood, 1996: 532)

The observation at the end of the Lockwood quote is very interesting: the social exclusion of people from full membership of society by the denial of civil, political and social rights because of race, gender, disability, sexuality or age may lead to quite different sets of political and social alliances from those predicted by class analysis. For Lockwood, class formation built around industrial and political polarisation is no longer as salient in late modern capitalist societies as it once was. The incongruities of power, authority and status which marked the possible fault lines for major transformations of the social and political order in earlier stages of social development are now highly unlikely:

> At the most abstract level the unity and coherence of market, bureaucratic and citizenship relations is to be found in the manner in which they combine to create a social universe of *individual* actors who are subject to *impersonal* rules which at the same time *legitimate* both the inequalities in the *rewards* attaching to (principally occupational) positions and the *allocation* of individuals to these positions. (Lockwood, 1996: 534)

The central issue in welfare capitalist societies has been the disharmony created between the *formal* nature of civil and political rights and the absence of *substantive use powers* to fulfil them without a corresponding range of *social rights* which could secure a basic level of health, education and material well-being for the poorest members of society. The principles of equality and social justice while underpinning the notion of citizenship in reality have been subordinated to the system integration needs of the capitalist economy. The social integration required to secure a civilised society at peace with itself has been and continues to be an elusive goal. The extent to which existing efforts to 'restructure' the welfare state either facilitate or hinder the evolution of equality between citizens is the substance of the contemporary welfare debate. Competing political vocabularies vie with each other to define welfare citizenship in terms of *entitlements, rights, opportunities* or *duties*. At any given moment there will be those in society seeking to expand their citizenship rights while others will be fighting either to make up what they perceive to be a deficit in their entitlements or to overcome their exclusion. Social integration and the possibilities of securing a welfare society are inextricably bound up with how these conflicts and struggles about the principles of access and exclusion will be resolved in the future. By examining the nature of the political debate about welfare and citizenship in the remainder of this chapter, I hope to point up the difficulties lying in wait for policy makers and political ideologues who fail to recognise the deceptively simple nature of the concept.

## Citizenship and welfare

Turner (1993) argues that historically the notion of *citizenship* has been linked to the development of abstract universal values which have helped to define modernity. By this he means that citizenship as a status safeguards the principles of achievement, rationality and social interdependence in the operation of social institutions and social policies. It acts as a bulwark against ascriptive, non-rational and divisive means of determining who belongs as a member of a society or who should receive a welfare benefit. The interpretation of these principles remains at the centre of the welfare debate. For this reason, I will intentionally place the contemporary political debate about citizenship and rights to welfare within the framework which I have set out in Chapter 1: the debate reflects the ongoing conflict between modernism, anti-modernism and postmodernism about what should constitute a welfare society in the 21st century. There are clear lines of argument discernible in the contemporary literature. First, the defence of the concept of citizenship is grounded in a welfare state discourse which suggests that without a sizeable contribution from the state to balance the vagaries of the postindustrial economy, the social order will increasingly be characterised by inequality, injustice, civil strife and social apathy. Defenders of the welfare state remain convinced that the project of modernity, and the social values associated with it relating to equality, justice and reason, are far from being a spent force. Second, there are those from the right who suggest that the very vocabulary we use to describe welfare provision should increasingly play down the notion of citizenship and instead emphasise the needs of consumers or clients rather than *citizens*. In advancing this claim it is argued that there ought to be a greater recognition of the duties and responsibilities which membership of a civilised society demands of the individual and which traditionally were grounded in family and community before the state assumed its current powers. The anti-modern discourse of obligation to society rather than oneself is, it is argued, too often neglected by supporters of a citizenship approach to welfare (see Marsland, 1996). Third, the view of the welfare state from the postmodern perspective is influenced by the apparent failure of welfare systems in the affluent OECD countries to alleviate increasing levels of poverty by bringing about a radical redistribution of resources. The reason behind this failure lies in the attachment to trans-historical humanitarian projects by the architects of state welfare which are both elitist and utopian in equal measure. They are wedded to outdated modernist theories about the amelioration of social and human behaviour, seeking to impose on those at the bottom of the social hierarchy not only material resources but also social values relating to altruism, social solidarity and collectivism which mean little to people in the early 21st century. The crucial weakness of modernist conceptions of citizenship is that they are attached to the notion of the nation state and cannot accommodate social and cultural diversity.

## *Citizenship and the welfare state: the modernist view*

Too often the concept of citizenship is understood as relating narrowly to formal legal and political rights and obligations. The origins of citizenship are to be found in the formal principles defining political membership of cities and polities as part of the transcendence of feudalism. It specified the rights and duties incumbent upon the participants in the emerging polities seeking to ground their social and political arrangements in the principles of legality, plurality and publicity, particularly in the emergence of the 18th-century public sphere (see Cohen, 1982; Habermas, 1989). However, the emergence of the Keynesian welfare state, and the growth in what Marshall (1950) has called social rights, have necessitated that a broader sociological perspective be developed.

Turner (1993) assists us in broadening this view to embrace a more sociological perspective by focusing attention on the social practices which affect social membership of the community and society at large. We are encouraged, therefore, to view the phenomenon as an integral part of what constitutes social solidarity and social integration in welfare capitalist societies. The sociological perspective fashioned by Marshall (1950) was based in this broader view. Citizenship in its various forms grew with the process of nation building. As Turner has observed, the classical sociology of Durkheim, Weber and Toennies, as well as Parsons, to name but a few, concerned itself with the social effects of the twin forces of industrialisation and modernisation on the social structure. Durkheim's concern about *anomie* was framed in the problematic of what bonds individuals to their communities and society: his sociology was pre-eminently concerned with the social divisions and social conflicts brought about by the modern condition and the steps necessary to minimise their destructive impact. The solution to the *anomic state* of asocial individualism which modernisation creates through unregulated market forces and exploitative industrial practices is the discovery of civil association through participation in the varieties of organisations and social institutions which are intermediary between the individual and the state: in short, by embracing a sense of social citizenship. Durkheim's concern was with how individuals can acknowledge their social interdependence in the face of forces which destroy their *collective sentiments* and undermine their religious commitment in an increasingly modern and secular social order. Toennies too was interested in how social membership could be cemented in societies which were no longer grounded in tradition (see Nisbet, 1970). As Turner (1993) argues, classical sociology developed an implicit theory of citizenship before Marshall through the analysis of modernisation. Citizenship, therefore, can be understood as the development of universalistic social values in conflict with, and always seeking to transcend, the particularistic values of traditional feudal societies. Returning to Marshall's evolutionary account, citizenship rights grew out of the process of institutionalising the legal, political, and social gains won by those social groups and interests fighting to gain membership of welfare capitalist societies. The struggle for social citizenship can, therefore, be understood as an integral part of the Enlightenment project and served the purpose of protecting and embodying the basic principles of justice, equality and rationality in the social practices which defined membership of modern society. The attack on this modernist conception of citizenship has taken a number of forms, and I will identify and discuss them later in this chapter. However, a concept of citizenship which links it to the growth and ultimate destiny of the welfare state ideal has a growing number of defenders in contemporary society. A good example of this can be found in Twine (1994). Central to his analysis is the very interesting distinction between social rights and *civil opportunities*. Marshall's pioneering work on citizenship focused on guaranteed social rights of access to collective resources and support in times of need. However, it neglects the civil opportunity route to welfare. By highlighting the concept of civil opportunity Twine seeks to clarify a conceptual confusion in Marshall's work. It is clear that there can be no guaranteed *right* to employment or to own property. The most that can be expected is that social policies will be constructed which will maximise the *opportunities* available to citizens to gain secure employment or own their house. In order to clarify the issues, Twine (1994) draws on the work of Titmuss (1958) here. At the core of Titmuss' analysis is an appreciation of the varieties of ways in which citizens are assisted with welfare support beyond public state welfare. Fiscal measures, creating what have become known as tax expenditures, can provide incentives for people to buy things such as private health insurance, take on large mortgages or invest in personal equity plans through tax exemptions granted to them by the state. And occupational welfare provided by employers can augment the welfare resources available to those in employment by providing them with a range of services such as free private health insurance and contributory and non-contributory pension schemes, depending on their status and seniority. Crucially the fiscal and occupational route to welfare is based on what Sinfield (1986) has called the *employmentship*, rather than citizenship, access to welfare. The general movement in all OECD countries today is to place a significant emphasis on the civil opportunity route to welfare through occupational benefits supported decreasingly by fiscal measures. The precarious security for all in the post-Fordist economy means that reliance on this type of welfare will be fraught with personal dangers for those who either cannot gain secure employment or experience frequent or prolonged unemployment. Titmuss identified what he called 'socially constructed dependencies' which are created by the 'restructuring' of the economy and the welfare state. These social changes which wreak such havoc on individuals' lives are rooted in the fluctuations of the economy and the construction of social policies which reflect cultural assumptions about the lifecourse: the institution of retirement is a socially constructed status effectively excluding people from membership of the economically productive community. In order to defend people from such 'socially constructed dependencies' beyond the individual's control, a social rights access to welfare will always be more secure than a civil opportunity route. Twine's (1992 and 1994) comparative analysis of occupational pensions and the State Earnings Related Scheme underlines the importance of maintaining a strong social rights conception of citizenship:

> Central to the debate about citizenship must be a recognition of interdependence and a consequent concern for those members of society who bear the costs of social changes which are thought to be in the interests of society as a whole: what Titmuss earlier called 'socially constructed dependencies'... Significantly, pensions which are provided through the civil opportunity of a labour contract cannot incorporate social costs of social change. Indeed the reverse is true. Members of such schemes who bear the costs of unemployment will also bear the added cost of losing membership of their OPS (occupational pension scheme) and having their subsequent pension reduced. (Twine, 1992: 171)

The modernist approach to citizenship and welfare is, therefore, fundamentally based on a recognition that dependencies remain socially constructed and only a collective response to social need which democratises the risks that all citizens will inevitably encounter in the post-Fordist economy can ensure social integration.

## Citizenship in a liberal society: the anti-modernist view

I have argued that the essence of the anti-modern perspective on welfare and society is rooted in an essentialist or naturalist view of social and human behaviour. Modern welfare institutions, it is argued, go against the grain of human nature and therein lies their weakness. At the heart of this argument is the belief that coercion rather than spontaneity characterises the social integration or social cohesion of modern welfare societies. In advancing this argument, Saunders (1993) concentrates on what he refers to as the 'fallacy of misplaced concreteness': welfare states are not the expression of the values of care, compassion or, as Titmuss would have it, altruism, because welfare societies can only be *moral* to the extent that the individuals within society are moral. Morality is only authentically expressed if it is freely chosen. For example, Saunders illustrates his argument by alluding to the treatment of deviants: forced community service meted out to a juvenile offender does not constitute a moral choice freely chosen by the deviant entrapped within the criminal justice system. Compulsion is a necessary part of the 'treatment'. Similarly, Saunders (1993) observes 'welfare state services and benefits do not derive from revenues gathered as a result of the free choices of individuals, but are rather financed through compulsory taxation and levies' (p. 75). People support taxation for welfare services which benefit them, especially the education and health services, but remain largely unsupportive of benefits which do not, particularly benefits which might be given to people that they consider undeserving. The welfare state is not an expression of altruism, as Richard Titmuss and the modernists would have it, but merely an expression of self-interest. It is expediency rather than morality which drives welfare policy and the welfare state is, consequently, *amoral*. It follows from this line of argument that a concept of social citizenship cannot provide a basis for maintaining social integration unless it is founded on a recognition of the inherent nature of people, namely, that they tend to pursue self-interest and the interests of family before those of the community and society. The naturalist basis of this argumentation is evident.

The critique of Marshall's concept of citizenship offered by those on the right, such as Marsland (1996), Green (1993, 1996) and Saunders (1993), draws on the vocabulary of responsibilities and duties rather than social rights. Saunders asks, is social cohesion best achieved by allowing everyone to claim a right to support without regard for the circumstances giving rise to material need? The negative answer proffered by the right allows a moralising dimension to enter the debate: wilful neglect of family responsibilities and an unwillingness to engage in either work or the seeking of employment are just some of the reasons why access to welfare should be restricted and based on duty and responsibilities rather than rights. If there is a concept of citizenship emerging from this analysis it is one that is based, not on social membership, but on social contribution through labour. The American conception of citizenship established by the anti-welfare rhetoric of the 1980s and 90s is one which stresses 'citizenship as practice' (see Hill, 1992). Shared commitments to work and to bear responsibilities and obligations emerged as an alternative perspective to the 'liberal individualism concept of citizenship as status'. The evolution of 'workfare' policies and the weaker rhetoric of 'welfare to work' strategies in the UK are grounded in this more active definition.

## *Citizenship and fragmented culture: the postmodernist view*

As with social theory more generally, a coherent postmodern perspective on citizenship has still to be developed. What is clear is that postmodernism has provided a useful vantage point from where we can at least fire critical arrows at 'modernist' views of citizenship.

Using postmodernism as a critical perspective, we should start from the ethnocentric flaws commonly identified in Marshall's concept of citizenship. Turner (1993, 1994) points out that the route to modern citizenship has been different throughout the modern West. Marshall based his analysis almost exclusively on the British case. Citizenship in America and France has been established by struggles from below to secure rights. The German case is characterised by citizenship rights being handed down. In the case of the United States, the stress on securing civil rights through the country's highest courts has meant that social rights through the evolution of a European-style welfare state have been almost totally absent (see Fraser and Gordon, 1994). And, of course, with different national and cultural trajectories for modern citizenship we also have to recognise that the evolutionary order may be altered. As the American case clearly shows, civil citizenship dominates and has largely hampered the development of social citizenship. More fundamentally, a central inconsistency in Marshall's evolutionary account is the tendency to treat civil and political rights as being of the same order as social rights. The problem with this assumption is that the former can be, and historically have proved to be, compatible with the growth and well-being of the capitalist system. By contrast social rights have as their central purpose the defence of citizens against the demands of the capitalist system. Contemporary theorists of the welfare state such as Esping-Andersen (1990) have described this as securing the status of *decommodification* for citizens as workers by providing them with an income and range of welfare benefits sufficient to allow their economic survival outside the labour market while also acting to raise their reserve price as labourers. Civil rights were originally granted as a purely formal principle in which bearers of labour power and owners of property were to be treated as free agents of bourgeois society against the restrictions and status-bound hierarchies characterising the traditional feudal social order. The wholly formal nature of civil rights meant, of course, that workers could be exploited mercilessly because they lacked the other necessary rights to defend themselves. As already indicated, civil rights were established first to secure freedom of association and the right of workers to combine. Political rights followed by social rights transformed the purely formal nature of civil rights by giving the citizen substantive use powers, first by establishing political participation and then securing access to minimum standards of health care, education and material resources. It is the granting of powers to citizens who can resist the excesses of capitalist exploitation through the welfare state that creates internal contradictions within capitalism and undermines it from time to time. Citizenship within the modernist perspective can, of course, also be seen as being supportive of capitalism by integrating workers and those at the bottom of the social hierarchy into society. This is how both Marshall and Titmuss would view the evolution of social rights: social solidarity, they would argue, is secured by the expansion of the welfare state into the provision of universal welfare services. Social divisions and class conflict would thereafter be minimised and so, it could be argued, social rights are compatible with the maintenance of the capitalist social and economic order.

However, Ignatieff (1989) claims that 'the rhetoric of citizenship is used, not to understand market society but simply to express moral distaste for the vulgarity of market values' (p. 66). When typically the left has resorted to the vocabulary of citizenship as a weapon against capitalism it becomes what Ignatieff would call *moral narcissism*. In the contemporary period, when the certainties of the modern age are no longer available, the misuse of the ideal of citizenship hinders its future development. What postmodernism as a form of critique can bring to the analysis of citizenship and welfare is the necessary element of debunking. The pretensions of the modernist view can be exposed by addressing realities rather than dwelling on mythologies:

> The civic pact of the welfare state was not between 'haves' and 'have nots'. Not between care-givers and care receivers. The break with Poor Law principles was explicit and deliberate. The basis of a citizenship of entitlements was the insurance principle and universality of benefit: everyone contributed and everyone benefited. (Ignatieff, 1989: 71)

Ignatieff continues by stressing that the middle classes have always done better from a welfare system based on entitlements because they know better how to gain their rights than the poor and ill educated. The welfare state is not about caring but about entitlements: it is an expedient recognition of the complexities which bring about social interdependencies. The history of the welfare state is not a history of compassion but rather the realisation that private satisfactions depend on the existence of shared entitlements. Modern conservatism has been slow to acknowledge these facts and the modernist left has been so distracted by its moral narcissism that the task of building a genuinely postmodern vision of citizenship in postindustrial society has barely begun.

The building blocks of a postmodern concept of citizenship will begin with the awkward political reality that loyalties to the nation state are today mediated by strong local community and regional loyalties on one level and integration into, and tentative loyalties to, supra-national communities at another level. The movement for devolution within the United Kingdom alongside wider forces for European integration is the obvious example of this. The postmodern condition is one in which local narratives and the globalisation of social and cultural life will undermine the coherence of the Marshallian and Titmuss vision of social citizenship (see Falk, 1994; van Steenbergen, 1994).

Ellison (1997) acknowledges that citizenship and social and political identity in late modern societies are being subjected to forces which fragment rather than integrate the subject. The problem which arises through the simultaneous political movements towards devolution and globalisation is that who is identified as being a citizen becomes highly problematic. Citizenship as a source of solidarity among people with communal interests is problematic in the postmodern age because the differences between people are politicised: the attachment of citizenship rights only to the dominant race, culture and religion is challenged. As Ellison (1997) observes, 'while citizenship continues to be employed to convey a sense of inclusion, what it means to be *included* is now a highly contingent matter' (p. 709). Citizenship becomes fragmented into varieties which are used to negotiate 'social change and new identities'. Some groups will be adaptable to taking up and using new identities and claiming rights while others will not. The postmodern condition will therefore lead to unstable political solidarities which will change and may undermine the regularities and traditions which cement the social order and which social citizenship was constructed to secure. Postmodernism is defined by the fragmentation of culture and so the common integrative status associated with citizenship and national political institutions will necessarily appear to be inappropriate. Indeed, Turner (1994) suggests the possibility that citizenship in the sense that I have been discussing it here, drawing on the concept fashioned by Marshall, may well become a remnant of history. It may come to be acknowledged as relevant for the 20th century and the period when the nation state was supreme but less relevant when global and supra-national forms of political organisation play a larger and more significant part in postindustrial societies. This is an interesting issue and an excellent point of departure for the next chapter which asks whether there is evidence that all welfare systems are becoming alike. Are there factors which determine growth and change in welfare systems leading to standardising effects on all systems within the OECD group of nations? Is there evidence that the institution of state welfare may be in decline in the face of standardising global forces? In the next chapter we need to examine the forces which determine welfare state growth and change in order to gain a better understanding of how, or if, they are likely to develop in the future.

## Citizenship, welfare and the decline of social capital

By way of drawing this chapter to a close, I will return to the theme of what constitutes a welfare society in the context of the competing views on citizenship. One very interesting way of looking at this issue is to introduce the concept of *social capital* into the analysis (see Coleman, 1988a, 1988b). Social capital is a relatively new idea when compared with the more commonly used concepts of physical capital and human capital. The former refers to the physical and material resources which are combined to yield productive capacity, and the latter refers to the creation of skills and knowledge in people through education and training which can also be used to improve productive capacity. These concepts are variations on the more widely understood notion of capital in economic theory and analysis which conceptualises the productive uses of money to bring about or realise profitable commercial enterprises. Social capital in the economic and commercial context refers to the relations between economic actors and expresses the degree of 'trust' necessary to conduct commercial transactions. A sense of duty and obligation built up over time, and based on a strong sense of being able to rely on other people, describes the concept of social capital. The social norms and sanctions which form part of any social community provide the basis of social capital. Strong civil associations, a strong sense of solidarity, a strong sense of communal obligation, a strong sense of duty to others – these are the building blocks of social capital and, one would expect, of a welfare society based on social citizenship. The strength of social capital in late modern and postmodern conditions is, of course, a highly interesting and contestable issue. As we have seen, there are a variety of perspectives available on the desirability of a welfare state and social rights to welfare: while one perspective suggests that social capital is enhanced by the welfare state through the cultivation of altruism and the creation of a sense of solidarity within the community, others have argued that social capital is destroyed by the welfare state because it supplants the networks of social, family and community relations which are said to exist 'naturally'.

Civic integration is another way of talking about social capital and citizenship. The degree of social cohesion and solidarity in society at both a national and local level is a crucial issue. I will return to this theme in Chapters 4 and 5.

# 3

# Is the welfare state in decline?
# Identifying the determinants

A central feature of contemporary debate regarding the welfare state is the confusion about whether the trend towards a declining role for state welfare is inevitable or merely desirable. Is there a declining role for the state in the provision of welfare because of structural changes to post-industrial economies and postmodern societies which are generating needs which are markedly different from earlier periods, or is there a declining role for the welfare state because political interests in government and the economy have decided that there *ought* to be a declining role for collective provision? This difference of viewpoint has been mirrored for some time in academic disputation about what causes welfare systems to grow and, indeed, decline. In order to gain a critical perspective on the broader issue of whether the welfare state, as a key social institution in late modern societies, is in decline, I will review the ongoing debate about the determinants of welfare state growth within the OECD group of nations. It will become evident that the answer to this question depends very much upon which welfare state is being referred to. Through the comparative analysis of whole welfare systems, rather than isolated social policies, a number of different welfare *regimes* have been identified. The focus of this chapter will be on whether national and international movements in politics, economy and society are leading to standardising effects on Western welfare systems. In a preliminary way this chapter will prepare the ground for Chapter 8 which explicitly addresses the issue of whether international economic and political movements might be undermining national welfare programmes.

There is now a widespread recognition that what were once considered to be rather specialist approaches to social policy analysis called 'comparative and developmental methods' are now regarded as mainstream and essential tools for acquiring perspective, both historical and international, on national welfare debates. The danger of addressing the large question of whether the welfare state is in decline from a purely British perspective is that we might confuse what is particular to the United Kingdom with what is happening more generally throughout the OECD. In any case, an ethnocentric approach to welfare state analysis is unsustainable in an increasingly global world. In order to know how the welfare state might be changing we need to know where it came from in the more particular sense of identifying the variables which typically bring about change to welfare systems. We need to engage in the controversy about which determinants of welfare state growth are likely to be influential in the future and, very importantly, we need to use a comparative perspective to check whether we can expect all welfare systems within the global economy to change in similar ways. If a commitment to state welfare is in decline, is it uniformly so in all or just some OECD countries?

## Determinants of welfare state growth

Variables with causal influence on welfare state activity involve complex social, economic and political processes. Nevertheless, it is instructive to identify those factors which research has shown to be implicated in shaping welfare state performance.

First, it is necessary to be clear about what is being examined. Often research on welfare state growth concentrates on the expansion of core social services and the public expenditure which supports them. Such approaches have tended to suggest that welfare systems will inevitably converge. Historically, most OECD countries with the exception of the USA followed a very similar trajectory. The southern European, or Latin rim, countries followed a different path and are only now addressing welfare issues comparable with North Western European countries under the auspices of the European Union. However, if we ignore the late developers we can identify distinct phases of evolution. There was an introductory phase of social insurance provision, starting with Bismarck's nation-wide compulsory insurance schemes for sickness, accidents and old age pensions in Germany throughout the 1880s, and continuing in other European countries up to the start of the First World War. The Liberal reforms between 1906 and 1911 represent the British piece of what became a wider movement to provide welfare cover for working people based on the social insurance principle. Between the wars the range of schemes was extended to cover new risks, especially unemployment and occupational diseases and culminating with European-wide cover for unemployment risk by the start of the Second World War. A phase of completion between 1918 and the mid-1950s saw all Western European countries develop compulsory insurance schemes underwritten by the state and covering all main occupational and health risks (see Flora and Heidenheimer, 1981). The period through the 1960s to the very early 1970s can be characterised as the phase of consolidation: rapid expansion had slowed, with the exception of Sweden and the Netherlands, and debate turned to qualitative issues. The oil crisis of the early 1970s marked a period of instability in all welfare systems within the OECD group of nations. Indeed the oil crisis signalled the start of a period of reflection within the rich Western countries which, in the context of welfare policy, has been variously described in terms of periods or phases of *crisis, retrenchment* and *restructuring* as well as *decline*.

What seems to be clear is that during the first part of the 20th century most welfare systems developed along very similar lines. As all welfare systems appeared to be converging towards a profile which differed only in minor details, the answer to the question of what causes welfare states to grow was sought in functional theories which favoured explanations of growth in terms of large-scale economic and industrial processes common to all modernising societies. Modernisation theory appeared to provide an umbrella under which a series of variables relating to levels of economic and industrial development were used to explain the emergence and rapid expansion of welfare throughout the 20th century. I have already stressed that the very idea of a welfare state is rooted in Enlightenment ideas about progress and modernisation, and in essence, it is one of the best political and institutional expressions of modernity. The industrialisation thesis extended this way of seeing the welfare state to the explanation of its development and growth. However, the variety of national responses to the period of crisis and retrenchment after the mid-1970s has called into question the neatness of structural theories of welfare state development (explanations which concentrate on structural features of the economy and society such as levels of economic growth and demographic change which appear to shape social change independently of attempts by people and politics to direct them). The emergence of the 'politics counts' school, however, has raised the possibility that the variations in welfare state regimes are far greater than was previously acknowledged and should, perhaps, be explained by the divergence occurring in political cultures. This is the debate I will briefly examine.

## Size of GDP and the industrialism thesis

Structural theories of welfare state growth tend to draw on three main variables: demography, the age of the social security system, and, most importantly, levels of economic and industrial development. The underlying thesis being advanced is that modernising societies must deal with imperative social and political problems relating to the dislocation of populations as industrial activity shifts from rural to urban production. Welfare provision grows to meet the social needs created by the social changes wrought by industrialisation but can only exist and evolve if there is first sufficient surplus economic wealth generated to pay for non-productive purposes. Without a developed industrial base the wealth creation necessary to pay for a society's welfare would be absent. Primarily, the thesis adheres to a *class neutral* view of the state: the use of the state as an instrument of political and class interest which might influence the outcome of social policy is rejected as a significant explanatory factor. Politics is only acknowledged as a feature of routine electoral processes. The argument is advanced by isolating those variables which can act as indices for industrial and economic growth. First, the level of national wealth is typically measured by gross national product (GNP) (taking account of all national resources globally) and/or gross domestic product (GDP) (which measures wealth creation within the confines of the national economy). GDP or GNP, whichever measure is used, is taken as a predictor of levels of health and welfare provision because only comparatively rich societies can afford to pay for welfare through the accumulation of large surpluses of wealth which can be redirected for welfare purposes by state taxation. An alternative measure of this variable might be the per capita income of the population. Second, the ratio of urban populations to rural populations, often combined with data on the proportion of the population employed in industrial and manufacturing enterprises, is taken as a good forecaster of welfare state activity. Analyses of contemporary welfare state restructuring have built on these basic insights by including measures of long-term unemployment as a structural variable. Unemployment is treated as a structural variable in two ways: first, as part of that group of social problems causing social dislocation, and second, within mature welfare systems with established legal and moral obligations to cover the risk of redundancy, every increase in the numbers of the unemployed claiming welfare support leads to an inevitable increase in welfare expenditure beyond the direct control of political elites. It is considered to be politically, and indeed morally, difficult to cut welfare benefits which are underpinned by the principle of legal entitlement. It is the stress on factors which appear to generate growth in expenditure and social needs beyond the immediate or direct control of political and policy actors which the industrialisation thesis first emphasised.

*Demographic* variables are identified by factors such as fertility rates, especially when an explanation is being sought for the variation between countries regarding their commitment to family policies and family benefits, and the proportion of the population in a given country over the age of 65. This latter index is particularly relevant when analysis turns to what is being called the 'ageing time bomb': growth in pension and health budgets will, it is argued, be largely driven by the imbalance between young productive and old unproductive members of society in the mid-21st century rather than the political will of politicians and the welfare lobby. Growing national wealth appears to bring about increases in the lifespan, although affluence also appears to create its own unique patterns of morbidity. Old people live longer but develop more chronic health conditions and disabilities which require social expenditure whereas in earlier periods, when the average lifespan was very much shorter, people tended to die before their degenerative conditions manifested themselves and required medical or social care. It is, therefore, demography rather than politics which is important. This line of argument is reinforced when the age of a country's social security system is brought into the analysis. The longer a welfare system has been established, whatever the branch of welfare, the greater will be the number of rights and entitlements established over the years. Expectations about the provision of a social service will, therefore, be heavily influenced by the sense of permanence which the population believes to be attached to old and well established social services. Once a welfare service is introduced it becomes politically awkward to remove it, especially those services designed for the elderly. A built-in dynamic is inserted into the welfare system driving up budgets which individual politicians find difficult to control.

Comparative analysis of rich with poor countries will undoubtedly highlight the importance of levels of industrialism and national wealth for welfare programmes. There is a common sense logic in the industrialism thesis. However, when analysis turns to the comparative analysis of countries within the OECD group of nations then structural variables and the industrialisation thesis appear to lack explanatory power. If the differences between the USA and Western European welfare systems are to be explained then a broader set of explanatory variables are required.

## The politics counts thesis

The *openness of the economy* is a variable which has been cited as a possible contributory factor in the growth of Scandinavian and British welfare systems. Countries such as the United Kingdom and Sweden, with very open trading economies, have partly developed welfare systems to protect their home populations from the downturns in the trading cycle. Social services and welfare benefits are, therefore, treated as a protection against the vagaries of the international market and as a form of compensation for loss of employment and income. However, with this factor we are beginning to move into the realm of political decision making because there is nothing inevitable about responding to downturns in the international trade cycle by introducing welfare programmes. That is ultimately a matter of political will. Other variables often cited with a similar structural quality which nevertheless point to the importance of politics are trade union density and left party strength within a country's political set up. The correlation of strong leftist or democratic socialist parties with the growth of welfare programmes is well understood but the influence exerted by trades unions and left political parties has to be organised and mobilised. A political explanation is required.

The presence of corporatist institutions which bring the main bargaining interests representing government, employers and trade unions together to shape policy is frequently correlated with strong and, it should be added, stable welfare systems. Austria and Sweden are clear examples of countries in the recent past with strong welfare systems founded on corporatist bargaining institutions which seek to control and direct political interests towards what are perceived to be common societal goals. Strong ideological forces such as democratic socialism, Christian democracy and Catholicism, which have a strong place in Swedish and Austrian politics and society, have also been strongly associated with corporatist bargaining over welfare in countries such as Germany, the Netherlands, Denmark and Norway as well as the United Kingdom throughout the 1960s and 70s, particularly under the Labour governments of Wilson and Callaghan.

Explanations for the weak commitment to state welfare in the United States have been sought in the absence of these very ideological and political forces from the political landscape of America. The United States is regarded as a welfare state laggard, exemplified by the passing of the Personal Responsibility and Work Opportunity Act of 1996 and the abolition of Aid to Families with Dependent Children (AFDC) which have ushered in a system of workfare, benefit cuts and time limits on the receipt of welfare benefits. In general there has been an ideological resistance in the USA to European-type welfare programmes such as universal free health care and universal old age and family benefits. Indeed the political climate in the USA has been hostile to state intervention in all areas of social and economic life. This preference for privatism and self-reliance rather than collectivism and federal or state support has been explained by the absence of a working-class-based political party and politically inward looking trade unions which have historically been linked with organised crime rather than a society-wide left political movement. The fragmented federalist structure of American politics has also made it difficult for clear guarantees to be given that social problems and social needs will be met by governmental action. State rather than federal government determines welfare strategies. Political variables more commonly associated with the introduction of welfare programmes in the American context are of the expedient type. For example, the *political business cycle* can lead to the use of resources for welfare purposes as part of an electoral bribe prior to elections and *non-institutionalised political action* such as urban rioting, demonstrating and civil rights actions may lead to welfare reform. While it is clear these are factors to be found in the political competitions of all countries, they appear to be a particular feature of American politics, with the Watts riots in Los Angeles in 1961 frequently being correlated with the 'great society' initiatives of the 1960s' war on American poverty associated with the Kennedy and Johnson administrations (see Piven and Cloward, 1972: Part 3). It is the struggle for civil rights through the American legal system that has led to progress in social justice, so leading to what we referred to in Chapter 2 as *civil citizenship* rather than *social citizenship* (see Fraser and Gordon, 1994).

## State-centred approaches to welfare state development

A distinctive perspective on welfare state development has concentrated on the role played by what Lockhart (1984) has called *significant political elites* which he divides into *pre-eminent* and *lesser* types. His argument revolves around the differentiation of welfare state growth into distinct parts by focusing on three types of question: Who decides to initiate a social programme through their control over the timing and rationale for a particular social policy or bundle of social policies? Who influences or decides that there can be an incremental change to welfare benefits and decides what those changes will be? Who decides what global sums of public expenditure can be devoted to welfare purposes. In short, who decides what a nation's *welfare effort* will be? Lockhart's answer to these questions is that structural problems with economy, society and political legitimacy cause problems for pre-eminent political elites who have the power to initiate welfare programmes as a response to perceived problems. Once the programmes have become established, a broader range of lesser political elites make decisions about incremental changes to those already established programmes. This is an attempt to integrate the expenditure and 'politics counts' approaches by focusing on their interaction. Structural problems occurring in economy and society create a framework which limits the possible actions that can be taken but the policy agendas which are constructed to deal with those structural problems will always be a matter for politicians and senior civil servants. Support for this view can be found elsewhere. De Swaan argues:

> Social security was not the achievement of the organised working classes, nor the result of a capitalist conspiracy to pacify them... a class struggle was involved, but the familiar alliances were reversed... The initiative for compulsory, nation-wide and collective arrangements to insure workers against loss came from reformist politicians and administrators in charge of state bureaucracies. (De Swaan, 1988: 9)

Various other scholars of welfare state development have come to the same conclusion, that interest groups and organised social class action have been crucial in shaping the kinds of social policies that have evolved in Western societies but the significant role played by political elites and bureaucrats has been prematurely discounted. Social policy development has not been about the exercise of power but about the 'politics of learning' and 'the principal agency and location of this political learning process has been the public bureaucracy' (see Pierson, 1991: 98–101).

## Explaining differences in welfare regimes

Research in comparative social policy has tended, therefore, to divide between two distinct approaches: one concentrating on the measurement of welfare effort and the other seeking to analyse *welfare outcome*. The former tends to concentrate on the aggregate sums of public expenditure allocated for welfare purposes, which invariably means examining the comparative performance of welfare systems as measured by the GDP spent on key welfare services such as social security and health. The latter centres on the qualitative factors involved in the measurement of welfare services as well as on benefits accruing to people. John Stephens (1979), for instance, makes the distinction between approaches to research which draw on International Labour Organisation (ILO) data on what is known as the *social expenditure ratio*, or the total amount of GDP allocated for welfare benefits, and his own preference for using all civil public expenditure excluding military funding (CPE) in his analysis of welfare in Sweden. The importance of these distinctions lies in their differential explanatory usefulness. Measures of welfare effort, such as GDP or GNP, explain structural features of welfare systems connected with levels of unemployment, and the age and sex composition of the labour force. Welfare effort concentrates on the growth in social transfers which increase because of the ageing of the population and because there already exist legal, moral and social expectations that all governments, irrespective of their political complexion, will meet social needs caused by structural changes in the economy. By contrast measures of welfare outcome based on all CPE attempt to assess all the ways in which social welfare is provided, including services not normally calculated as welfare such as transport provision and environmental services. An excellent example of this approach can be found in the Swedish case of active labour market policies (ALMP).

Central to the Swedish conception of welfare is the view that there is a collective responsibility to intervene early to ensure the retention of *commodity* status for its citizens. In other words, the Swedish approach to welfare has reasoned that there is no better way to secure welfare than by pursuing a full employment policy which attempts to provide an income from employment for as many people as possible. If a full employment strategy should fail then the welfare state combines with active labour market intervention to maintain the highest level of buying power for its citizens as can be achieved by linking ALMP with a universal welfare state: laws on minimum wages, legislation affecting the bargaining power of unions as well as state intervention into labour markets to subsidise employment and provide sheltered employment for the disabled and educationally disadvantaged were all considered to be primary objectives of the Swedish welfare state throughout the 1970s and 80s. Universalism in welfare benefits and services were harnessed to ALMP to create a fairly unique conception of the welfare state which most other countries in Europe did not or could not emulate (see Korpi, 1980).

The distinctive focus on *outcomes* within the Swedish conception of welfare suggests that social policy is driven by active political and moral objectives. Research using CPE, modelled on the Scandinavian variant of welfare state, concentrates on welfare outcomes and has, therefore, tended to highlight the influence of politics and political mobilisation in the policy process. Research has tended to show that such political activities have a greater influence on social assistance and means tested benefits and, in general, are better at explaining the incremental growth of benefits already in existence than the global amounts of public expenditure allocated for welfare purposes. Politics matters, it appears, but only to some extent and in some ways (see Uusitalo, 1984; O'Connor and Brym, 1988; Pampel and Williamson, 1988).

Expenditure-oriented approaches to comparative analysis of welfare have been weak in demonstrating a relationship between spending levels and quality of benefits. For example, it is now widely acknowledged that the United States spends a much higher level of its GDP on health than any of the Western European countries, in fact 13.4 per cent in 1991 compared with the United Kingdom's 6.6 per cent, Sweden's 8.6 per cent and the Netherlands 8.2 per cent. The quality of health care in the United States, while at the frontiers of knowledge in some fields and for some people, is for the population as a whole very much inferior when compared with the nationalised and universal coverage of the typical European system. In excess of 30 million Americans own insufficient health insurance in a system based almost entirely on private insurance (see Hill, 1996). More generally it has been found that there is variation between countries with respect to matters such as the coverage of welfare schemes (or the proportion of the population covered by a particular benefit), income replacement ratios, with pension levels generally being higher in Scandinavia and continental Europe than in the United Kingdom, and the number of waiting days that must elapse before a benefit can be claimed. This last factor can also be related to the criteria of eligibility demanded by a welfare system which may be wider or narrower depending on the ideological complexion of the policy makers.

To a large extent research on comparative welfare patterns has been very revealing about the difference between the form and the content of the welfare state: the *form* of welfare system which has evolved in Western countries has, largely, been a product of industrialisation and demographic changes linked to the shift of populations from rural to urban settings and the increasing globalisation of economic and productive processes, the *content* of welfare programmes has reflected the political cultures, bargaining institutions and class structures of different countries. We can illustrate the emergence of differences between welfare systems by briefly exploring the subject of *models of welfare*.

## Models of welfare

Analysis of modern welfare systems has been advancing beyond the increasingly sterile debate about expenditure and politics in the past decade by collecting data on the determinants of welfare state growth and decline in order to identify and classify national welfare systems into distinct models of welfare. Richard Titmuss (1974) began the process of developing models of welfare by distinguishing between *institutional* systems founded on the principle of universalism and social citizenship and *residual* systems shaped by the market and, crucially, family and individual self-reliance. Other social scientists have built on this basic distinction in recent years (see Higgins, 1981; Mishra, 1984, 1990; Jones, 1985). Esping-Andersen (1990) has done more than most to reveal the theoretical usefulness of models of welfare for comparative analysis. His classification of welfare systems is based on their capacity to provide support for citizens outside of the market by the provision of access to health care, social security assistance and social housing. The principle measure of a welfare system is decommodification, taken from the Marxist notion of the commodity nature of labour power which must be exchanged in the market place in order to realise value. Systems which provide universal access to welfare benefits are described as measuring high on Esping-Andersen's decommodification scale. By contrast countries which rely on the market and have very low benefit levels, tight eligibility rules and means testing as the main mechanism for distributing welfare, score low on his decommodification scale. The data gathered to assemble the models of welfare for this analysis have been varied, drawing on both the welfare effort and welfare outcome traditions: the division of countries into liberal, conservative/corporatist and socialist/social democratic variants of welfare states follows from the empirical differences to be observed in how countries meet their welfare commitments. The liberal model is found in the USA, United Kingdom, Australia, New Zealand and Japan and is characterised by comparatively ungenerous replacement ratios, increasing use of means testing and long contribution records for eligibility. The conservative model is found in Austria, France, Germany, Italy and Belgium and is characterised by the strength of the work achievement and earnings-related principles for access to welfare rather than universalism. Catholicism and institutions of corporatist interest mediation between the main bargaining groups in society which simultaneously limits the role of the state in the organis-ation of welfare are also features of this model, although corporatist structures can also be found to be a feature of large welfare systems such as social democratic Sweden. The socialist or social democratic model is characterised by the principle of universal access, equality of provision between the social and occupational groups and a strong commitment to social citizenship and is found in Scandinavia, particularly Sweden, with residual elements of it remaining a feature of the United Kingdom. The exact fit of any country into any particular model is not possible. The United Kingdom and New Zealand cause most difficulty because they were once pioneers in welfare provision but throughout the 1980s in the United Kingdom and the 1990s in New Zealand there have been attempts to move their welfare systems from a socialist to a more liberal variant.

Castles and Mitchell (1992) move beyond this type of analysis and attempt, explicitly, to link what they call instruments, outcomes and poli-tics in the shaping of welfare regimes. By this they 'seek to explore the degree of fit between a simple partisanship model and typologies elabo-rated by combining both expenditure and welfare instruments' (Castles and Mitchell, 1992: 14). They therefore combine expenditure and polit-ical analyses to generate a configuration of welfare state regimes which is slightly different from, but nevertheless compatible with, those found in the work of Esping-Andersen and others. Their analysis is based on highlighting the significance of *benefit equality, income and profit taxation as a percentage of GDP* (taken as a proxy to measure the progressivity and redistributive potential of a nation's tax system) and *political configurations* (specifically the degree of non-right incumbency in government) for classifying welfare state regimes.

There is undoubtedly a correlation between the two main variables in the welfare debate, namely, high public expenditure and what Castles and Mitchell call a strong non-right hegemony in politics. Countries such as

Austria, Belgium, Denmark, Finland, Norway and, of course, Sweden have committed and continue to commit comparatively large proportions of GDP to welfare. They have experienced left political party strength over time combined with historically weak right-wing anti-welfare alliances. Countries with high benefit equality between social classes, high taxation levels based on progressivity and high social expenditure ratios also have strong left political parties and strong dense trade union membership. The fourfold typology generated from this work modifies that of Esping-Andersen slightly: the *liberal* variant consisting of Canada, France, Ireland, Switzerland and the USA is characterised by weak left party strength and low trade union density, although on some measures Canada is radical (taxation) and France is conservative (low benefit equality); the *conservative* variant of Germany, Italy and the Netherlands is characterised by a strong left party strength but weak trade union density and influence (Catholicism rather than left politics appears to flavour welfare provision in these countries); the *radical* variant of Australia, the United Kingdom and New Zealand combines high levels of benefit equality and progressivity in taxation with weak non-right incumbency. The *non-right hegemony* model of Scandinavia and Austria scores high on all three variables with high benefit equality, progressive taxation yielding a good redistributive potential and strong left political strength combined with very weak and fragmented right-wing political parties.

To return to the central issue of this chapter, the question of whether Western welfare states are in decline: it is clear that this is not a simple issue. There are complexities involved here because of the distinctive histories, political and cultural structures of countries, and, it should be emphasised, the variations in political will to support and develop a commitment to state welfare rather than market- and informally driven systems.

The really interesting issue that must be confronted in the closing section of this chapter concerns the changing nature of politics in late modern or postmodern societies. We have isolated the importance of political organisation and left party strength in determining the consolidation and growth of welfare systems in the advanced societies: in complex societies cultural and political factors will have more explanatory power than variables which explain the origins of welfare states in terms of their industrialisation trajectories. However, what is the nature of politics, and in particular, class politics in postmodern societies? The debate in the social sciences, especially sociology, in recent years has been about the decline of social class as an explanatory variable. Gender, ethnicity, age and *new social movements* with an interest in the environment and new ways of organising social and family life are increasingly acknowledged as important. What then of the traditional dynamics behind welfare state development?

## Postmodernity and the politics of welfare

The challenge being made to the defenders of state welfare today comes packaged in the form of both anti-modernist and postmodernist discourses. We have witnessed throughout the 1980s and 90s an increasingly strident call for welfare reform which has, by increments, shifted the political centre of gravity in all Western countries with large welfare systems to the right: markets, families and communities are no longer peripheral providers of care but are now considered to be pivotal sources of welfare as we enter the 21st century. Modernity is under attack on two fronts and Chapters 4 and 5 will return to the issue of whether the sources of care favoured by the right and the left can fulfil the role increasingly allocated to them by examining in turn the right-wing stress on self-reliance and the project of 'remoralising' society and the left-wing view which stresses collective values through communitarianism and the rediscovery of civil association. For the present, I wish to explore a little further the question of the political dynamics behind welfare state development. We have acknowledged that left political movements and left political parties have been very influential in creating and supporting welfare state development. However, as we move into the 21st century, the nature of politics and political organisations may have changed markedly, even when contrasted with the early 1990s. Class in contemporary politics may be a less significant influence on the policy process than it once was.

We have already acknowledged the impact of post-Fordism on the occupational structure. The social changes which have altered the industrial landscape and the principles underpinning economic activity in late modern societies have also transformed the social structure in Western societies. Traditional working-class communities have been dispersed as the decline of primary industries such as coal, steel and shipbuilding has led to their replacement by smaller industrial units located on green field retail and industrial parks adjacent to new housing developments. The transformation of the Chrysler car factory at Linwood in Scotland into a retail park containing a multi-screen cinema together with Asda,

McDonald's, Burger King and Pizza Hut, to name only a few of the new household names to occupy the site, is an excellent example of how the economic and industrial scene has changed in many parts of Europe and North America. High skilled permanent male jobs have been replaced with part-time low skilled and low wage insecure jobs mainly for young people and women. Meanwhile the middle classes continue to abandon the main metropolitan areas in search of a lifestyle free from urban congestion and crime as they use their education to obtain work in highly skilled technical jobs in small non-unionised enterprises in the new towns and green field industrial parks. This description might be rather truncated but in essence it conveys the general nature of economic and industrial change giving rise to the postindustrial society. I will return to these particular issues in Chapter 6. In Britain and the United States the long run decline of the manual working class has been notable. Ashley (1997) observes, for example, that in 1964 25.8 per cent of the workforce in the United States was employed in manufacturing declining to 19.6 per cent in 1982 and further to 18 per cent by 1992. In Britain the decline of the manual working class as a proportion of the population decreased from 41 per cent in 1984 to 33.8 per cent by 1992 (see Taylor-Gooby, 1997). In political terms these changes have caused the industrial working class to shrink and so the natural constituency for left political parties advocating pro-welfare state policies has also dwindled. Political sociologists have described the political consequences of these social changes in a variety of ways. The loss of support for traditional left parties, such as the British Labour Party, among traditional working class voters has been described in terms of *class dealignment*:

> Britain has demonstrably changed... from being a predominantly blue-collar society to a predominantly white-collar one making the pool of 'natural' labour voters shallower while simultaneously swelling the pool of 'natural' conservative voters. In 1964, the working class amounted to 51% of the electorate... In 1992 it had fallen to 35% (Heath *et al.*, 1994: 281)

In actuality what appears to have been happening throughout the developed capitalist economies has been the withering of the main forms of working-class organisation because of what Ashley (1997) prefers to describe as *deindustrialisation* of labour rather than *deproletarianisation* of the working class. It is labour that is being shed rather than production, because GDP remains comparatively high when the 1990s are compared with the 1980s. As the workforce is *deindustrialised* it loses its collective strength through the demise of the large and powerful industrial trade unions. In terms of the welfare state debate, what has been striking is the growing weakness of those social and political forces which have traditionally fought for welfare services:

> The decline in the absolute numbers of a relatively well-organised working class nonetheless has had a significant effect on national culture and on political structures within the nation state. But what has had the greatest overall impact in the developed capitalist economies is not so much the absolute fall in the numbers of industrial workers... as the weakening or dismantling of the political structure through which organised labour historically expressed itself.
> (Ashley, 1997: 138–9)

The changes described here appear to have led to further alterations in traditional attitudes and lifestyle choices. Consumption patterns have changed and the 'embourgeoisement thesis', which was popular in politics and sociology in the 1960s as an explanation for those industrial workers who adopted middle-class lifestyles and political attitudes at the height of the Fordist boom, is regaining popularity (Watt, 1997; Goldthorpe *et al.*, 1968–69). There has been a discernible shift in political attitudes resulting from the economic and social changes of the last three decades. First, some sections of the skilled and semi-skilled working class, especially those with marketable industrial skills which can procure reasonably secure employment, have tended to vote to the right and support anti-welfare policies designed to reform social services which were not perceived as being of benefit to them in their new status as mortgage holders and house owners. This issue is, however, complex because there appears to be popular support for some aspects of the welfare state, such as social insurance benefits, child benefit and the health service, but less support for those benefits which lie outside of the social insurance framework (see Taylor-Gooby, 1985a, 1985b; Papadakis, 1992). The success of the Thatcher governments of the 1980s can be partly explained by their success in winning the votes of natural Labour supporters among the securely employed skilled working class. Second, there appears to have been a movement towards postmaterialist values and new social movements organising around issues of gender, ethnicity, age and the environment and away from traditional class politics centred in the large industrial trade unions. This appears to be a feature of all Western countries. The tendency for labour markets to fragment and divide into core and peripheral sectors, with the former consisting of highly paid secure career jobs and the latter consisting of low waged semi- and unskilled work of a part-time nature which episodically feeds people into welfare dependency, has meant that the class structure in postindustrial societies has become more complex, especially in terms of reading off political attitudes.

Women, unskilled male workers, especially those over the age of fifty, ethnic minorities, lone parents, the disabled, the retired and those adhering to green values have tended to occupy the peripheral employment sector and form, overwhelmingly, the foundation of a claimant class in the modern welfare system. The politics of welfare in the postmodern age will, inevitably, revolve around the organisation of these disparate interests and the defence of their stake in society as the movement for reform gains momentum in the 21st century.

The politics of postmodernism is a politics of fragmented interests and lost legitimacy. The decline of the traditional working class organisations and industrial interests means that the modernist voice which defended the welfare state and struggled for its growth in the 20th century is weak against the anti-modernist and postmodernist critics currently seeking to 'reform' or 'restructure' it. On the one hand, the politics of the welfare state is about the middle classes and their stake in it. Should they pay for a welfare system through increased taxation which is predominantly for the benefit of others and, in any case, in the European and Antipodean contexts, should they derive universal benefits from a welfare state when they have high and secure incomes? And, on the other hand, it is about the integration of gender, ethnicity, age and postmaterialism as bases for uniting claimants in defence of welfare. In the absence of a unifying political interest and organisation how can the pro-welfare state voice be heard and be influential in the policy process? It is the growing diversity of political interests which appears to be a particular feature of postmodern politics. The discourses of markets and individualism confront the discourses of stakeholding and communitarianism as possible strategies through which the apparent excesses and shortcomings of the state welfare system can be reformed in the 21st century. Central to this entire political and policy process is how the idea of civil society should be interpreted and organised. This returns us to our main theme of how a welfare society is to be fashioned in the 21st century.

Postmodern societies will be faced with the problem of how they can include highly politicised, but largely unorganised, interests in the policy process while also setting limits on the state as a controlling force. A new consensus is emerging throughout the OECD countries around the theme of 'the mixed economy of welfare': this unanimity is based on the view that welfare is not primarily a responsibility of the state, and where collective provision has evolved it should be returned to the market, the family and the community. However, it is less than clear how justice and fairness can be secured in those Western countries with a colonial heritage which has bequeathed them societies of great cultural and social diversity unless there is a role for a strong interventionist state which can provide public goods when needs demand it. O'Sullivan (1993), writing about postmodern politics, asks if it is necessary to deconstruct and validate any and every difference in society, and if it is, how can legitimacy be established and chaos and despotism be avoided? In mature liberal democratic societies there are a variety of lobbies variously based on gender, ethnicity and age seeking to stake a claim for their piece of the welfare cake. However, moral choices have to be made about who gets hurt. This is particularly the case in welfare reform. Can a strong state be avoided? In attempting to address this problem, O'Sullivan (1993) suggests that political theorists with a postmodern tendency could do worse than take note of John Gray's (1988) comments on Hobbes. Strangely he characterises Hobbes as the first postmodern political theorist because in order to understand how a social and political order can be maintained he conceptualised a 'deconstructed' state of nature. He concluded that civil association backed by a strong political authority is the only way to ensure that a diversity of interests be accommodated. A postmodern polity with an attenuated state would be unable to deal with the chaos.

However, it is the acknowledgement of that authority which is at issue in the postmodern political competition. If the state must fulfil a reduced role in the field of welfare, and civil society or civil association must take on an increased role, then the foundations of a welfare society must be based primarily on having established rules of participation which facilitate an open and accessible civil society. O'Sullivan (1993), for example, argues that there are confusions about the nature of civil association which social and political theory must address if the state is to be replaced as the dominant source of authority in the field of welfare in the postmodern age. First, the gendered nature of civil society must be transcended. Women, particularly women who deviate from the familiastic model underpinning social and public policy by being divorced, lone parents or seeking collective solutions for their child care problems, must be included in public as well as private spheres of civil society. They need to have their voice legitimated. Second, those of the political left inspired by the enlightenment tradition, but hostile to *bourgeois* political institutions because they are invariably dominated by the interests of the capitalist economy (Gramsci, Habermas and Arato and Cohen are cited as tending towards this view), must accept that the idea of a civil society which is organised around 'an unending seminar about policy' may be inefficient in a complex society. The idea that policy can be determined by a process of democratic discourse in civil society is considered to be challenging but largely unworkable. Without the authority of law and the state how can any serious business be conducted? Third, the liberal right must also acknowledge that civil society cannot be reduced to the capitalist market. While 'an unending seminar about policy' is to be avoided there should be recognition by the right that the enlightenment tradition championed by Habermas, in which the public sphere is the location for reason, debate and education, is an important democratic check on secretive decision making and commercial dealings. Fourth, the idea of the minimal state may have established the principle that the state need not be the monopoly provider of welfare services, but how we organise our social services and meet our caring obligations are matters that must be subjected to a discursive rationality that is public and accountable. In Chapter 5 I will return to some of these themes in my discussion of communitarianism and associational democracy.

In the following chapter I intend to examine the argument that society has become 'de-moralised' and that a return to Victorian virtues is the best way to recover a sense of civil association and achieve the welfare society.

# 4

# Society in decline? Social virtues and social capital

As a reaction to what some conservative analysts perceive to be the value pluralism of the 1960s and 70s, the two decades ending the 20th century have seen the rise of a conservative critique of modernity. At the heart of this anti-modern critique is a rejection of what Novak (1995) has called 'vulgar relativism':

> Vulgar relativism is an invisible gas, odourless, deadly, that is now polluting every free society on earth. It is a gas that attacks the central nervous system of moral striving. This most perilous threat to the free society today is neither political nor economic. It is the poisonous, corrupting culture of relativism. (Novak, 1995: 19)

Novak also observes that we live in an age of 'arrogant gullibility': it is the variety of 'passionate beliefs' pursued today which troubles the anti-modernist. The value pluralism of late modernity means that the very notion of what constitutes 'truth' is also relativised and in place of moral certainties we have only nihilism which, he maintains, is the enemy of freedom:

> Freedom needs clean and healthful habits, sound families, common decencies, and the unafraid respect of one human for another. Freedom needs entire rain forests of little acts of virtue, tangled loyalties, fierce loves, undying commitments. Freedom needs particular institutions and these, in turn, need peoples of particular habits of heart. (Novak, 1995: 19–20)

This critique hits out at both the collectivist impulse underpinning welfare provision in modern society and the fragmentation of social institutions and belief systems which appears to be a characteristic of the emerging postmodern age. There are two inter-related dimensions: an attack on the welfare state idea, which has focused on the overly generous and profligate nature of welfare systems in the OECD, and the 'moral hazard' which such public munificence is claimed to have for work incentives, character and social behaviour. By way of setting the scene for the analysis being offered in this chapter, I will return again to the theme of competing conceptions of modernity and the welfare society which were discussed in Chapters 1 and 2. The conservative critique of welfare can be characterised as anti-modernist if we contrast it with what I believe is the important distinguishing feature of modernity.

Therborn (1995b) reminds us that the notion of the 'modern' emerged from the Latin word *modernus* which was used to distinguish the present in medieval times from antiquity. In the contemporary understanding of modernity, however, it is not the present which is important but the discovery of the *future* as something to be shaped, constructed and controlled. As has already been stated, it is the systematic application of science and technology to the understanding and control of society and nature which distinguishes modernity. The future is 'discovered' in the modern era as an 'open, unbuilt site never visited before, but a place reachable and constructible' (Therborn, 1995b: 126). The optimism of modernism is based on this forward looking gaze which retains confidence in a linear concept of progress and the belief that improvement in the human condition is, and will remain, possible. This emphasis on futures and linear progression is precisely what is lacking in both the anti-modern and postmodern perspectives. The failing confidence in the great 'isms' of modern society is what has led to the 'vulgar relativism' of the postmodern age: the nihilism and cynicism about which Novak despairs. I wish to restrict my observations to the anti-modern perspective on the welfare society at this point.

What I am choosing to call anti-modernism is clarified by Therborn's stress on the future orientation of modernity. The conservative critics of contemporary societies with strong welfare states view the present as a corruption of the *past*: as the end product of ill-advised departures from tried and tested practices, sound axioms and, as we shall see, social virtues. Stability is always preferred to that which is novel. In the field of social welfare, anti-modernists have a distrust of modern political constructions and policy interventions which appear to undermine the 'natural' order of things. For example, the transfer of responsibility for welfare from the family to professional practitioners, such as social workers, operating from within state bureaucracies is particularly disliked. The anti-modernist position is one which remains strong in contemporary politics, particularly in the libertarian and anti-welfare lobbies of American politics and the intellectual right in British social policy analysis. George (1998), for instance, has observed that just as governments of the right pursued expansionist welfare policies when the social democratic model was in the ascendancy from the 1950s until the early 1970s, governments of the left throughout Europe have pursued policies of containment and contraction since the 1980s. The political centre of gravity in welfare politics has moved rightwards so enhancing the apparent relevance of anti-modern themes in the contemporary welfare debate.

The foundation of this intellectual movement is the rediscovery of the Victorian conception of 'virtue' as a critical tool for censuring the relativism of social values in contemporary Western societies. In claiming a partial return to Victorian ethics in Anglo-American philosophy, a point on which I will retain a position of agnosticism, Himmelfarb (1995) quotes approvingly from liberal American philosopher Martha Nussbaum (1992). The following quote underlines the essence of the anti-modernist perspective which is said to characterise the contemporary critique of late modern societies:

> Anglo-American moral philosophy is turning from an ethics based on enlightenment ideals of universality to an ethics based on tradition and particularity; from an ethics based on principle to an ethics based on virtue; from an ethics dedicated to the elaboration of systematic theoretical justifications to an ethics suspicious of theory and respectful of local wisdom; from an ethics based on the isolated individual to an ethics based on affiliation and care; from an ahistorical detached ethics to an ethics rooted in the concreteness of history. (Nussbaum, 1992, quoted in Himmelfarb, 1995: 250–1)

What is sociologically interesting about this anti-modernist philosophical perspective is that at its core is the claim that an authentic vision of a 'welfare society' can be found. In contrast to the *anomic* state of late modernity, we are offered an appreciation of the 'virtues' which secured social harmony and mutual aid in Victorian times and which modern policy makers should and can learn from. At the centre of Himmelfarb's analysis is the view that Victorian 'virtues' were supremely dominant throughout the English-speaking world and where they were acknowledged there was also a recognition that self-help, self-interest and individualism were inextricably connected to a sense of duty and responsibility for family, community and the general interest. It is the failure to acknowledge this inheritance which, she argues, has led to the increase in incivility and to the *demoralisation of society*. What is distinctive about this analysis is that it uses the concept of 'moralisation' in a very particular way. For example, 19th-century philanthropy is often characterised as a mode of welfare intervention aimed towards 'remoralising' a subset of the poor, often referred to as the residuum or the dangerous classes (see Morris, 1994; Lewis, 1998). The thrust of the argument offered by Himmelfarb (1995) and Davies (1987) is that, in fact, Victorian society was very 'moral' and it is modern society that requires to be 'remoralised'. The full thesis should be examined.

## The demoralisation of society thesis

The notion of 'virtues' in Victorian times had a broader meaning than today. According to Himmelfarb (1995), who has provided the most articulate account of the demoralisation thesis, virtues in Victorian times relate to more or less fixed standards of behaviour which were commonly acknowledged even though they were often violated. The kinds of virtues that are being considered are wisdom, justice, temperance and courage as well as the Christian virtues of faith, hope and charity. In addition to these more widely recognised virtues, the Victorians added work, thrift, cleanliness and self-reliance to the list. The demoralisation thesis, therefore, points to the social and political embeddedness of these virtues in the social structure of 19th-century Victorian society as its grounding for an historical and comparative critique of the relativism which distinguishes postmodernity. It also decries the tendency to trivialise the Victorian concept of virtue by mutating its original meanings, reducing a sociologically interesting aspect of social cohesion 'to a prurient interest in sexual laxity'. Indeed on this particular issue Himmelfarb has an interesting point to make about the nature of Victorian society by reminding us that to focus singularly on the sexual dimension of the word 'virtue' leads us to the false view that it illuminates the Victorians' puritanical obsession with chastity and fidelity when in reality it points to a broader feature of 19th-century culture and social fabric. The central characteristic of Victorian 'virtues' was that they provided an explicit measure of prevailing social norms which all social classes acknowledged. The 'small morals' relating to manners, dress and conversation which shaped routine daily interaction built up to provide a framework within which all social encounters could be reliably regulated. An interesting interpretation is given to the supposed hypocrisy of Victorian times by Himmelfarb when she quotes La Rochefoucauld: 'Hypocrisy is the homage vice pays to virtue' (p. 23). She puts the point very clearly. 'The Victorians thought it no small virtue to maintain the appearance, the manners, of good conduct even while violating some moral principle, for in their demeanour they affirmed the legitimacy of the principle' (p. 23). The guilt-ridden angst suffered by the Victorian deviant was balanced by a censorious attitude to others' frailties.

The thesis being developed here is one in which morality in the form of 'social virtues' acts as a mechanism for binding the social order, even in the face of conspicuous differences in wealth, power and moral probity. Victorian society was very hierarchical yet it also appears to have been very orderly. Why this was so has, of course, led to academic debate at the level of social theory as well as social history (see Femia, 1981; van Krieken, 1992). Concepts such as 'moral hegemony', 'contradictory consciousness', 'false consciousness' and 'labour aristocracy' have all been applied by various Marxist analyses to explain the lack of revolutionary zeal within the bulk of the working class. These concepts point to the institutional and ideological mechanisms which work to secure the social order and undermine attempts to disrupt it. And it must be noted that the advocates of the demoralisation thesis overlook, or prematurely discard, the significance of social and economic power in maintaining adherence to the exaggerated social divisions which marked 19th-century industrialising societies. However, the contrary perspective, and the one favoured by the demoralisation thesis, is to reject such 'social control' theories as being condescending to the working class. Himmelfarb asks whether working people in Victorian times were gullible dupes or rational people? Her answer is that the Victorian working class itself used distinctions between 'rough' and 'respectable' members of the community and employed 'moral' rather than 'economic' criteria to create social distance from those who might be regarded as lacking 'social virtues'. The fundamental argument being advanced is that people from the bottom of the social hierarchy do not prefer to be drunk and work-shy rather than sober and industrious, and the Victorian working class was as *morally* robust as its middle and upper class counterparts. The whole of Victorian society was a *moral society* in which social virtues were acknowledged in everyday life and constantly used as a yardstick to measure appropriateness and deviance in social conduct. Respectability was a function of character and employability, especially for the labouring classes, and was dependent on the individual demonstrating that behaviour was consistent with 'good character'. Himmelfarb cites the example of workers who carried testimonies to their character from former employers with them wherever they travelled as a sign of their worthiness.

The social indicators of this respectability and social cohesion are, predictably, to be found in the crime statistics and the declining rate of illegitimacy in the latter half of the 19th century. With respect to the decline in the rate of crime, Himmelfarb observes that between 1857 and 1901 the rate of indictable offences declined by 50 per cent from 480 per 100,000 population to 250 per 100,000 population. And she underlines her argument that Victorian Britain was law abiding by stating that:

> The absolute numbers are even more graphic: with a population of 19 million in 1857, there were 92,000 crimes; with a population of 33 million in 1901, there were 81,000 crimes – 14 million more people and 11,000 fewer crimes. (Himmelfarb, 1995: 39)

The case on illegitimacy revolves around the view that the family anchored notions of respectability and social virtue. Respectability was, in other words, a family enterprise. First, there was a high degree of sexual licence in the 19th century but pre-marital pregnancy invariably led to marriage because there existed a strong sense of moral obligation for men to take responsibility for their progeny. This particular argument is one which is also used by Fukuyama (1997) to describe the more modern distinction between pre- and post-1960s sexual and moral behaviour. I will return to the contemporary version of this point later. Second, marriage problems and breakdown among the poorer sections of the community arose from irregular employment, drunkenness or ill health and premature death rather than extra-marital sexual encounters.

Social virtues were, therefore, a feature of all social classes and shaped behaviour, admittedly within a hierarchical and unjust social order, around notions of self-reliance, self-help and family and community responsibility for care. The upsurge in philanthropic assistance in the Victorian period was geared to augmenting rather than replacing this moral infrastructure of caring and sense of duty which resided primarily in the family. (The underlying assumption of the Victorian approach to welfare was that human beings were rational moral beings and that the social order was inextricably dependent on everyone acknowledging this.) The anti-modernist perspective suggests that contemporary Western societies have lost sight of this principal feature of 19th-century social structure, hence the assertion that modern societies are 'de-moralised' societies. In late modern societies there appears to be a worrying paradox: the more affluent a society becomes the more crime ridden and demoralised it becomes. Referring to the notion of a U-curve model of deviance to describe the fall and rise of crime, violence and illegitimacy between 1850 and the late 20th century (see Davies, 1987 on this point), Himmelfarb prefers to describe it by a different letter:

> The curve is actually more skewed than this image suggests. It might more accurately be described as a 'J-curve', for the height of deviancy in the nineteenth century was considerably lower than it is today – an illegitimacy ratio of 7 per cent in England in the mid-nineteenth century, compared with over 30 per cent toward the end of the twentieth; or a crime rate of about 500 per 100,000 population then compared with 10,000 now. (Himmelfarb, 1995: 234)

Despite the acceptance by the demoralisation school that there is, to some extent, a correlation between material conditions and rates of deviant behaviour, the central paradox remains for them that the largest upsurges in deviant behaviour from the 1960s onwards appear to correspond with periods of comparatively low unemployment and rising affluence.

Davies (1987) offers another version of the same basic thesis. He claims that many of the features which have stimulated debate and concern in contemporary society, such as rising levels of incivility, anti-social behaviour, rising levels of violent crime and rising levels of illegitimacy, can *only* be explained by a 'demoralisation' model. We are urged to judge the usefulness of theories and models in social science by their effectiveness in explaining the widest range of phenomena. Alternative theories of criminality and anti-social behaviour fail this basic test. For example, arguments which claim that there has not been a real rise in crime and incivility, but only the orchestration of a succession of *moral panics* to distract attention from a strategy of strengthening the state to better manage capitalism, are rejected. Davies may have a sound point when he protests that while increased levels of crime and anti-social behaviour may indeed have led to the expansion of the state apparatus, nevertheless it does not follow that the rises in the rates of criminality have been 'unreal' (see Kinsey, Lea and Young, 1986; Young and Matthews, 1992; Walklate, 1998 for a discussion of the realist debate in criminology). Further, social control and social class models which treat criminal and anti-social behaviour as being 'anti-hegemonic', or what Taylor, Walton and Young (1973) called pre-political action in their 'new criminology' of the early 1970s, must explain the internecine character of most contemporary crime in which working class and poor people rob one another. And finally, accounts of criminality in terms of the increased opportunities afforded to criminals by poor architecture and badly designed housing estates (see Felson, 1994 for an elaboration of this broader criminological theory) must also explain why the individuals concerned act in such an 'immoral' and anti-social way in response to those opportunities. Material disadvantage and crime may be correlated but not necessarily causally related. At the heart of Davies' (1987) analysis lies an epistemological premise that human beings have free will, are capable of making moral choices and are not wholly determined by social and structural forces outside their control. It is the tendency in modern society to deny personal responsibility, and accept too readily that human beings are not truly free but instead their actions are determined by biology, economics and the social and physical environment, which Davies considers has had a 'pernicious influence' on contemporary thinking. Without making the assumption that society is populated by 'moral beings', the case for 'remoralising' society is difficult to make. Free will is exercised in a social and material context, but people make choices within a culture which increasingly seems to be morally neutral. A moral community should promote moral and virtuous behaviour by developing institutions in civil society which support rather than undermine respect for persons, life and property.

Davies (1987) is able to draw on the same historical data used by Himmelfarb (see Gatrell, 1980; Gatrell and Hadden, 1972). The decline in criminality and incivility in the Victorian and Edwardian periods, when social change was rapid and social dislocation an ongoing problem for all social classes, is contrasted with conditions of affluence and security today which coincide with high levels of criminality and incivility (see Kinsey *et al.*, 1986; Young and Jones, 1986). Both Himmelfarb and Davies, therefore, provide the foundation for a critique of welfare which is distinguished by its stress on the 'de-moralisation' of society by social policies which undermine personal responsibility and the principle of mutual aid, especially after the First World War.

Moral progress, it would appear, does not automatically stem from material progress. Contemporary societies, it is argued, have lost sight of the importance of maintaining moral sanctions and incentives. They have developed a culture of 'moral neutrality' by divorcing the institution of welfare from the incentive to work and contribute to society. The liberal 'momentum' which has been a dominant characteristic of modernity has tended to undermine bourgeois ethics and, in particular, the bourgeois institutions which provide the substance of civil society, such as families, churches, voluntary associations and the like. An interesting counter to the 'demoralisation' perspective is alluded to by Tester (1997) in his analysis of Himmelfarb's thesis. In reference to the work of Bauman (1985), Tester points to the important distinction between *civilisation* and *culture* with a capital 'C'. Tester comments 'Civilisation is about pragmatic civility, but Culture is about what are taken to be the deeper, non-rational, aspects of what it means to be human' (p. 66). Civilisation identifies the unruly and pointless as harmful whereas Culture accepts them as expressions of humanity. Bauman argues that modernity is founded on principles of order quite different from those of traditionalism: modernity replaces the morality of virtues, discussed by Himmelfarb, with the rationalities of business, bureaucracy and markets. Demoralisation is the inevitable end product of the process of modernity: the 'moral neutralisation of the bulk of human conduct' (Bauman, 1990: 34). Perhaps a further note of clarification is called for here in relation to Margaret Thatcher's admiration for Victorian values and Gertrude Himmelfarb's admiration for Margaret Thatcher. The contradictions within the project of Thatcherism referred to in Chapter 1 are again highlighted by Bauman's observation that modernity replaces the morality of virtues with the morality of markets: Thatcherism was not libertarian in the sense that absolute market freedom was its essential core, it also contained strong elements of what I refer to later as 'old conservatism'. It is this contradictory tension which gave Margaret Thatcher her distinctiveness and which Himmelfarb found to be worthy of admiration.

A common theme in contemporary social policy analysis which can be found to accompany this historical line of argument is the growth of the 'contract culture'. This concept has been used to describe the transformation of relationships between the state and voluntary and charitable organisations on the one hand, and the changing character of voluntary effort on the other. Whelan (1996), for example, frames his critique of the welfare state in terms of the many ways it has acted to undermine the 'social virtues' of charity and voluntary aid giving characteristic of the 19th century. In place of the social infrastructures of mutual aid created by private citizens and innovative service provision by genuinely independent charitable organisations in the 19th century, today we have a system of government subcontracting to the voluntary aid system. The decline of civil society is hastened by this process. Indeed the type of osmosis between state and society brought about by the incorporation of private charities and voluntary organisations into the state-controlled welfare system appears to be a conspicuous feature of many contemporary European welfare systems accustomed to having a *strong* and centralised welfare role for the state. This was described in the introduction in reference to Kraemer's account of Dutch welfare state development (see Kraemer, 1966). In the British context, Whelan (1996) talks about the blurring of the boundaries between *civil society* and *political society* as voluntary organisations are increasingly reduced to nothing more than pressure groups fighting to win government grants and service provision contracts to survive. Whereas the charities and voluntary organisations of the Victorian and Edwardian periods relied on government to fill gaps in welfare assistance which they were unable to supply, today the reverse occurs: voluntary organisations are caught within a welfare system described as the 'mixed economy of welfare' distinguished by the state's attempt to withdraw from the field of direct provision in order to become the *enabling* authority. Consequently, social needs which are rights based and must be met by statutory guidelines, but which increasing numbers of governments are unwilling to resource from state funds, are being put out to tender. The voluntary organisations are, therefore, often cast in the role of supplicants rather than partners as they vie with each other for lucrative government contracts. Lewis (1993) has pointed to the possible implications of this trend. She remarks that there may be a tendency for the voluntary agencies to 'go where the money is' and this means, in some circumstances, abandoning or scaling down their important non-service provision. With reference to her own research into the practices of voluntary organisations she observes: 'In the case of the organisation running the day care contract, advocacy, innovation and research, which are set down by the national body as basic functions to be performed by all affiliated groups, were receiving relatively short shrift' (Lewis, 1993: 189–90). Loss of autonomy appears to be a particularly worrying aspect of the 'contract culture' for many voluntary organisations but also, crucially, their role within the communities in which they operate and the volunteers they attract may also be affected by the changing character of the organisations. This raises questions about the nature of civil society in the late modern period.

There are two main aspects to this issue. First, there has been a growing interest in what has been called the 'theory of social capital' which focuses attention on the bonds of trust and solidarity which form the cement of the social structure. Second, there has been a growing interest, mainly from within the conservative tradition of politics, in seeking ways to bolster the institutions of civil society against the pressures of modernity, including the welfare state. I will examine each issue in turn.

## The theory of social capital

For Himmelfarb, the Victorian and Edwardian periods in British history were distinguished by the reliability and trust evident in social relationships both at an interpersonal level and in the way commerce was transacted. The *social virtues* so admired by her constituted the foundation for a society based on *social capital*. It is the apparent absence of this intangible social resource which has led an increasing number of sociologists to begin to develop a more systematic appraisal of this phenomenon.

There is a sense in which the founding fathers of Western sociology such as Marx, Toennies, Weber, Durkheim and Simmel were all engaged in an enquiry into the changing nature of social capital. The central questions addressed by that intellectual tradition were fundamentally about social change and social cohesion. How is society possible? How is the social order maintained and transformed? Does modernity destroy the foundations of the social order?

The clearest description of the concept of social capital as it is being used in the contemporary analysis of family, community and welfare is provided by American sociologist James Coleman (1988a, 1988b). The theoretical problem addressed by Coleman is how to develop a coherent sociological perspective which can illuminate how interpersonal relationships between social actors and the general properties of social systems are connected: what makes the 'social virtues' described by Himmelfarb evolve into an intricate web of taken-for-granted expectations about behaviour upon which everyone could rely and which would provide a foundation for a social order with distinctive stable civic qualities? Sociology has tended to view the social actor's behaviour as being governed by norms, values and social rules about duty and obligation which are inculcated into the raw members of society by a process of socialisation. It is these normative structures which shape behaviour in given social contexts. By contrast, the economist is fond of treating the *economic* actor as someone who acts independently of such social influence, pursuing individual rather than collective interests in order to maximise their personal utility. Whereas sociology has from time to time lapsed into an over-socialised conception of the social actor, neo-classical economics and some political philosophies, such as contractarianism, utilitarianism and the natural rights tradition, have nonsensically ignored all social shaping of behaviour, an issue we will return to in the next chapter. The theory of social capital is situated in the theoretical space which attempts to resolve these problems by examining how networks of relationships between social actors can contain properties which can facilitate or hinder productive activity at the level of the social system. It accepts the principle that actors are rational and purposive but that purposiveness is always shaped by social contexts.

As described briefly at the end of Chapter 2, social capital is distinguished from both human capital and physical capital, which might also include financial capital in the form of money, bonds or shares. Physical capital relates to the assembled material and technological resources to be used for the production of wealth. Human capital relates to the individual property of the social actor who has acquired education and skills training to enhance her or his market value. Social capital, by contrast, inheres in the structure of relations between and among actors and is not possessed by any one person. The crucial distinction being made here is between the tangible nature of physical and human capital and the intangible nature of social capital. Coleman defines social capital by its function: its ability to be used as a resource which can be drawn on in a variety of social contexts. It makes visible the crucial importance of trustworthiness, obligations and expectations as resources which make stable social interaction possible in social encounters and commercial transactions. It allows social actors to realise their interests because it yields value which can be used in a variety of social and economic contexts. The excellent example used by Coleman (1988a) to illustrate the import of trust in building social capital is that of the wholesale diamond markets where it is common practice for one merchant to allow another to examine a bag of stones in 'private at his leisure' in the sure knowledge that inferior stones will not be substituted. These transactions are conducted without formal insurance. A slightly different way of understanding the workings of social capital would be to consider the case of crime control when it operates to censure undesirable behaviour. Braithwaite (1989) points to what he calls 'integrative shaming' of deviants within a community as the basis for a more enlightened approach to punishment. The more tightly knit the community, the greater the likelihood that the delinquent individual will be exposed to the disapproval of his or her neighbours and peers in ways that affect their self-concept. Embarrassment, shame, guilt and remorse are emotions which the delinquent only has when he values his inclusion within a community: the potential to mobilise community censure depends on the existence of social capital. I will illustrate this further later. To anticipate the analysis a little, a number of writers have argued that social capital has atrophied in late modern societies (see Putnam, 1995; and to a lesser extent Fukuyama, 1997). In order to assess that argument we need to know a little more about the nature of the phenomenon.

A central feature of social capital is that it is based on trust, reciprocity and the expectation that obligations held by people and parties will be repaid: Coleman describes obligations as 'credit slips'. Social communities founded on self-sufficiency also tend to be communities low on social capital. In hierarchical communities and families where an autocratic leader distributes favours by virtue of their concentrated power and resources, and can therefore forcibly oblige the recipients to return the favour at a later date, there will also be an abundance of 'credit slips' which the autocrat can 'call in' at any given moment. This would clearly be an example of social capital underpinned by the power and threat of enforcement characteristic, for example, of the Mafia. There has to be more than naked power and violence behind social capital. The thrust of Himmelfarb's analysis suggests that there has to be a degree of embeddedness of social values and norms in the community as well, perhaps combined with a need for reciprocal support. Where needs are met overwhelmingly by government welfare services we might expect social capital to be weakened. In the midst of affluence there is also likely to be little need for the help and assistance of others within a community. The notion of social virtues which prevailed in Victorian times articulated the sociological reality of people behaving 'honourably' because they had internalised the expectations of their culture and confronted daily the forbidding consequences of punitive and negative reactions from peers, family and community if they violated the taken-for-granted rules of the time. What was it about community life in Victorian and Edwardian society that facilitated effective normative constraints?

A particularly insightful aspect of Coleman's analysis is the attempt to sketch the shapes of social structures within which norms and obligations can be effective. Clearly, if the moral bind of public censure, or, indeed, publicly acclaimed approval, is to be expressed or made known to the social actor, then the structure of relationships which carry the social capital must facilitate this. The crucial concept here is what Coleman calls 'closure'. If norms are to shape behaviour internally then there must also be an effective normative and structural framework to influence behaviour externally, especially to mark out publicly and explicitly what Durkheim called the moral boundaries of society. What makes normative sanctions effective and underpins social capital is the 'closure' of social networks. Behaviour is more effectively sanctioned if social actors can combine together in a situation where all are known to each other. Social networks without 'closure' are less effective, and will experience weaker social capital if some of the social actors are unknown or are only peripherally or tangentially related to a community. The analysis is illustrated by Figures 4.1 and 4.2.

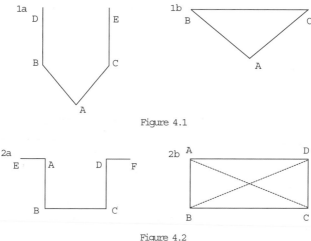

Figure 4.1

Figure 4.2

Social networks and social capital

Source: Adapted from James S. Coleman 'Social Capital in the Creation of Human Capital' American Journal of Sociology, 94 Supplement, 1988, S95–S120

In Figures 4.1a and 4.1b the idea of 'closure' is illustrated. In Figure 4.1a the letters represent social actors within a network. The point of the figure is to illustrate that actor A can affect B and C because A has a relationship with both, but if those relationships result in negative, harmful or annoying effects on B and C, they cannot combine to sanction A because they are unknown to each other. B and C have a relationship with D and E respectively but D and E are not known to each other and neither has a relationship with A. There may be individual encounters between B and A or C and A to exert influence but there can be no collective assembly of social capital to weigh against A. Figure 4.1b illustrates a network with closure where all three social actors have a relationship with each other and can combine to generate social capital to guide and shape behaviour. They can generate collective sanctions or communal approval and, crucially, build trust.

Figures 4.2a and 4.2b illustrate the same principles but in the context of what Coleman calls 'intergenerational closure'. The purpose of these examples is to outline the presence or absence of social capital in a family or school context. Figure 4.2a represents the relationship across generations by the vertical lines such that parent A is related to child B and parent D is related to child C. The two horizontal lines at the top of the figure represent two additional adults by the letters E and F, one known only to adult A and the other known only to adult D. Neither of the adults E or F knows the children B and C and adult D does not have a relationship with child B neither does adult A with child C because A and D are unknown to each other. Figure 4.2b seeks to illustrate intergenerational closure where the two adults A and D are known to each other and can discuss the children's behaviour together, so adding closure and 'come to some consensus about standards and about sanctions'. An aspect lacking from Coleman's figures, and a feature which I have added by inserting the broken diagonal lines, is the direct relationship between adult A and child C and adult D and child B. While the relationships represented by the broken diagonal lines are not as strong as the vertical lines, which we can interpret as parental, the broken diagonal lines finalise closure by creating a social situation where all adults are known to all children within a given community and would, therefore, act as influences on their behaviour. The relationship between a teacher and pupil or an adult in charge of a youth organisation within the community might be appropriate examples.

To conclude this part of the argument we can acknowledge that social capital can be conceptualised as a public good which is a necessary, if not sufficient, aspect of communal life facilitating civic engagement. The benefits of social capital are distributed throughout a network of relationships rather than experienced individualistically. The formation of concerted action within family, community, and in society more generally, is assisted by the presence of social capital without the necessity for already existing formal, public and bureaucratic channels through which that organised action can be expressed: individuals can effectively draw out of a bank of goodwill, certainty and trust that may have been established over time and know that they in turn will be called on to support and contribute to that bank of goodwill. Social capital emerges, therefore, out of the 'trustworthiness' buried in social structures which 'allow the proliferation of obligations and expectations' of support, or indeed censure. Coleman's discussion of 'appropriable organisations' as a further illustration of the central theme involved in the theory of social capital is instructive. It draws our attention to the notion of discovery of collective support and common interest that can occur in community or family life in the midst of a conflict or struggle. An ad hoc organisation of individual interests mobilised to deal with one issue may discover that the same grouping and organisation can be used, or appropriated, for others. Once the certitude in others' reliability has been established, a reservoir of trust and reliance can be used as the foundation for subsequent activity with a common purpose.

Woolcock (1998) and Fukuyama (1995, 1997) have extended the sociological interest in social capital through their analysis of economic development theory and, in Fukuyama's case, the changing structure of management forms in modern capitalist organisations. He argues that flat, or networked, forms of management which are increasingly common in newer technology fields facilitate more efficient and flexible work patterns because of the social capital which such organisational structures enhance. The downside of this, and the one which returns us to the demoralisation thesis and the critique of modernity, is that there are many areas of social and economic life which have experienced only the decline of social capital. Putnam (1995) has conjured up the sharpest imagery in the attempt to capture this idea when he writes about 'bowling alone': the decline of civic engagement has resulted in the privatisation and the individualisation of what were once social activities. The technological transformation of leisure through television, videos and now, increasingly, home computing connected to the internet is leading to a very introverted population increasingly moving towards withdrawal from the public sphere. The experience of life through simulation and second-hand experience is a common theme in the work of postmodern thinkers such as Jean Baudrillard (see Ashley, 1997; Městrović, 1997) and one that I will return to in Chapter 7 when its implications for welfare and caring are explored. Social and geographical mobility, demographic transformations such as fewer marriages, more divorces and fewer children and the decline of community-based enterprises have all contributed towards the attenuation of social capital, according to Putnam.

The focus on the changing structure of family relationships has been a particularly strong theme in the anti-modern critique of welfare and also in the theory of social capital. Coleman (1988a, 1988b) Putnam (1995) and Fukuyama (1997) in particular have pointed to what they see as a clear correlation between the growth in single parent households and the decline in social capital. The nature of their respective analyses differs slightly. Coleman (1988b) argues that the possession of human capital (education, skills and material resources) by parents can assist their children to do well educationally, especially if they devote time to building trusting relationships with them through shared educational and leisure experiences. Additionally, networking with significant others in the educational and occupational spheres can have major gains in terms of building family solidarity and enhancing career advancement. By contrast, Fukuyama locates his analysis in the more tendentious notion of 'the great disruption' resulting from the changing balance of power between men and women since the 1960s brought about by the discovery of the contraceptive pill and the improving ratio of female to male earnings. Increasingly women have been able to survive independently of men. The loss of masculine identity resulting from this development has, it is claimed, stimulated a sense of sexual irresponsibility and withdrawal from commitment to marriage and family life on the part of men. In short, social capital is destroyed by men who can no longer be *trusted* to support family life by marrying the women they impregnate. The widespread acceptance by everyone in society of male responsibility for pre-marital pregnancy prior to the 1960s meant that social capital was high and family life more secure (although Fukuyama acknowledges that obligation to marry occasionally needed to be enforced by the shotgun). Phillips (1999), writing in a similar vein, attacks trends in social policy which encourage welfare to work programmes which effectively coerce lone parents into the labour market consequently destroying the fragile social capital remaining in families without a male breadwinner. Fukuyama, perhaps more pragmatically, also sees social capital increasing in some areas, particularly, as already noted, in modern high technology industries with co-operative management structures. Putnam (1995) also observes that in one particular sense the decline of social capital has been good, namely, the fading of intolerance, discrimination and prejudice which are often features of overly close knit communities.

## Rebuilding social capital and the contradictions of anti-modernism

The conception of a welfare society which emerges from the anti-modern critique of the welfare state is one which looks backwards for its foundations to the orderly arrangements characteristic of Victorian civil society. A strong welfare society is one in which mutual aid, social virtues and strong communal bonds create the conditions for social capital to 'do its work' independently of bureaucratic state interference. It is to the institutions of civil society (the voluntary organisations, the churches, the charities, and the community-based self-help groups) that we are urged to look in order to find an alternative reality to state welfare. It is being claimed that caring and social support can thrive best if they emerge as an organic feature of social relations rather than as something orchestrated by professional welfare practitioners (see Robertson, 1988 for a brief discussion of the concept of 'organic' in this context). Green (1993, 1996) has conceptualised this idea as 'community without politics'. By this he means to convey the notion of a public sphere consisting of civil associations rather than corporate associations. A brief outline of his central arguments will help to clarify this.

What is termed 'the welfare problem' by Green is not a financial but a moral issue; a welfare system which is organised along collectivist state lines 'impairs human character'. It does this by undermining and eventually crowding out the tradition of mutual aid originating in Victorian times. Welfare state provision 'diminishes opportunities for us to be of service to each other' by encouraging dependence on statutory authorities rather than on family and community. The argument turns to the market both as a source of moral education and as the most effective mechanism for ensuring freedom. Adam Smith, who viewed liberty as a moral ideal, provides the intellectual grounding for Green's perspective. The habits of hard work, which Smith and other 18th-century philosophers and political economists believed could only be rewarded by an unencumbered liberal economy, must be combined with a compassionate and responsible attitude to fellow human beings. It was considered to be the social and moral duty of the well off to attend to the needs of the less fortunate, so long as those in need had also been accustomed to moral strivings to better themselves and society. In defending the central theme of liberty in relation to those 18th-century liberals such as David Hume, Josiah Tucker, Edmund Burke and Adam Smith, Green (1993) observes that the conception of *liberty* which prevailed was liberty under the law rather than the liberty of free abandon: 'It was liberty guided by conscience rather than naked wants' (p. 13). Corporate association is a concept which emanates from collectivism. Society divides into political elites and those willing to yield control of their welfare to those elites who direct policy and distribute 'resource rights' (the right of the *citizen* to make claims on the money of others through taxation). This hierarchical political arrangement releases the citizenry from cares, responsibilities and duties towards each other: 'the tendency of such doctrines is to weaken human character by diminishing opportunities for us to develop our skills and our virtues through direct participation in overcoming the hazards of life' (Green, 1996: xii). Civil association is rooted in non-political co-operation and assists in the building of mutual aid through the formation of social capital, although this is not a term Green uses.

There have been many concerns expressed about the decline of civil society, or the deficit of civil society, over the years. Knight and Stokes (1996) writing under the banner of the *Foundation for Civil Society* provide a quantitative audit of the main indices of civil society in contemporary Britain: churches, trade unions, charities and voluntary organisations, mutual aid, political participation both in voting and party membership and social networks. A brief summary of their findings indicates:

1.  The membership of the Church of England has declined from a peak of just under 4 million in 1930 to just under one and a half million in 1995. Other denominations within the Trinitarian tradition experienced similar declines, with the Catholic Church experiencing a 200,000 decline in the number of people attending mass between 1988 and 1995. There has been a slight increase in the congregations of the non-Trinitarian churches such as Jehovah's Witnesses, Mormons, Spiritualists and non-Christian faiths, but only slight.

2.  The percentage of union members among workplace employees has declined steadily from 50.6 per cent in 1976 to 33 per cent in 1995. Unionised jobs were falling four times faster than jobs in the economy as a whole. Knight and Stokes also point to the TUC's Affiliated Membership List for 1995 which shows that the number of member representatives has declined from just over 12 million in 1980 to just over 7 million in 1994.

3.  The data on the charities and voluntary organisations are mixed, with notable declines in membership of established organisations such as

the Scouts, the Boys' Brigade, the Guides and the Brownies. The Women's Institutes and the National Association of Round Tables have also witnessed their memberships decline. However, the membership of environmental and educational organisations such as Greenpeace, Friends of the Earth and the National Confederation of Parent Teacher Associations has increased. Formal carers have, of course, increased as a by-product of changing social policies, especially with the emergence of a 'contract culture' which has encouraged many caring charities to supplant services previously provided by the state. Informal carers, however, often perform their tasks unrecognised and with only rudimentary formal organisation.

4. Mutual aid went into 'steep decline' from 1945 onwards. The working-class organisations which combined to provide services such as burial clubs, deposit societies, mutual aid insurance schemes and building societies in the 19th century have all vanished as the state has taken over responsibility for these matters.

5. Political participation in voting and party membership is often taken as a measure of the vitality of democratic politics and a vibrant civil society. Turnout at local elections is very low, averaging about 43 to 44 per cent of the eligible population. General elections are averaging a turnout of just over 70 per cent and this is being interpreted as an indication of falling interest and trust in politics and politicians. Membership of political parties has been in decline since 1945. The Conservative Party has seen its membership fall from 2.8 million in 1952 to 400,000 in 1994. Labour Party membership has declined from 1.1 million in 1945 to 304,000 in 1994.

These trends are part of a general movement in the interests and priorities of the population as a whole. They are also taken as important indices of changing attitudes to activity within the space we call civil society. How this apparent public political malaise can be reversed does, of course, exercise the minds of all political groups. Green has a particular slant on this problem. The idea of depoliticising law making lies at the heart of his strategy to rebuild and *reinvent* civil society. The project amounts to a recovery of the social virtues and welfare practices of the 19th century, and for that reason I term it anti-modern. There is little in the way of engagement with the practical difficulties involved in the constitutional restructuring required to return the organs of civil society and the political institutions in contemporary Britain back to their pre-welfare state days. The main thrust of the analysis is to point disappointingly towards what many might recognise as a neo-liberal social policy agenda in which marketisation prevails where it is most profitable, the philanthropic ethos fills in where it is not and the statutory authorities wither to extinction in order to facilitate the burgeoning solidarity of communities untainted by political interference. Green's vision of a welfare society is one in which lone parents will be coerced into work and the unemployed, the disabled and the sick must rely either on private social insurance or, more likely, on the re-energised voluntary and charitable organisations which would be free of government grants and authentically free to offer aid on whatever basis the organisations' trustees chose.

A fundamental contradiction emerges from the anti-modernism of much conservative criticism of the welfare state: it attempts to run seamlessly together views which both celebrate capitalism and fundamentally distrust it at one and the same time. This results in an argument which seeks solutions for the problems of modernity by appealing to the very forces which have created them. The contradiction arises from the failure to confront the competing traditions and theoretical understandings of capitalism within conservative thought. For example, Giddens (1994) distinguishes between old conservatism, philosophical conservatism, neo-conservatism, in both European and North American formats, and neo-liberalism, again in European and North American variants. The anti-modern perspective on welfare contains elements of each type.

Old Conservatism is associated with the work of Louis de Bonald, Joseph Maistre and Edmund Burke. It is explicitly anti-modern in its wariness of rationalism and in its opposition to the Enlightenment. The stress upon harmony and tradition within this political paradigm can be contrasted with its sense of disorder which historically it associated with the twin revolutions. The French Revolution which transformed thinking about social and political relations and the Industrial Revolution which ushered in capitalism both undermined established institutions and patrician culture rooted in the aristocratic strata: parliaments and commerce disrupted traditional social structures. The bourgeoisie were perceived as enemies who were sullied by money and commerce with a particular penchant for novelty and change rather than tradition and stability. However, old conservatism relies upon the existence of a strong state to ensure the continuation of tradition and hierarchy. This is an aspect of its philosophical foundations which appears to have survived various attempts to 'modernise'. Philosophical conservatism rescues conservative thought from the inertia of tradition. It introduces an empirical theme into political thought. Traditions can be supported because they are tried and tested: it is knowledge that is 'saturated' with practice rather than knowledge which is abstract and untried that we are encouraged to seek and acknowledge. Giddens identifies Roger Scruton and Michael Oakeshott as two contemporary advocates of philosophical conservatism (see Oakeshott, 1962; Scruton, 1980). Oakeshott, in particular, argues that reason must always work from within a tradition: the tradition provides the social and political context which guides thinking and human action. Importantly, this variant of conservative thought eschews the unchanging and static forms of old conservatism. Politics is likened to a conversation in which movement and change are possible. However, the modern versions of conservative political thought increase the sense of contradiction and discontinuity with earlier paradigms.

What has been labelled neo-conservatism has found a more sociological form of expression and draws attention to the impact of modernity on the key institutions of society providing continuity and stability, especially the family and the main organisations of civil society. In its North American variant, Giddens claims that it comes from the old left 'free from nostalgia' which nevertheless wishes to protect and, where necessary, revive tradition in the face of the postmodern, postindustrial and post-Fordist onslaught. Daniel Bell (1973, 1979) observed that capitalism develops according to a secular puritan logic whereas culturally it is undermined by the 'imperative of pleasure' and consumption. The liberalism of the market flows over to impact on art, literature and sexuality. Moral individualism invades family life and in place of stability and continuity we experience self-gratification and *anomie*, which Durkheim first identified as a particular problem of the *abnormal forms of the division of labour* but which has come to be recognised as the condition of late modern or postmodern society. In Britain similar themes have been explored through the guise of what is known as 'ethical socialism' (see Halsey and Dennis, 1988; Halsey, 1996). The popularity of the 'ethical' version of socialism with the right may be an indication of its close affinity with American neo-conservatism, although it should be noted that Halsey (1996) and Young and Halsey (1995) do appear to retain their connection to left-of-centre politics. Neo-conservatism is against government and the state, except where it acts in its traditionally strong role of enforcing law and social order. The neo-liberal version of this perspective, which found political expression in the 1980s through the policies of Margaret Thatcher and Ronald Reagan, shifts the gaze again to argue that capitalism is not the problem but the solution. A strong state which enables and secures social and economic activity but is also minimalist regarding market interference provides the framework for the neo-liberal's conception of society. Moral decay is a strong theme and an emphasis on bolstering both patriarchal family life and the key voluntary and charitable organisations of civil society is seen as contributing immeasurably to rectifying this problem. Family life and family break-down are, of course, treated as being largely autonomous from the vagaries of the market: in the midst of the ebbs and flows of economic cycles but somehow not fundamentally affected by them.

## Concluding observation

Returning briefly to the theme of social capital, Edward Banfield (1958) undertook a study of Montegranesi in the south of Italy which is often cited as an exemplar of a society in which social capital is absent and the sense of civic culture very weak. The key concept identified by Banfield is that of *amoral familism*. The term describes a situation in which Banfield found southern Italians living their lives according to a principle of family centredness: maximising the short-run interests of the nuclear family and assuming that others would behave likewise. The absence of community projects, community facilities or community organisations was a feature of the region which Banfield was particularly struck by. He later extended this analysis to account for the decline of the American city (see Banfield 1970, 1974; Katz, 1989). The fundamental dilemma confronting contemporary policy makers, especially those of an anti-modern bent who are much taken with the notion that market forces can solve the anomic malaise of postmodern society, is that amoral familism rather than a vibrant civil society may be the end product. Anti-modernism has a very under-theorised understanding of social cohesion because it does not acknowledge, as Coleman clearly does, that social capital cannot be understood or built if the premise of policy making is that the actor is only motivated by individualism. (Durkheim understood this in the 19th century.) The normative frameworks of social action do not flow automatically from market processes, neither do they flow auto-matically from static traditions. They invariably require a more social grounding. It is with that problem that the next chapter deals.

# 5

# In search of community: communitarianism and stakeholder welfare

I concluded the last chapter by suggesting that the moral basis of society, in particular its welfare ethos, required a social grounding. The anti-modernist perspective discussed in Chapter 4 develops the claim that there is no contradiction between the free market founded on the liberty of the individual to act independently of collective and state interference and the emergence of a more responsible and caring society: after all, it is claimed that the Victorians created a society based on the free market which was industrious, productive and 'moral', both in its central values and norms and in its approach to welfare and caring. The so-called rediscovery of this idea in neo-liberal and neo-conservative political thought and policy throughout the 1980s and 90s in Britain and the United States succeeded in establishing a centre right hegemony within many of the OECD countries which shifted the political centre of gravity towards an anti-welfare stance, or at least to an acceptance of the mixed economy of welfare. In response to this the modernists of the centre left in contemporary times have been intent on finding an alternative and equally popular political theme for the start of the 21st century. The Clinton and Blair administrations have labelled this project a search for the 'third way' between the free market and state socialism. The concept itself has been stolen from the Swedish social democrats, and in particular their theoretical gurus Rudolf Meidner and Gosta Rehn (see Meidner, 1980; Rehn, 1984) who characterised the Scandinavian approach to welfare as a 'third way' between the command economies of Eastern Europe and the market capitalism of the Western nations in the post-Second World War years. The definition of what constitutes the 'third way' has had to be revised with the demise of East European communism. Now it appears to be centred on the concept of 'communitarianism' and the strengthening of civil society without necessarily abandoning a role for the state; stressing individual responsibility more and collective rights less (see Giddens, 1998).

I will return to the popular political meaning behind the 'communitarian' theme in contemporary politics and its association with the notion of stakeholder welfare later. I first want to explore the philosophical and sociological foundations of communitarianism which Etzioni has described as a contemporary social movement (see Etzioni, 1993). There are a number of intellectual roots to the current interest in communitarianism. Philosophers such as Michael Sandel, Alasdair MacIntyre, Charles Taylor and Michael Walzer have provided the most sophisticated discussion of the idea, mainly in the form of an attack on liberalism (see Mulhall and Swift, 1996). Sociologists such as Paul Hirst (1994, 1997), and perhaps at a less theoretical level, Amitai Etzioni (1993), have provided what amounts to a socio-political manifesto for postmodern society, raising important questions about collective life and the relationship between *statism* and *pluralism* in the postmodern age. The concept preferred by Hirst, and a number of other political theorists concerned about the current condition of the political institutions in the West, is *associative democracy* (see Cohen and Rogers, 1995). This idea has been examined explicitly in the welfare field by Hirst (1994) and Hoggett and Thompson (1998). The concept emerging from these analyses is of a welfare society based on a network of associational chambers and consociational councils. I will examine this notion later under the heading of associational democracy.

## Communitarianism and the critique of liberalism

The detail of the debate between communitarianism and liberalism in political philosophy need not detain us for too long. There are details in the debate between the communitarianism of Sandel, MacIntyre, Taylor and Walzer and the liberalism of Rawls regarding the nature of justice and the significance of the social which would prove to be too distracting for my purpose here. However, there are also important insights emerging from the philosophical exchanges which assist in clarifying what it is that drives the search for a more communal way of living in postmodernity. The contemporary reaction against neo-liberalism and the stress its advocates place on unfettered market forces is beginning to find expression in a call for a rediscovery of community. For example, the movement towards the devolution of power within the nation state and the European Union; of shifting control and accountability downwards to localities; and the creation of new levels of community awareness through increased participation in re-energised institutions within civil society could be interpreted as a desire to regain a sense of community. The unease about the globalisation forces also at work in the contemporary world is something I will return to in Chapter 8.

The most useful context within which to place the communitarian critique of liberalism is, therefore, as a reaction to the conservative and, in some forms, anti-modern analysis of society articulated by advocates of the free market. The arguments discussed in Chapter 4 for reinventing civil society and building 'social virtues' are based on the premise that only free market forces can provide the mechanism for securing social order and individual freedoms: the freedom of the individual is given priority over other social entities in the neo-liberal perspective. This view is rejected by those philosophers and sociologists who find the weight placed on individual freedom and market forces as a solution to the modern world's ills unconvincing. It neglects the fundamental social nature of people and their need to be gregarious.

## Philosophy and community

The communitarian critique of liberalism in philosophy, by people such as Sandel, MacIntyre, Walzer and Taylor, has been aimed primarily at John Rawls (see Mulhall and Swift, 1996). There are other representatives of the liberal tradition who are, perhaps, even more natural foes of the communitarian position than Rawls, such as Robert Nozick (1974), but the access which Rawls' notion of 'the original position' provides for those who wish to argue a more socially grounded case for justice and morality appears to be the preferred point of entry for the communitarian view in philosophy. The particular methodological issue which stimulated the critique was Rawls' use of the counterfactual device of the 'original position' which asks us to imagine what principles of justice would be agreed between people who were free and equal acting 'behind a veil of ignorance' (the clearest illustration of the *veil of ignorance* is that of a person who cuts a cake into scrupulously equal parts because they do not know in advance which piece they will get). This manner of proceeding is not uncommon in the liberal tradition of political philosophy and leads back to the notion of contracts within a 'state of nature' which was a

common mode of reasoning in the work of those social thinkers associated with the Age of Reason prior to the 19th century, such as Hobbes,
Locke and Rousseau. And in his *Theory of Moral Sentiments* published
in 1759, Adam Smith argued that the correct way to discern the morally
correct path was to posit the existence of a hypothetical impartial spec-
tator and then imagine what he would regard as the appropriate course to
take. It is the pre-eminent focus on individualism which such models of
reasoning lead to at the expense of factoring in an understanding of social
constructionism that communitarian thinkers have challenged. Rawls
appears to have moved towards the communitarian position in recent
years, and has acknowledged through his writing that many of the premises of his communitarian critics form background assumptions in his
thinking (see Rawls, 1993; Mulhall and Swift, 1996), nevertheless his
earlier seminal work *A Theory of Social Justice* (1971) remains a target
for those challenging the principles of liberalism in philosophy. In any
case, Rawls' acceptance of communitarian principles should be qualified.
For example, Frazer and Lacey (1993) point up an important distinction
drawn by Michael Sandel (1982) between *constitutive* communitarianism
and the weaker notions of *sentimental* and *instrumental* communitarianism. The stronger version of communitarianism which Sandel calls
*constitutive* treats the idea of community as a reality which is not
'optional': it is impossible to conceptualise an individual divorced from
the social values, culture and community practices which shape his or her
life. By contrast *sentimental* or *instrumental* communitarianism relates to
people's desire to further collective interests and promote common
purposes and values. These latter versions of the communitarian idea are
compatible with liberal philosophy. The construction of meaning and
identity through inter-subjective interaction is missing, therefore, in the
weaker versions. There are four dominant themes emerging from the
debate. I will briefly discuss each.

## Conception of the person

A recurring premise in liberalism is that of the freely autonomous individual who is born with all the essential characteristics defining their
humanity: the moral status of the person is not dependent on their embodiment in a matrix of social relationships and social institutions, they are,
in short, 'antecedently individuated'. Rational individuals are held to
enter into agreement with other rational individuals about the most desir-

able social and political arrangements to institutionalise, and to pursue goals and values that they, as pre-social beings, consider through their reason to be worth striving for. Communitarians, such as those I have mentioned, have great difficulty in accepting this concept of the 'disembodied self'. People are constituted by, are what they are because of, the social values, social institutions and cultural life which communal living creates. The priority given to the asocial individual by liberalism ignores the ontological, or material, reality that we live in communities with pre-existing meanings. From the start of our existence we are social beings whose lives are shaped by social relationships and, very importantly, socially constructed inequalities and injustices.

## Asocial individualist conception of society

As an extension to the theme already described, liberalism can be criticised from the communitarian perspective because it does not possess an adequate notion of the social order as something which Durkheim called *sui generas*, or separate from the sum of the individual parts which constitute it. Liberalism tends to accommodate to the idea of society by treating it as the by-product of contractual agreement: 'a co-operative venture for the pursuit of individual advantage' (Mulhall and Swift, 1996: 15). Society, within liberal theory, becomes reduced to a private association formed by individuals pursuing their selfish projects which from time to time require ad hoc co-operative arrangements. The contract is the source of this co-operative behaviour but communitarians would argue that people are attached to the *content* of values and social goals: social bonds are of value in themselves not just as a means to a selfish end.

## Universalism

One theme I touched on in Chapter 4 which I regard as a central aspect of the anti-modern view is that of *essentialism*: the treatment of human behaviour and people as the bearers of a human essence which makes all human beings the same. The idea of an unvarying human nature which can only be meaningfully supported by social, economic and political arrangements which go with the grain of that human nature predisposes conservative political thought, and much of the liberalism which fuels it, to regard its conclusions as *universally* applicable. Communitarians, however, insist on the appreciation of the cultural particularity of communities. Communitarianism is certainly more relativistic than liberalism and, it might be added, this suits it well as a philosophical remedy for the fragmenting and devolving tendencies which might be associated with the postmodern condition. The local and community social values and institutions will, therefore, be more influential in shaping the outlook, behaviour, and attachments to social institutions than broader loyalties and commitments.

## *Anti-perfectionism, neutrality and subjectivism*

The liberal stance on matters of social and public policy is that the state should not interfere unduly, if at all, in the expression of the individual's subjective preferences. It is, therefore, the job of the public authorities to remain neutral about matters of taste or morality which people express through their participation in the market place: the state should be anti-perfectionist with regard to a whole range of concerns which are, according to the logic of the liberal position, properly matters about which only individuals can make choices. This position obviously opposes the view that the state apparatus can be used as a non-neutral instrument to bring about social change and desired goals such as the redistribution of income and wealth, the provision of welfare for all regardless of income or the advocacy of public health policies. As indicated in the last chapter, there are real contradictions in the position adopted by the neo-liberal version of conservative thinking on the role of the state: anti-perfectionism regarding matters of market behaviour often conflict with perfectionist attitudes to family life, individual morality and sexuality. The 'strong state' aimed at controlling incivility and maintaining law and order can appear to contradict the neutral and anti-perfectionist stance regarding participation in the marketplace.

## Sociology and community

The foundations of sociology were also concerned with the tension between individualism and community, indeed Robert Nisbet identifies the concept of 'community' as one of the building blocks of the sociological tradition; initially more significant than the idea of society itself (Nisbet, 1970). Toennies' *Gemeinschaft und Gesellschaft, 1887* (see

Toennies, 1963), Le Play's *Les Ouvriers Européens, 1855* (see Herbertson, 1950) and Weber's *The City* (see Weber, 1958) are three examples of the way in which the community theme permeated 19th- and early 20th-century European sociology. The sociological issue in the 19th century was precisely to challenge the broad attack on *all* forms of community during the Age of Reason. The Enlightenment took its strength from its increasing success in challenging traditional forms of community: feudal remnants in the 18th century were the object of relentless intellectual hostility from the Philosophical Radicals, particularly Jeremy Bentham.

Durkheim's sociology can be understood as a reaction against the utilitarian thinking of his contemporaries and the 'individualist perspective of self, mind and personality', especially in the work of his chief critic Gabriel Tarde (see Nisbet, 1970: 95–7). The sociological tradition emerged to reinstate the importance of the concept of the social in the idea of community. However, in the work of Durkheim, we see the very contemporary concern about balance between the individual and the social which one might detect in attempts to pursue the idea of a 'third way' in modern politics. Strong (1995), for example, argues that the Enlightenment project rests on what she calls two 'intuitive premises': a principle of separateness, that all individuals have a distinctiveness which must be acknowledged, and a principle of togetherness which specifies 'that these differences are, in and of themselves, never morally adequate reasons for the domination of one person over another' (Strong, 1995: 70). Locating this insight in the debate between liberalism and communitarianism, she claims that we should see the principles as being in tension with each other, but a necessary tension which we must acknowledge. The danger is that those engaged in the debate have overlooked this insight leading to an unnecessary polarised exchange of views. For example, Nozick's version of liberalism maintains that the qualities we have as individuals are accidents and that the possessions that we have flow from those qualities so establishing our natural claim of entitlement; they make us what we are. By contrast, the communitarianism of Sandel and Taylor suggests that the qualities and possessions we have as individuals are the product of our embeddedness in a particular socio-historical tradition and our entitlement to those properties derives from our *collective* participation and social membership in it. Durkheim, however, understood the dilemma now facing modern political architects and policy makers well: the divide occurring between the interests of the individual and the social can, within the logic of his sociology, only lead to a weakening of social integration and the onset of *anomie*. This classic sociological idea draws our attention to the breakdown of balance between our sense of ourselves as social beings and our egoistic tendencies encouraged by a society which is hierarchical and based on unfettered market forces. The social bonding of the individual to his or her social group is destroyed by survival strategies which stress competition and the self rather than community, family and society. Modern industrial societies depend upon the emergence of both individuality *and* social co-operation because the mechanism for ensuring coherence is a social division of labour: the principles of *togetherness* and *separateness* identified by Strong (1995) are, therefore, both essential. Durkheim was concerned about the weakening of the institutions of civil society because they performed a crucial integrative function mediating between the state and the individual, binding the individual to the social group and society and protecting against pathological forms of social structure such as *egoism* and *anomie*.

This issue returns us to the very contemporary concern about what our society and its welfare future will be in the 21st century, in particular, how to reconcile principles of *universalism*, associated with the Beveridge welfare state, with the emerging *particularism* which seems to be a feature of postmodern advocates for radical restructuring of welfare, both on the right and the left. The anti-modern approach to this problem, which was discussed in the last chapter, looks backwards to the Victorian period in search of the principles and organisational structures which might provide an alternative script for living. That quest has offered us a future with a very much diminished role for the state, an enhanced role for the market and a plethora of friendly societies and organisations for mutual aid. The modernist view associated with the Beveridge–Keynes welfare state has difficulty conceiving of welfare other than in statist terms. Planning and bureaucratic delivery have been its key features throughout the post-Second World War period, and that is also true of the varieties of other European welfare states such as the French, Dutch and German systems which have grown since the 1960s. State or market appears to be the only choice considered in recent years for welfare reform. The concept of a 'third way' emerging today eschews the left–right framework within which that type of thinking is organised. Both the Beveridge welfare state based largely on the institutional model and the principle of universalism and the residual market-based system founded on *selectivism*, borrowing its moral economy from the Victorian system of philanthropy and self-help, are now considered by those attracted to communitarianism to be inappropriate for the new millennium. The diversities of social needs in contemporary Western societies mean that there must be a reconciliation in policy and social life between principles which until now have been treated as mutually exclusive: universalism and selectivism; communitarianism and particularism; individual and society; state and market provision.

## Postmodernity, universalism and particularism

Since 1997 the battle ground has shifted in the politics of welfare in Britain and Europe. The political conflict is now between the defenders of the welfare state idea shaped by a commitment to the enlightenment project of modernity and the champions of postmodernity inclined towards postmaterial values and a radical deconstructed conception of a welfare society. Central to an understanding of this politics is the modernist's defence of the principle of universalism in social policy in the face of their postmodern welfare state critics who argue the case for particularism in a context of growing social and cultural diversity in Western societies. At the start of the 21st century policy makers can no longer plan social policies as if they will meet some unspecified general human need. What this means is that social policies should reflect the reality of variance in ethnic, cultural, sexual and gender interests within nation states as well as supranational organisations such as the European Union, and respond with sensitivity to the *particular* social needs which disparate social groups express in a pluralist world.

In a sense what is being opened up for examination is the very notion of what constitutes *community*. The key welfare objective at the heart of modernity is to integrate excluded groups into a common national culture; a common national community. The poor and socially excluded are to be incorporated into society so that they can enjoy the same opportunities and, hopefully at some point, the same equalities of outcome that the more advantaged in society benefit from. The welfare state project is, therefore, an important instrument through which that key goal can be obtained. It presupposes a common, integrated, social entity in which the underlying rationale for a welfare state is to meet *universal* human needs (see Doyal and Gough, 1991). The suggestion that the underlying principles and rationale which have guided social policy, especially in the post-1945 period, must be re-examined is causing concern among those committed to a state collectivist or Fabian approach to welfare. Taylor-Gooby (1994) makes a strong case for resisting the critique of universalism issuing from the postmodern school. His concerns appear to be that in the fight to defeat poverty and injustice postmodernism will only succeed in undermining the state's necessary role as the co-ordinator of rational social policy planning: trends towards greater inequality and social exclusion in the 21st century are indicated in many OECD countries and strong concerted action by policy makers will be required to reverse their direction. Indeed there remain existent universal needs for improved health, better education and material well-being which may be obscured by theoretical movements which talk about diversity and particularism and so underestimate the scale of the effort required to overcome injustice in a society that is postindustrial, post-Fordist and postmodern. The implication of the modernist defence of state welfare is that no institutional arrangement other than a strong welfare state can design and manage such an important task.

However, the new 'reality' is that the social transformations which have been taking place in the industrial, occupational and community life of many Western societies appear to be creating social diversities and political fragmentation where there once was, or appeared to be, unity and consensus about how social policy should be fashioned. Questions have been raised by postmodern theory about the appropriate institutional and political structures required to deal with the social polarisation in society and, very importantly, the cultural pluralism which is demanding recognition. The suspicion is that the main objection to postmodern theory is that those rooted in the Fabian social administration tradition of social policy analysis have failed to acknowledge the new social conditions which postindustrial, post-Fordist and poststructuralist perspectives are attempting to describe. The ultimate test of any theoretical system is whether it can adequately grasp the changing economic and social landscape and identify possible policy responses.

The dispute about principles of social policy is merely another dimension of the broader debate between liberalism and communitarianism. The universalism which is a feature of the liberal position is often regarded as being opposed to the particularism favoured by communitarian theory. Thompson and Hoggett (1996) and Spicker (1994) provide a useful clarification of the debate. The underlying premise of their analyses is that there has to be some acceptance of universalism by communitarians and postmodern theorists of the welfare state: the respecting of social and cultural diversity and the right for communities and regions to take responsibility for the lives of their members, are universal principles, even if very basic ones. Without the acceptance that there have to be ground rules about what can and cannot be tolerated the unwelcome possibility would remain that racist, sexist and totalitarian tendencies could surface which would succeed in exacerbating divisions and diminishing everyone's freedom. However, the traditional defence of universalism by modernists and Fabian welfare state theorists must also be challenged. Thompson and Hoggett (1996) make a distinction between general universalism, which depends on 'procedural impartiality' to justify its operation, and specific universalism which compensates everyone for the negative impact of industrial change and socially constructed problems. Both positions should be criticised. The former principle allocates welfare goods without discretion, treating all applicants alike, and is stigmatising and insensitive to social and cultural difference; the latter principle assumes an imagined community which is invariably white, male, able bodied and heterosexual. In treating all members of a society or a community in the same way significant inequalities can be overlooked. Both forms of universalism are charged with being clumsy, remote, invariably bureaucratic and centralist and, ultimately, disempowering. Spicker (1994) and Thompson and Hoggett (1996) wish to reconcile the competing demands and contradictions which postmodernity poses for contemporary social policy. They would wish to see particularism, positive selectivism and universalism all contributing to a more humane and receptive social policy. While rejecting the means testing associated with selectivism there nonetheless can be a recognition of the importance of some measure of positive selectivism targeted on disadvantaged groups, if for no other reason than to promote a sense of inclusion within society. Spicker (1994) rightly observes that often our main responsibilities are particular for family, friends and community and are not universal. However, particularism must be exercised with attention given to its limits: its tendency to widen inequalities by generating divisions between in and out groups. The issue is whether we can conceive of a form of political organisation which can accommodate these conflicting demands. We can approach this problem in two ways: the first is to explore the theoretical dimensions of a democratic framework capable of dealing with the fragmentary social and political realities of a postmodern world, the second is to examine the concrete policy initiatives emanating from contemporary government. The notion of associational democracy will provide insight into the former and an examination of New Labour's policies on combating social exclusion will address the latter.

## Associational democracy and welfare

At the end of Chapter 1 I briefly described the project which Peter Leonard (1997) identified for an emancipatory postmodern welfare system. The condition of postmodernity which he draws attention to is, as we have noted, the fragmented character of social and cultural norms and the growing pluralism of social ideologies, identities and attachments. These changes appear to be a feature of all Western postindustrial societies. Within such a social environment it is no longer feasible to embrace a *statist* welfare system based on centralised planning and founded on a post-Second World War Beveridge understanding of universalism and social need. There has to be a recognition of the social and cultural pluralism which characterises contemporary Western societies. The racist, imperialist and ethnocentric principles which have governed the growth of most European welfare systems, especially regulations governing immigration and access to welfare support, have to be challenged in a postcolonial era when there is a growing movement towards supra-national integration (see Gordon, 1983; Jacobs, 1985; Gordon, 1986; Williams 1989). Leonard, therefore, wants to supplant centralised bureaucratic welfare by community-based systems which work from the bottom up. The dilemma for the postmodernist is, of course, how to reconcile social, cultural and ethnic diversity while also avoiding schism and conflict. The answer increasingly appears to be to recover a sense of community solidarity in the aftermath of free market fatigue, but one which does not jettison a pivotal role for the state. A key issue will be how the institutions of government are related to the institutions of public opinion formation.

### State and civil society

To reiterate a point made earlier, in reference to an observation made by John Gray (1988), O'Sullivan (1993) argues that in a context where there is a diversity of interests and conflicting parties within a political community, the answer to their pacification can be found in the work of Thomas Hobbes who, O'Sullivan unusually claims, was the first postmodern political theorist. Hobbes deconstructed the social and political order likely to be found in his imagined 'state of nature' and concluded that the only way to accommodate diversity in a stable social and political order was to build a model of civil association but one which acknowledged a common political authority or sovereign. In a more modern context Victor Perez-Diaz (1998) has advanced the same point regarding the varieties of theories about civil society that are currently circulating. He makes a distinction between 'maximalist' conceptions which cannot accept that civil society can operate independently of the state and 'minimalist' views which visualise a sphere of public political activity and civil association separate from the influence of the state. A number of social and political theorists including Durkheim (1964), Gramsci (see Femia, 1981: Chapter 2) and Habermas (1989) have articulated the 'minimalist' position. The concepts of civil society or public sphere which we identify with these major figures in sociology and political theory imply a strong sense of community and popular public participation in social and political life but the exact nature of the relationship between 'the public' and the state has been unclear and remains a perennial debating point in political theory. Habermas, Durkheim and Gramsci have, in their different ways, conceptualised civil society as an institutional complex which is set apart from the state. They view civil society as an institutional space for ideological struggle and resistance to state power. John Keane (1988) articulates the key idea. His vision of civil society is shaped in the context of a critique of the inflexibilities and bureaucracy of the Keynesian welfare state:

> Civil society... has the potential to become a non-state sphere comprising a plurality of public spheres – productive units, households, voluntary organisations and community-based services – which are legally guaranteed and self-organising. (Keane, 1988: 14)

The problem identified by O'Sullivan (1993) with this type of characterisation is that civil society may be conceptualised as 'an unending seminar on the nature of the public good, from which the reality of power is to be scrupulously excluded' (O'Sullivan, 1993: 39). In this regard, Habermas and Keane could be accused of lacking clarity about how the deliberations of civil society will influence policy and decision making. The danger of a politics which neglects the significance of power is a real one. The concept of civil society emanating from the right, and in particular the work of Green (1993, 1996), is one which is explicitly of a depoliticised space where state interference would be limited to the most abstract forms of legal regulation, mainly about behaviour, with only the minimalist legal constraints being placed on market activity by the state. Civil association in this version is almost entirely about the nourishing of self-help, mutualism and voluntarism rather than collective welfare provision. However, a 'maximalist' view of the state/civil society relationship would stress the continuing importance of the state as a source of funding, law making and organisation in a system of civic association. I think Hirst ultimately holds to this 'maximalist' view.

A good starting point to assess Hirst's (1994, 1997) advocacy of associational democracy is to recognise his sympathy for the project of seeking to reinvent or re-energise civil society or civil association articulated most clearly by Green (1993, 1996) and discussed in Chapter 4. However, it is the anti-modernism of Green's approach, looking backwards to the voluntary associations, mutualism and co-operative movements of Victorian Britain which Hirst objects to. He makes a number of observations which prepare the way for his substantive thesis. First, the Conservative perspective fails to acknowledge the scale of the problem. Economy and society are dominated by state bureaucracies and large multi-national private corporations which have marginalised voluntarism and mutualism relentlessly throughout the 20th century. Such large organisations are, according to Hirst, top down and managerialist. Second, and most importantly when considering the support of the right for voluntarism and mutualism, such movements were, historically, products of workers' struggles with reluctant employers and governments. It is with some irony that we now witness neo-liberal and neo-conservative interest in them. It was the failure of the labour movement and, in Britain, successive Labour governments, to nurture the friendly societies, the co-operative movement and the workers' mutual organisations in favour of centralised, nationalised and bureaucratised welfare which has resulted in the collapse of many key institutions of civil society. The labour movement's obsession with state welfare has systematically silenced those voices for decentralisation and pluralism. The consequence of this has been that the 'Labour Party largely threw away these assets, abandoning voluntarism for bureaucratic "modernity". The problem now is that the tradition represented by the friendly societies or the co-operative movement is more or less dead' (Hirst, 1997: 140). The right, of course, has been able to equate socialism with state collectivism and appropriate the voluntary idea as its own. A fundamental difference between Hirst's concept of associational democracy and the right's notion of a market-based society dominated by voluntary welfare, a community without politics, is the need for state supervision and public money to support the rebirth of organisations which were systematically destroyed throughout the 20th century.

## Associational democracy and a confederal welfare system

Associational democracy as advocated by Hirst (1994) effectively seeks to demonstrate the relevance of a 19th-century idea for the 21st century. The concept rests on the principle that the primary means of governance in the postmodern age should be through self-governing associations. There should be the devolution of the performance and administration of welfare services to publicly funded but constitutionally independent voluntary associations or bodies. Central to this model is the idea that the properties of markets, such as the right not to buy from one supplier and transfer to another, would be foundational for the workings of self-governing associations: in place of contracts and markets there would be a legal entitlement to *exit* from one association and join another but within an overall political structure based on state funding of welfare services. It is the notion that such freedom of choice for the individual can be secured in a non-market, community-based, and largely collectivist, system, which makes Hirst's model iconoclastic in the contemporary welfare debate. A key assertion by Hirst is that such a devolved system would not reduce social provision or lead to weaker political and economic governance. The objective would be to establish a manageable and accountable state but not an under-governed society. This would be achieved primarily by revitalising civil society and by the creation of what has been called a 'confederal welfare system'. The vision emerging is one that explicitly rails against the rigidities of right–left thinking about constitutional reform and ideological conflict. There would be a reversal of the key designation given to our political institutions: the state would be considered a secondary association, although remaining a very important institution, and the voluntary associations of the confederal welfare system would become primary associations. However:

> The public power in an associationalist system... would not be a marginal entity. While power should be as localised as possible... there must be a common public power. Such a power should be based on representative democratic principles, deriving its authority from a federal constitution that prescribes and limits its powers. (Hirst, 1994: 33)

Associations would require a common legal framework to set down common social standards and regulations governing the limits of their functions. But rather than substitute individualism for society and state, as we might envisage in a classical liberal theory of the state, associationalism in the form advocated by Hirst attempts to reconcile the tensions between individualism, collective responsibility and the need for a common political authority in a pluralist society. Communication about policy and decision making would be enhanced by devolving activities from the state to the associations, and, most importantly, by allowing the individual the right to join and leave the association at will: the right of *voice*, to express views about matters of policy and provision, and the right of exit, should the association fail to deliver adequate services, would be guaranteed.

There would be a division of responsibility and function between the federal, regional and municipal levels of governance, with taxation and macro-economic management remaining as a responsibility of the federal government. Welfare services would be organised, planned and delivered at the regional and municipal levels. Basic income and a range of welfare benefits would be distributed through the associations and based on the allocation of public funds determined at the level of federal government. However, Hirst acknowledges that there will have to be what he calls 'a residual bureaucratic collectivist system' funded out of taxation and 'top sliced' from the formula-based funds allocated to the associations to cover services such as private psychiatric practices and social workers' co-operatives. Individuals would register with an association of their choice and receive their welfare benefits from their chosen association. In addition to the right to join and exit from associations freely, citizens would be entitled to allocate up to 5 per cent of their tax payments to services or associations of their choice: the freedom of the market would be combined with collectivism and public funding in this model. Voluntary self-governing associations would be the main mechanism through which social services would be obtained in a postmodern society.

A number of substantive problems with the model can be identified. First, questions must be raised about the right of exit. In the case of people who are welfare dependent because they lack the material resources to survive independently of a self-governing welfare association, the right of exit would be purely nominal. Residents of sparsely populated rural areas may not have the range of choice enjoyed by urban dwellers. In such a situation the likelihood of monopolies emerging is a strong possibility. Citizens such as the frail elderly and the mentally ill suffering from physical and emotional difficulties may not be able to make judgements about their needs without advocacy assistance. Second, we must acknowledge an important distinction between a 'community of fate' into which people are born, such as a nation state, which can command loyalty from citizens in a fairly unique way by requiring them to die in war for an abstract national cause, and a 'community of choice' such as a self-governing association, which would find loyalty potentially fickle. The management of boundaries and the question of attachment and loyalties to an association rather than a state are key issues. Third, the exercise of the right of participants in the association to voice, or the right to influence policy by democratically articulating criticism, would remain a problem, as it is for all democratic processes. The contribution of the educated and informed professional classes to decision-making would inevitably dominate proceedings. And, fourth, and related to this issue, is the tendency towards particularism within self-governing associations: the hi-jacking of associations by those seeking to advance a partisan political and social agenda. This raises an important concern about what rules of inclusion or exclusion would be permitted. The phenomenon of NIMBYism (Not in My Back Yard) may be a by-product of imperfect democratic processes. The concept coined to describe this phenomenon is the 'mischief of factions'. This becomes a problem when a mechanism for encouraging community participation and empowerment succeeds only in exacerbating division and heightening social and political conflict. Hoggett and Thompson (1998), however, depart from Hirst on the degree to which such difficulties can or should be resolved by the state. Hirst's solutions ultimately lie in the residual legal, administrative and political powers retained by a federal government. For Hoggett and Thompson this would inevitably undermine the self-governing status of the system. Their claim is that administrative and legal interventions would be used when educative and political argument would be more in keeping with the system's ethos.

A final and brief note should be made about the apparent abstractness of the concept of *associational democracy*. There are elements of the Dutch welfare system which have echoes of associationalism. The Dutch *pillarised* structure of devolved service provision underpinned by state funding which operated between the 1930s and 60s was not dissimilar to the model outlined by Hirst. Founded on the principles of sphere sovereignty and subsidiarity (theological and liberal beliefs seeking to deny state authority over people's lives), the Dutch system has been able to handle the tension between principles of universalism and particularism in social welfare better than many other Western countries including Britain (see Cox, 1993; Engbersen *et al.*, 1993).

## Community and stakeholding in the contemporary politics of welfare

The arguments for some form of associational democracy could be detected in the British devolution debate. As Scotland begins to make its Parliament work and Wales its Assembly, the idea of creating a layer of devolved assemblies for the English regions becomes a strong possibility. A future decision to devolve responsibility for welfare to such regional assemblies and parliaments would make Hirst's ideas less abstract. He provides a clear alternative vision of what a genuinely welfare society might look like to that proposed from the anti-modern right by David Green.

In the British context, two 'big ideas' circulating prior to the 1997 General Election were 'communitarianism' and 'stakeholding'. In particular the ideas which Amitai Etzioni was advocating in his book *The Spirit of Community* (1993) were being grasped by the Labour Party as a useful political device to counteract almost two decades of free market celebration under successive Conservative administrations (see Etzioni in the *Sunday Times,* 9 October, 1994 and 19 March 1995; Phillips in the *Observer*, 24 July, 1994). And in an attempt to keep pace with the new orthodoxy, William Hague appears to be warming to the notion of 'civic conservatism' as a way to modernise the British Conservative Party in the wake of the Party's 1997 electoral defeat. The key axiom in this 'new' Conservative vision is that the institutions of civil society are *as important* for his political project as the releasing of unencumbered market forces. A similar set of ideas was, of course, discussed in the last chapter with an anti-modern twist (see Green, 1993, 1996). It remains to be seen whether British Conservatism can steer a course which can embrace a forward looking process of modernisation without succumbing to the lure of policies which are backward looking and anti-modern which has been its natural tendency in the past.

### New Labour, stakeholding and community

With respect to the Labour Party and the Labour government, the ideas of 'community' and 'stakeholding' are beginning to merge. The two ideas were bonded together in a variety of policy documents said to be influential in shaping New Labour's political thinking (see Field, 1996;

Radice, 1996; Hutton, 1997). In a book containing an introduction by Tony Blair and edited by one of his staunchest supporters, Giles Radice MP (see Radice, 1996), the two themes of 'community' and 'stakeholding' are clearly brought together. Tony Blair, before becoming Prime Minister, outlines the key themes and their meaning:

> I believe in a 'stakeholder economy' in which everyone has the opportunity to succeed and everyone the responsibility to contribute. It is based on the idea that unless we mobilise the efforts and talents of the whole population, we will fail to achieve our economic potential... A stakeholder economy is one in which opportunity is extended, merit rewarded and no group of individuals locked out. (Radice, 1996: 10–11)

The vocabulary implies another closely related theme, and one which is essential to underpin the theme of community, that of social inclusion. This concept is set off against social exclusion resulting from a lack of economic, educational and training opportunities for those at the bottom of the social hierarchy. Stakeholding and community are policy themes which are contrasted with the social polarisation linked to free market economics and the formation of an 'underclass'. The government's social exclusion unit established in 1997 is fundamentally about driving forward the 'inclusiveness' theme and ensuring that it permeates a wide range of policies, although it remains disinclined to pursue the policy strategy through a redistribution of scarce public resources. The rhetoric can also be found in the way New Labour talks about business. In a chapter discussing the reform of capitalism, Handy says:

> There should be a middle way. We should think of business not as a piece of property owned by someone but as a living *community* [my emphasis] in which all the members have rights... Companies are *communities of people* [my emphasis] united by common aspirations rather than a bundle of assets owned by shareholders... The case for the 'stakeholder' company, in which all the players have formal rights, is a powerful one. (Radice, 1996: 28)

The problems arise more clearly when the key ideas are translated into the context of welfare reform. The tensions which we have identified earlier between *individual* and *society* become evident because *stakeholding* seeks to combine in one concept the idea of everyone participating in welfare provision but doing so as individual owners rather than as welfare recipients of collective resources. In setting out the concept of 'stakeholder welfare', former Social Security Minister Frank Field comments:

> The scheme which I propose is based primarily on self-interest. You not only save for your own pension and pay into your own unemployment benefit but you also have a stake in how the system is run. (Radice, 1996: 145)

Elsewhere Field (1996, the *Sunday Times* 2 August 1998) talks about constructing a welfare system that 'goes with the grain of human nature' and acknowledges 'self-interest' as a human motivation. He also talks about the corrosive effects of welfare on social character. The Green Paper on welfare reform published on the 26 March 1998, *New Ambitions for Our Country, A New Contract for Welfare,* attempts to straddle the difficult line between a welfare strategy which assures people of support and the pooling of risk but explicitly shifts the burden of insuring against hardship back to individuals and away from the state. In the subtext of the Paper, the 'coercion' of lone parents and welfare dependants back to work is discernible and remains a major source of criticism of the proposals. The obvious conclusion here is that what Ferge (1997) has called the 'individualisation of welfare' has a greater priority in policy terms than the community. It is ownership of personal welfare capital which defines 'stakeholder welfare'. Despite the attempts to weld the communitarian and stakeholding themes together they appear, at least at the current state of policy development, to be antithetical to each other.

Page (1999) characterises New Labour's stakeholding policy as rooted in what could be called *endowment egalitarianism*: equality of opportunity through access to education and skills training for a highly volatile postindustrial employment market is stressed. Governments under this scheme no longer *guarantee* citizenship through the pursuit of egalitarian social policies but promote *the active society* through welfare to work strategies, a stance which is consistent with OECD and European Union approaches to welfare and employment as I have indicated elsewhere in the book. It is the era of *conditional citizenship* in which a willingness to work and contribute to society is the normative expectation imposed on those claiming benefit.

Catherine Jones Finer (1997) acknowledges that the meaning of the concept of stakeholding is fundamentally consensual in its origins: a society founded on 'shareholding' in which everyone should gain something from membership even if the shares are unequal. However its origins in 'Asian values' found in 'self-styled national corporations in Singapore and Japan' means that as a social principle it jars with European ideas about solidarity and collective security. It is the attempt to reconcile stakeholding and communitarianism through the social inclusion initiative which lies at the heart of the New Labour approach to welfare. The notion of stakeholding appears to have provided a subheading for the Labour government to demonstrate continuity with past Conservative social policies in the areas of education, social security, health care and social care (standards and league tables in education are refined rather than abandoned; the work ethic and the crusade against scroungers remain at the heart of the new deal social security policy; internal markets and self-governing trusts in the NHS are *adjusted* the better to meet the supposed needs of patients; and social care remains a defining policy area of what has become the new orthodoxy of welfare pluralism). In September 1998 the New Labour government published *Bringing Britain Together: A National Strategy for Neighbourhood Renewal*, describing the paper as pointing to a 'new deal for communities'. However, in reviewing the policy document Ginsburg (1999) perceptively observes that of the many reasons identified by the document as contributing to the collapse of poor neighbourhoods and communities, the impact of structural economic changes, the breakdown of family life and the rise in predatory crime are effectively dismissed as the focus for policy intervention in favour of attending to 'the fragmentation and critical gaps in urban programmes'. The stress is on revitalising and improving local management and government administration not on redistributive policies which are deemed to have been a failure.

The Labour government has, since 1997, failed to transcend the conservatism of its political predecessors. Despite the tag of 'new', the Labour government has been insufficiently modern. The version of communitarianism borrowed from Etzioni is what can best be described as 'moral communitarianism': it talks of responsibilities, duties and the need to reinvigorate civic association but the stress is upon social behaviour rather than material disadvantage. It is people changing rather than social structure changing which is on the agenda. Through a variety of policy initiatives it is the responsibility of the citizen to adopt a more civic-oriented stance regarding work, claiming welfare, supervision of children and the building of strong communities. And meanwhile the tendency to slip into an anti-modernism by evoking the imagined past of robust communal living and solidaristic neighbourhood support, as Blair and Straw's ethical socialism has a tendency to do, appears to inform the social policy of the 'third way' (see Hughes, 1996).

However, the main confusion in the Labour government's policy strategy revealed itself when the Chancellor, Gordon Brown, announced to a meeting of News International executives in Idaho in July 1998 that the left had concentrated too much on 'the good society' instead of the 'good economy'. Labour, he assured his audience, was committed to 'entrepreneurial values' and 'economic dynamism' (*Guardian*, 18 July 1998). Where does this leave the pursuit of community and welfare?

The question always remains when politicians turn their attentions to communities: whose community?

## Whose community?

A distinction has to be made between the postmodern acceptance of diverse communities and the modernist assumption of state collectivism which pursues the idea of 'one nation'; of a sense of national or regional identity through assimilation and, in its most worrying moments, of 'the people', as if society consisted of a homogeneous mass of like minded souls. The concept which best describes the 'new' Labour project in social policy is 'new realism'. Developed in the field of criminology, 'realism' purports to base policy on the method of the social survey: by asking and listening to 'the people' about what their experience has been and what they want to happen. It is fraught with difficulties because the authoritarian often mixes with a sense of community partic-ipation to produce illiberal yet populist social policies grounded in the notion of the government being responsive. The idea of 'critical communities' in which excluded groups such as homosexuals, ethnic minorities or radical environmentalists struggle for citizenship rights and against their marginalisation is largely overlooked in the 'new realism' of moral communitarianism. Universalism rather than particu-larism informs modernist social policy and its communitarian rhetoric. From such a position the 'deviant' communities must struggle to be 'included', often not on their own terms. What we may be witnessing in contemporary British politics at the start of the new millennium is a policy model best described by the roof metaphor I referred to in Chapter 1 (see Bagguley, 1994) to describe the condition of late moder-nity: social policies will contain elements of the modern, anti-modern and postmodern simultaneously like 'an imbrication of layers'. However, before consensus can genuinely be built the real deprivations of contemporary living must be addressed. The breakdown of community in the inner cities and peripheral housing estates often generates the call for a 'new realism' in policy. It is to the nature of that 'new realism' that the next chapter turns.

# 6

# When community breaks down: urban change, social exclusion and criminality

The most damning charge laid against the welfare state is that, despite the messianic claims made by its early liberal and social democratic prophets, it has failed to deliver a promised land in which poverty has been eliminated. It was the visibility of that failure as the 21st century approached which stimulated the anti-modern and postmodern critiques of the postwar welfare settlement. All advanced industrial countries have experienced problems relating to social cohesion and increasing criminality. One very important underlying cause of these problems today is the urban concentration of poverty and disadvantage in our major cities. This poverty has a discernible spatial form, typically occupying core or inner city and peripheral areas of the urban conurbation, which combines with social, economic and cultural factors to make social exclusion from mainstream society for the residents of these marginal areas a visible feature of contemporary urban life. When discussion turns to imagining the contours of a 'new' welfare society, urban policy, which has as its main focus the relationship between social and spatial forms within the built environment, must be a very important area of concern.

The rhetoric of communitarianism, in whatever political form it is offered, cannot disguise the reality that urban poverty and dilapidation provide poor conditions for residents of a neighbourhood to build a sense of community. There are competing analyses to explain why the inner cities and peripheral housing estates appear to have replaced traditional working-class solidarity with an internecine state of war characterised by criminality, incivility and a breakdown in community spirit. The anti-modernists from the political right tend to view the problem in behaviourist terms and, as we have discussed at various points in the analysis so far, blame a profligate welfare state for the destruction of social char-

120

acter and the incentive to work. An integral part of their critique is to blame the modernists, manifesting themselves as municipal socialists, for the misconceived social engineering associated with large-scale urban renewal programmes in the 1950s and 60s which, it is claimed, destroyed communities and built social problems into badly designed high rise blocks and crime ridden soulless social housing estates. Community spirit is palpably absent from our large urban centres. The interesting question is, why is this so? The underlying economic dynamic behind contemporary urban processes needs to be addressed. It may be conceded that ultimately individuals make choices about how they adapt to their living environment but in order to appreciate the nature of those choices we must first have some understanding of the structural conditions which shape social action. This chapter will examine the place of urbanisation in the process of shaping those choices and creating the conditions within which survival strategies which we might deem to be deviant nevertheless are a product of our changing economic and social structure.

The analysis being offered here focuses attention on the impact of post-Fordism on a number of interrelated aspects of urban living: first, the built environment, especially the *restructuring of space* within the large urban conurbation; second, the emergence of 'new' forms of urban poverty which are associated with these changes, particularly the processes and experiences of what has come to be labelled 'social exclusion'; and third, the changing *forms of survival* which appear to be part of the post-Fordist city, including changing forms of criminality.

## Post-Fordism and the city

A key to understanding the urban form of today in Western societies is to appreciate what Rosemary Mellor (1997) has called the major transitions in urbanisation: periods of decisive change in state–society relationships which fundamentally altered the nature of urban forms and governance. For our purposes we need dwell on only a few limited historical transitions. In Britain from approximately 1880 until 1920 the power of the rentier classes, the middle class or petite bourgeoisie who profited from the *laissez-faire* principles governing the property markets, was challenged by a host of political groups including the trade union and labour movement. This resulted in the creation of a new moral framework grounded in what Mellor (1997) calls 'family welfare urbanisation'. Public health reform, new standards for infant care and maternal responsibility and, crucially with respect to housing, the setting down of minimum standards for construction and occupation established a new welfare-oriented agenda for urbanisation which found expression in the growth of low density social housing and urban renewal policies in both the inter-war and the post-Second World War periods. The idea of a social economy underpinned by the rule of law in the public interest restricted the unbridled use and abuse of housing and town planning by the rentier class. As ideas about family welfare dominated thinking about urban policy, there was a drive to provide good quality and affordable housing for the poorest classes and a commitment by the state, through the authority of a reinvigorated local government, to invest in the urban form by constructing roadways, parks, town centres and theatres. An environment free of the rentier motive was established. However, the weaknesses of the British economy in the postwar period became evident during the 1960s and early 1970s giving rise to another major transition.

The movement from Fordism to post-Fordism in the period after the early 1970s has been described as an attempt to resolve the contradictions and tensions within welfare capitalist systems whose reliance on Keynesian economic theory and institutional welfare policies was discernibly failing. The goal of full employment associated with Fordism relied on a state commitment to demand-led public expenditure policies which came to be regarded as a brake on economic growth. In addition, industrial strife and an expanding welfare bill gave rise to what many identified as the classic visible symptom of a system in trouble, 'stagflation': inflation combined with low or even negative growth. The problem of welfare dependency increased throughout Europe in the 1970s and 80s for large numbers of the population, the majority of whom were male, as they were thrown out of work by declining primary manufacturing industries and experienced a slow absorption back into the labour market following the end of recessionary periods. An ongoing social and economic problem was stimulated by subsequent periods of economic restructuring, namely the persistent concern about 'social exclusion' and 'underclass' status for those unable, or unwilling, to re-enter the labour market for insecure, un-unionised employment in the burgeoning service and retail sectors at wage levels much lower than they had previously enjoyed in the old, male-dominated manufacturing sector. The post-Fordist order has several distinctive characteristics when compared with the Fordist regime which preceded it. Full employment is given a much lower priority in state economic policies and is displaced by a determination to enhance the nation's economic competitiveness in an increasingly global economy.

From this emerges a social and economic strategy to promote enterprise, innovation and flexibility among the population. It is UK PLC which becomes the central idea driving economic and public policy. Mellor (1997) observes that effectively the 'national interest' is redefined by the domination of non-national capital in the British economy, especially the 60–70 per cent dominance of manufacturing industry by the top one hundred companies, all of which are multinationals. The state comes to mediate between the external interests represented by the multinationals and its own population.

The change towards a more explicitly mixed economy of welfare by bringing in commercial and voluntary sources of provision has been seen as an example of how these changes have been working themselves out in the welfare sphere. As the economy relies less on large primary manufacturing industries such as shipbuilding, coal and steel, there is a shift towards service industries, small batch production rather than economies of scale and the growth in small and medium sized enterprises. The marketisation of state welfare provision can be interpreted as part of the process of 'hollowing out the state': described by post-Fordist theory as the shift of the costs and responsibility for welfare away from the state and into civil society. The expansion of female participation in the labour market in the post-Fordist era (approximately 50 per cent of the workforce) is combined with flexible work practices and a tendency for deunionisation. Again, we see these trends very clearly in the growth of the social care industry. However, perhaps one of the most visible signs of the post-Fordist changes can be seen in the urban and industrial landscapes of our major cities. The term 'post-Fordist city' is often used as shorthand to describe a range of changes transforming urban space. While I recognise that cities, like societies and cultures more generally, contain elements of the old, the new and the novel, the concept of 'the post-Fordist city' encapsulates the essence of contemporary urban life better than most other designations and will be used here.

## The post-Fordist city

The most immediate factor to note about the contemporary city is that compared with the various financial pathologies suffered in the 1970s and early 1980s, the post-Fordist city is presented as a healthy and vigorous centre for enterprise and leisure. Seldom do we hear about the fiscal crisis of the city (see Alcaly and Mermelstein, 1977), the loss of population and employment, the erosion of the tax base and the 'sump city' of poor and ill-educated households, although these problems have not vanished. What is more likely to be at the forefront of economic and local government publicity today is a celebration of the revival of the city centres, the growth of employment opportunities in the new green field industrial units within the city boundaries and the growth of the arts and leisure as a source of wealth, employment and enjoyment.

In contrast to what we have referred to as 'family welfare urbanisation', which rests on strong state support and a collectivist orientation to social and public policy, post-Fordism has as a primary principle the withdrawal of the state from active involvement in economic and regional development. The idea of 'local partnerships' between central and local government and commercial interests supplants proactive state intervention in urban change and planning. Private finance provides the necessary development capital and pursues projects in housing, community centres and other urban schemes in conjunction with public authorities. The role of local government, or development corporations formerly state managed but now likely to be independent agencies, is to ensure that the city is transformed in ways desired by private capital but kept in line with general urban policy guidelines. In reference to the transformation of Manchester into a desirable post-Fordist city, Mellor (1997) observes that:

> In the cycle of property investment the moment has come for reclamation of previously developed land and buildings: a rent-gap has opened between potential, or speculative, values and the values conferred by previous use. The role of the state agencies has been to facilitate a transition which will further the restructuring of the regional economy which led to the demise of the archaic city. (Mellor, 1997: 65)

The interesting political feature of the reorganisation of urban management and policy making is that the state is no longer directly responsible for urban and regional development. It is its partnership with the private sector and accommodation to the market which now drive public policy. The result is that the family welfare model is compromised, if not entirely jettisoned.

The development of the post-Fordist city is uneven. The effects of postindustrial change leave some areas of the city suffering from decline as the old manufacturing industries give way to the new, cleaner, service and high technology enterprises (see Turok and Edge, 1999). The city centres become spaces for regeneration as the old built fabric is bulldozed to make way for shopping malls, conference delegates, tourists and affluent consumers. For example, the canals of Birmingham and Manchester are transformed into areas where restaurants and pubs can be located to support the growth in the arts and leisure facilities being built. However, in some towns the centre and periphery become entangled in a commercial war as national retail outlets relocate to out-of-town green field shopping centres and the city centres begin to decay through a loss of commercial activity (although, with the opening of the £600 million Trafford Centre in Manchester in September 1998, the expectation is that such developments will no longer be permitted in Britain in the future). The preparation for these changes took place in the 1950s and 60s when major urban renewal programmes transferred the populations of inner city working-class areas close to the old disappearing manufacturing industries to the outskirts in green field social housing estates. Those that remained in the inner city became entrenched in a built fabric which was in need of renewal, but for as long as it continued in poor repair it could provide a home for those unable to escape its grim boundaries and a source of cheap housing for immigrants (see Power and Mumford, 1999). Race has to be added to poverty as a problem which has taken on a distinctive spatial form, especially in the United States. Residues of the leftover industrial dereliction which are deemed to be of cultural interest in the now unused industrial landscapes may be reclaimed either for exclusive housing or for heritage parks for the leisure and tourist industry. London's dockland is a prime example of redevelopment illustrating the former. Wigan Pier and the 1980s' garden festivals in Glasgow and Stoke on sites formerly used as docks and steel works are good examples of the latter within the United Kingdom.

The globalisation of markets and enterprises creates a competitive situation in all countries in which city regions in one country compete with similar city regions in others. Cities compete for investment, for the right to host prestigious conferences or sporting events and for the location of major branch and manufacturing plants. The mobilisation of assets to compete effectively in this competitive international market means that all cities reallocate their scarce resources to present the best face to the world. As some cities, regions and towns benefit from success in this race to secure inward investment, others fail. Development is not only uneven but can lead to major disparities in income, wealth and future prospects. What is distinctive and new about the post-Fordist city is the marked polarisation which occurs between the winners and the losers.

## The dual city or the quartered city

The most expressive concept to emerge in urban sociology to describe the growing disparities in wealth and well-being associated with modern urbanisation was that of the 'dual city' or the divided city (see Mollenkopf and Castells, 1991). The notion of towns and cities having rich and poor areas is not new, and a number of commentators on urban affairs have questioned the value of using terminology which tends to oversimplify a complex pattern (see Marcuse, 1989, 1993; Mooney and Danson, 1997). Nevertheless, the value of the concept lies in its concentration on social polarisation within urban space, indeed on the marked variations between regions, cities and towns and, crucially, areas within cities and towns which appear to have grown along with postindustrialism. Marcuse (1989) recognises that with two exceptions, the European quarters in the colonies of the Third World and black and white cities in apartheid South Africa, there are few historical examples where a city can be depicted in such literal terms, but he also acknowledges the initial value of describing the post-Fordist city as a 'dual city'. Therefore, before prematurely dismissing the idea of a 'dual city', we should investigate examples of urban forms today where the description appears to illuminate at least one feature of the changes affecting the city which have been brought about by post-Fordism.

Two British examples can be described to highlight the social and economic processes which have already been noted, namely the transformation of city centres and city images as a marketing strategy to compete in the global economy of service and leisure.

Mellor (1997) has described the transformation of Manchester from a city and regional hinterland suffering badly from postindustrial decline into what she refers to as a 'cool' or 'vibrant' playground. For example, between 1978 and 1988 Manchester lost around 300,000 industrial jobs and 70,000 public service jobs, with 500,000 redundancies being announced in the same period. Why did this happen? Manchester's world position in the cotton textile industry declined and its position as a provincial business centre diminished. This industrial decline also meant that the city witnessed the loss of service and support jobs for those same dying industries. Mellor comments that it ceased to be a town centre for the local population. The problems which were frequently being discussed in the 1960s and 70s – eroding tax bases, depopulation, an ageing infrastructure and the growth of a shabby urban centre – applied to the city. Between 1984 and 1989 Manchester witnessed the beginnings of a building and marketing process which is now being labelled post-Fordist: museums, exhibition centres and the G-Mex mass forum were built. There was increased investment in hotel provision. Granada Studios began to market itself as a major tourist attraction and there was the rediscovery of Salford Quays and the canal areas as a suitable focus for an expanding leisure and heritage industry. Manchester was marketed as 'the 24 hour city'. There was effectively the creation of a new public sphere catering for young affluent professionals, many from the highly paid financial service sector. However, the fall in property values between 1989 and 1994 coupled with a still declining and weakening industrial base undermined the marketing gloss. Mellor points to the continued fall in recorded full-time employment. The vacant office space and, most significant of all, the poor inner city envelope surrounding the commercial areas which houses the unemployed and unemployable testify to the precarious economic foundations of the 'new' Manchester. The superficially pleasant environment of the inner city regions (made pleasant by housing improvement and landscaping) cannot disguise the reality that, for many living in the city, life is about surviving poverty and, regrettably, predatory crime within their own impoverished community. While the city image of Manchester is enhanced by projects such as the Olympic Games bid and the construction of sports stadia supported by stylistic transformations in the leisure industry, postcode discrimination, where whole city neighbourhoods are effectively labelled as deviant, ensures that those most in need of employment are systematically screened out of the labour market. The 'dual city' idea points to the tendency among marketing agencies to present a very partial front to the commercial world of potential investors. This place marketing is considered a demeaning but necessary feature of the international competition for inward investment. In this evolving urban mosaic the city centre is not a place for the unemployed and poor who lack the spending power to make use of the increasing numbers of restaurants, night clubs and bars. The urban promiscuity of the economically excluded becomes a matter for policing and surveillance to ensure that the 'excluded' spend their time in and move through the urban space appropriately. I will return to this issue later.

Mooney and Danson have undertaken a similar analysis of Glasgow (see Mooney and Danson, 1997; Danson and Mooney, 1998). Indeed Glasgow was one of the earliest British cities to manifest tendencies towards 'dualism' in urban development. A succession of culturally driven and image creating campaigns aimed at raising the national and international profile of Glasgow as a business, tourist and leisure centre was begun in the 1980s: the Miles Better Campaign, the National Garden Festival in 1988, the European City of Culture in 1990 and the *fin de siècle* status as city of architecture and design in 1999 are the prime examples. The creation of the Merchant City as an up-market residential area for young upwardly mobile and successful people is a further example of the *gentrification* of an area which had remained uninspiring and undeveloped for many years. Mooney and Danson contrast these developments with the consequences of the Fordist boom of the 1950s and 60s that ushered in major slum clearance and urban renewal programmes which transformed the city centre by decanting the residents of the poor inner city areas to the four main peripheral housing estates at the four corners of the city boundaries. These estates were hastily built and extremely under-serviced. Easterhouse, despite being the size of a major Scottish town such as Perth, contained no centre, few shops and very little in the way of leisure facilities. While Mooney and Danson and Mellor may have difficulty in accepting the broad usefulness of the 'dual city' model, nevertheless their descriptions of contemporary Glasgow and Manchester serve the purpose of highlighting the growing divisions between the participants and the excluded in the post-Fordist city. They have drawn attention to the way that urban space has contributed to the poverty of large numbers of the population.

An alternative conceptualisation of the urban process has been found in the idea of 'quarters' (see Marcuse, 1996). Within a context of asymmetrical development, some areas of the city increase their value and status while others decline: a zero sum game appears to be in process. In the United States, extreme divisions are becoming apparent with the growth of 'outcast ghettos' and 'advanced homelessness' alongside the flowering of areas of conspicuous opulence protected by 'militarised policing' (see Davis, 1992). Marcuse's argument is that the post-Fordist city is quartered rather than dualistic. By this he means that the divisions are more complex than the 'dual city' concept permits. In fact, Marcuse identifies at least five 'quarters' rather than four with the presumption that cities are fluid and constantly changing forms which have at any given time or period in history a fairly identifiable pattern which is discernible. His divisions are:

- *luxury housing spots*: enclaves of isolated buildings and blocks occupied by the rich and top hierarchy

- *the gentrified city* for those professional and managerial groups that are 'making it'
- *the suburban city* for single family housing, the middle professional and managerial groups and the skilled artisans which can be found both at the outer reaches of the city or near the centre
- *tenement city* which is constituted by the cheaper single family areas and includes areas of social housing occupied by lower paid workers
- *abandoned city* where the 'victims', the poor, the unemployed and the excluded congregate, constituting an area of 'advanced homelessness'.

In addition to these areas of divided residence, Marcuse argues that the urban centre has a distinct pattern within what he calls 'the economic city'. First, the areas with prestigious office blocks are the locations where 'big decisions' are made, often located in areas with rising property values within the city centre. Wealth and power are mobile and those who make decisions about a city or region invariably have no residential attachment to it: the office block is for convenience rather than a stake in a local business community. Second, there may be an area which Marcuse calls the 'city of advanced services'. These areas are characterised by 'downtown clusters' of professional offices enmeshed in a complex communicative network. Again the lack of attachment to the location by the main business actors and the mobility of power, wealth and service provision is stressed. Third, we might identify the city of unskilled work located in relatively cheap industrial units, warehouses and sweatshops providing goods and consumer services in the city. It is an area where informal or irregular economic transactions often lubricate the business cycle. Fourth, adjacent to the city of unskilled work is *the abandoned city* where those expelled from society can be found. It is an area coloured by a retreatist sub-culture in which drugs, alcohol and street crime occupy a central place.

The erection of spatial and social barricades segregating the areas of poverty from those more integrated into the global economy is a constant process in terms of everyday life and politics. The process of social exclusion of whole categories of people and activities is captured in this more complex model. As one area advances with the ebbs and flows of the postindustrial economy, other areas decline and shrink in population and functional significance for the local city economy. It is the politics of survival in such divided cities that we must examine. The issue of social cohesion which lies at the heart of a welfare society is extremely problematic when we consider the realities of the contemporary urban struc-

The tendency to view these divisive processes as beyond human and tical intervention becomes seductive, especially in an era when the pitalist market place is in the ascendancy.

## Social exclusion and welfare in the post-Fordist city

The role of the welfare state has been to intercede on behalf of the poor and dispossessed with those who structure space and lifechances in the urban process and to ensure that social boundaries between the people who inhabit neighbourhoods, towns, cities and regions do not become social barriers. The task of building and maintaining social and economic integration in society has depended on social policies being grounded in a sense of solidarity, pooling of risk and collective provision. However, the post-Fordist welfare state is a 'hollowed-out state', with the main responsibilities for the welfare state infrastructure increasingly being renegotiated by governments with their citizenry and devolved to voluntary and commercial supply. How effectively the state can fulfil its traditional welfare role in the new economic and political conditions of post-Fordism, employing an 'at arms' length' form of supervision of private decision making, becomes an interesting question. In place of intervention in the direction of policy, governments have resorted to enunciating social and moral principles with the expectation, or hope, that they will at least have a declaratory effect, setting the moral and political parameters for the many devolved centres of decision making.

One principle which has remained dominant in welfare discourse, because it appears to reconcile the principle of state welfare with a collective sense of social justice, is the 'work ethic'. With respect to this, Bauman (1998) has directed our attention to the changing rationale behind the welfare state idea as we move from the modern to the postmodern era: from a 'society of producers' to a 'society of consumers'. Social security was *always* conceived of as residual assistance and premised on the existence of, or potential for, full employment. Now that work has become scarce, especially for the unskilled and ill educated in a postindustrial society, the presence of the work ethic remains a source of political friction and policy confusion impeding the modernisation of welfare in the 21st century. While the work ethic has remained an obsession with the managers of contemporary welfare systems, the important question to be posed is, what relevance does it have in a time when full employment is no longer possible? Setting benefit levels to maximise the incentive to work was an integral part of the welfare state in its early days, certainly in those systems influenced by Beveridge. What appears to be happening in the post-Fordist period is that the work ethic is undergoing a mutation, transforming the welfare state into what has been called the 'workfare state': the emphasis is no longer on structuring benefit levels to avoid creating poverty or unemployment traps but on making labour cheap and flexible in order to maximise its absorption into a postindustrial economy saturated with low paid, low skilled and insecure part-time jobs. Welfare to work strategies (vocational guidance, training schemes and subsidised employment underpinned by the threat of benefit withdrawal for non-participation) underline that 'work' is expected of claimants, but they also heighten the sense of being deviant for those unable or unwilling to accept employment at a minimum wage level.

With consumption rather than production being the key feature of the post-Fordist economy, those excluded from the consumer society because of low income, insecure income or no income are presented with a major human problem. Their consumer choice is limited, as is their access to social networks and activities which only money and a secure income can provide. Hutton (1995) has described our society as the 40:30:30 society: 40 per cent have secure employment, 30 per cent have insecure employment and 30 per cent are unemployed or living on extremely low incomes. It could be argued that 60 per cent of the population at any given time experience great difficulties with the demands of the consumer society because their material confidence is undermined by insecure employment or low and decreasing welfare benefits. In order to minimise the exclusionary potential of the workfare state a number of social analysts have advocated the abandonment of the work ethic and its replacement by a basic income policy (Paul Hirst's (1994) perspective on this notion was discussed in the last chapter) which can at least ensure that all citizens, irrespective of their capacity to contribute to the productive process, can secure sufficient resources to retain a foothold in postmodern society (see Jordan, 1987; Parker, 1995). Others have argued for a reorientation of social policy towards understanding the issues surrounding consumption: shopping, travel, viewing and playing are just some of the themes so far under-researched and largely ignored by the social policy discipline (see Cahill, 1994). With respect to the mundane, but crucial, problems contributing to a sense of social exclusion, Gilroy and Speak (1998) describe the social, psychological and organisational barriers which fix the non-workers and non-consumers marooned on a Newcastle housing estate into a mental state of feeling cut off. The constant failure to find employment, often exacerbated by postcode discrimination; the constant lack of money to buy goods and services for family members; the absence of crèche facilities, affordable child care and play schemes to be able to take up job opportunities all combine with a parsimonious welfare system to ingrain a sense of exclusion for many in the spatially isolated housing estates. The everyday experience of being poor in a materialist and consumption-oriented society remains a phenomenon often discussed but little understood from the perspective of those who are poor themselves.

The 'consumer society' presents an equally large and difficult problem for those managing and directing the welfare state. Bauman (1998) is correct to suggest that 'in a world populated by consumers there is no place for a welfare state' (p. 93). The uniformity of provision which aimed to ensure 'equality' in the Beveridge welfare state is replaced by a demand for choice, not just in the growing diversity of products provided by the market but also in the public goods provided by the state. The clearest expression of this movement can be found in the transformation of British housing policy. In Britain it is the market and the 'right to buy' which have begun to shape the urban settlements and have given rise to a concern about the *residualisation* of some housing estates where 'work poor' households remain trapped in a deteriorating built environment without either work or a welfare state to assist them to gain a 'stakehold' in the 'new' society. The scope of social and public policy in the post-Fordist city is also limited by the changing agenda which favours social partnerships with private capital to make things 'happen'. The 'private finance initiatives' being used to build NHS hospitals is a controversial British example of this. The movement towards a post-Fordist welfare posture by many European countries may be exacerbating the economic and social processes which structure 'social exclusion'.

What do we do with the 'unneeded, unwanted and forsaken' who present image problems for the 'marketers of place'? The answer provided by the policies issuing from rapidly reducing welfare systems is to place them 'out of sight'. They must be removed from the streets and public places: a process which the post-Fordist 24 hour city accomplishes with the help of private as well as public security forces and the *panoptic* surveillance of closed circuit television (more on this later). The other tendency is to isolate the poor, disadvantaged and workless by what Bauman (1998) has termed 'mental separation': by banishing the poor from the world of 'ethical duty'. This is accomplished by transforming the concept of citizenship from an idea which recognises the rights of the disadvantaged to access services and benefits when in need to a notion which is primarily concerned with their obligation to the community and their contribution to productive activity. In such a context the portrayal of the poor as indolent, immoral and criminogenic becomes part of a process of redefining the problem of poverty in an epoch when the welfare state idea is gradually being played down. The retention of the work ethic becomes part of an expedient justification to characterise unemployment as chosen idleness: the logic which follows suggests that as the poor and the unemployed do not contribute to the community because they have 'chosen' to remain idle, they cannot expect to make moral claims on society. The extent to which this process of public denial will progress ultimately depends on the degree of political will to institutionalise it as the 'new' concept of welfare.

In general, the economic and market forces which have transformed the western economies, altering their occupational structures along with their urban and industrial landscape, are presented as being necessary, inevitable and largely uncontrollable. However, in Chapter 3 it was concluded that 'politics counts' when considering what determines welfare state development. It was noted that European welfare systems have displayed marked differences in their capacity and willingness to intervene in the workings of the market economy and facilitate the decommodified status of their citizens: they have varied in terms of the range and generosity of their social security provision allowing people to survive outside the labour market and, as in the case of Sweden, have extended the scope of welfare intervention to include active labour market policies. Part of this variation in welfare regimes will be manifested in the differences to be found throughout Europe and North America in the way poverty, disadvantage and social exclusion are defined and treated. Indeed, there will be variation between welfare systems with respect to whether an issue such as 'social exclusion' is regarded as a significant policy issue at all, reflecting the political and ideological complexion of a nation state. Welfare regimes embody a mix of political and ideological forces which lead to the evolution of distinctive 'narratives' or 'paradigms', picking out particular features of society for their citizens which are regarded by the political elites, state bureaucrats and career politicians as the objects for policy intervention. The character of the political debate in a nation state will shape the way such a social problem will be tackled. With respect to the international differences in the way disadvantaged groups in Western societies are defined, in European Union countries the definition of 'social exclusion' driving policy initiatives is derived from French politics (see national paradigms of poverty discourse set out later). However, in the United States, a quite different political debate has shaped the way poverty is viewed and understood, in particular what Kantor (1993) has called 'a Jeffersonian notion of urban politics' in which the federal government has tended to abrogate its responsibility for urban development by devolving block grants and decision making to states and local city governments. Thomas Jefferson extolled the virtues of what Europeans now understand by the concept of *subsidiarity*: political questions are best resolved by governments closest to the people. The implication of this idea in contemporary America has been that many states have effectively abandoned the inner cities in favour of 'common interest developments' (CIDs) which amount to exclusionary middle-class settlements on green field sites, so called *edge cities*, which have acquired their own municipal government along with pay-as-you-go public services and policing. Kantor (1993) points out that 'only a few hundred of these associations existed in 1960, but there are more than 125,000 today and they may soon rival the 39,000 elected local governments in numbers and power over individuals' (p. 38). The racialisation and spatiality of social exclusion in the United States is not, therefore, unconnected with the growth of what Kantor calls a 'dual political system'. The consequence of the CIDs is to 'separate the business of generating money from the realities of social polarisation'. By this he means that one set of government institutions deals with welfare, schools, law and order and the consequences of social polarisation, 'mostly concerned with providing social therapy' and operating on tight budgets, and another set of institutions are concerned with 'money-generating government': facilitating the needs of private capital and controlling taxation. These are the unelected public benefit corporations and independent public authorities 'to wage the city's economic warfare by planning, financing and operating public projects with as little interference as possible from citizens and their city halls' (p. 39). It is the movement away from community-building politics by deliberate political choice which distinguishes the United States. In order to understand this process, we need to examine the variations in what Silver (1996) has called 'national paradigms of poverty discourse'. Although the European Union appears to be a standardising influence on these issues, especially through the adoption of the French analytical discourse, there remain significant political differences between the members of the Union.

Cousins (1998) has attempted to relate the idea of 'national paradigms of poverty discourse' to the notion of welfare state regimes.

Following Silver (1996), she identifies four paradigms (solidarity, specialisation, monopoly and neo-organic) associated with different welfare state models:

● *Solidarity* is associated with the Durkheimian tradition in France which understands exclusion as an integral part of the breaking down of social bonds. As Silver (1996) has observed, the French tradition has differed from the Anglo-Saxon, or Lockean liberal, view of solidarity which has understood social integration in terms of 'social contracts based on political or market relations'. In contrast, the social bond between the state and the poor lies at the heart of the French concept. Cousins differs from Esping-Andersen (1990) by characterising France in this way as a representative of a conservative-corporatist model. Policies aimed at promoting solidarity such as the horizontal distribution of family benefits from the childless to those involved in child rearing is a feature.

● *Specialisation* is associated with the liberal or Anglo-Saxon welfare model, of which Britain and the United States are the best examples. The central idea here is that society, politics and the economy consist of a network of voluntary exchanges and that 'social exclusion' derives from 'discrimination, market failures and unenforced rights'. The conservative interpretation of this view leads to policy devices aimed at fighting market blockages including restrictive practices in the labour market. The removal of wages councils can be understood as part of this model. As Cousins observes 'the specialisation paradigm, however, associates dependency on welfare, long-term unemployment and the *underclass* with failings of personal characteristics' (Cousins, 1998: 139). The continuation of this underlying liberal model in New Labour welfare policy means that there has been little impact on reducing the polarisation between those in work and those out of work which was a strong feature of the 1980s and early 1990s. The adoption of this fundamental model in Britain continues to justify the shift towards means testing and a 'coercive' stance behind 'welfare to work' policies. The United States expresses these tendencies in even sharper contrast, restricting eligibility for and duration of welfare benefits. The assumption is that people exclude themselves through their deviant behaviour and attitudes.

● *Monopoly* models are associated with the Scandinavian countries, in particular Sweden. Exclusion within this paradigm results from the use of class, status and power to ensure social closure for the benefit of those doing well from the system. Cousins comments that Marx and Weber have been influential architects of this concept. A stress on universalism and social citizenship underlies welfare state strategies to combat social exclusion.

● *Neo-organic* models have been associated with conservative countries with an authoritarian heritage. Germany, Spain, Italy and Portugal are identified. Silver (1996) originally tied this paradigm to countries which have privileged hierarchy and tradition as foundations for the social order and welfare obligations. Social exclusion will tend to be gendered and ageist. The dominance of patriarchy and male bread-winning combined with a very weak welfare state, as can be found in the Mediterranean rim countries, have resulted in high levels of youth and female unemployment in countries such as Spain. However, further differentiation is required here. The placing of Germany into the neo-organic model should be qualified because the social polari-sation associated with the Mediterranean rim countries cannot be found there.

The important insight which this work reveals is that the shape of poli-cies to deal with 'social exclusion' will reflect the political and ideolog-ical forces which are in the ascendancy within a nation state at any given time. What is clear throughout Europe and North America is that the poli-tics of welfare have accommodated to the pressures of the market and post-Fordism. The workfare state is beginning to emerge even in a country such as Sweden with a strong social democratic heritage (see Gould, 1996). At the centre of the 'workfare' idea, as has already been mentioned, is the view that idleness is chosen behaviour. The problem of 'social exclusion' will be difficult for governments to tackle effectively as long as the behaviourist paradigm remains strong in policy circles. The corollary of the behaviourist paradigm in welfare politics is that the stress shifts from social policy to social control.

## Post-Fordism and criminality

The transition to post-Fordism... involves a return in some respects to pre-Fordism, to the generalised surveillance and disciplining of the working class. Crime control thus becomes 'actuarial'... concerned with risk assessment, incapacitation and management of delinquency. This takes a juridical – as opposed to a welfare – form, as it did in the early nineteenth century... The relationship between the workfare state and actuarial criminal justice continues to be that of reciprocity: the criminal justice picks up those who are unwilling to bend to the new flexibilities of the workfare state. (Lea, 1997: 52)

The quote from Lea encapsulates the fundamental changes which have taken place in the criminal justice stance in relation to post-Fordism. The real consequence of the economic and political processes shaping the post-Fordist city is that those who have been marginalised have been finding a strategy for living which often absorbs the predatory and competitive ethos of postindustrial economics (individualism), but their sense of outrage at the existing arrangements (relative deprivation) encourages them to embrace methods of survival which are deviant and perceived as threatening to the social order. It is this combination which generates a *criminogenic cynicism* among the marginal populations.

There are three aspects to the changing pattern of criminality which should be recognised. First, there is what Miller (1958) called the 'generating milieu' of crime and delinquency which draws our attention to the insecurities wrought by working-class unemployment on community life in the inner cities and peripheral housing estates. Second, the organisation and character of crime itself has changed in relation to broader economic forces, including globalisation. And, third, in terms of policing and punishing the 'excluded', the response of society appears to be the abandoning of the pretence of rehabilitation in favour of more efficient methods of incarceration and incapacitation.

## Community and crime

Perhaps the most notable feature of life in the inner cities, both in North America and in Europe, is the internecine character of crime. Residents of certain working-class communities are more likely to be burgled by their neighbours than by someone from outside their area. Middle-class residential areas typically have lower victimisation rates than adjacent working-class areas. Young (1998) describes this as the implosion of the working-class area. Aggression and incivility seem to be widespread and the reality for many people living in areas with high crime rates is that the informal community structures and controls appear to have broken down. The reasons for this weakening of community controls are many. Lea

(1997) draws an insightful distinction between working-class communities which are employment based and those which are unemployment based. In the former, which generally characterised what we have described as Fordism in the post-Second World War period, community life was not free of petty criminality and deviant values but was grounded in working-class conservatism buttressed by informal community relationships. Lea refers to its base in an ethical moral economy of solidarism with a strong sense of social and moral boundaries. It was characterised by community sanctioned deviance against the bosses (petty pilfering was acceptable) and it was hostile to outside forces, particularly the police interfering in scams and 'hidden economy' dealing ('grassing' to the police was absolutely forbidden). However, predatory crime against people from the same community and neighbourhood was unacceptable. Its presence is witness to the destruction of the informal community controls which history and established residence build up. The urban renewal programmes of the 1950s and 60s combined with high concentrations of long-term unemployment to *disorganise* working-class areas. In the absence of material resources and marketable skills the only means available to many working-class youths are their aggression and sense of territorial control.

Classical sociological concepts of deviance assist in understanding what is happening in this transformation of working-class communities. Edwin Sutherland's (Sutherland and Cressey, 1966) theory of differential association makes the simple point that criminality is learned behaviour: the pattern of our associations shapes the values we acquire and the techniques for committing crime that will be available to us. The greater the frequency, intensity, priority and duration of associations favourable to the violation of the law over those favourable to upholding it will influence an inclination towards deviance. What is learnt in these associations is what C. Wright Mills (1940) called a 'vocabulary of motive' or what Sykes and Matza (1957) relabelled 'techniques of neutralisation': the motivation to commit crime and neutralise the moral bind of conventional society is learned, and supported by peers and community contacts through the acquisition of commonly accepted and socially validated linguistic devices to justify, rationalise and so motivate criminality ('they can afford it', 'nobody will get hurt', 'they're insured', 'everyone is out for themselves so why not me'). The destruction of working-class communities through urban renewal and mass unemployment has meant that the established parent culture rooted in labourism and collectivism ceases to be as effective in a climate of declining trade union and working-class strength. The vocabulary of motivation which is now influential emerges from the street life in the anomic habitats of housing estates and inner city ghettos controlled by unemployed and unemployable youths. They are organised into gangs because delinquency is typically a group enterprise, and plugged into a hedonistic and consumerist youth sub-culture but without the means to be lawful participants in it. It is the materialist nature of the sub-culture, rooted in the desire for clothes and fashionable (lifestyle) accessories, coupled with long-term youth unemployment which determines the most influential vocabulary of motive. In a context of social isolation from law abiding associations, the combination of individualism and relative deprivation becomes a potent impetus for criminality.

The other aspect of differential association is learning the techniques for committing crime: the skills and the knowledge, especially about informal markets for the exchange and disposal of stolen goods. Cloward and Ohlin's (1960) classic study of delinquency and opportunity, despite its weaknesses as a contemporary analysis of gang delinquency and sub-cultures, identified the concept of 'illegitimate opportunity structure' to describe the variations in access to tutelage in criminal techniques and deviant values throughout the social structure. Affinities with people who understand about cars can lead to the acquisition of knowledge and skills appropriate for a criminal career in car theft. Similarly, those with associates in white collar occupations will discover a whole range of possible deviant careers involving embezzlement and selling frauds. Those young people living their lives in the impoverished conditions of the post-Fordist city ghetto or estate will confront the availability of illicit drugs as the main 'illegal opportunity structure' to be negotiated.

## Post-Fordism and the irregular economy

In post-Fordism the conventional economy has gone global, with capital and markets now worldwide and transcending the limits of local trading. So, too, has the drug business, becoming more organised and inserted into a global division of labour involving producers, financiers, distributors and local salesmen. Lea (1997) observes that one of the great motivations for the barons of organised crime earlier in the 20th century was to gain respectability through the acquisition of criminal wealth. While this may remain an important motivation for some international drug capitalists, it is less likely to be a motivation for significant players in the illegal markets who are simultaneously 'respectable' entrepreneurs in the legitimate economy. Crime mirrors the global post-Fordist city. It is a bazaar (Ruggiero and South, 1997) or an emporium (Young, 1998) in which drugs of all kinds are available, where the boundaries between the open and the hidden economy are separated by only a thin membrane and where, as Ruggiero and South (1997) state, the class and racial divisions found in the respectable market are mirrored in the practices of the hidden economy. The big money to be made by the financiers and distributors well away from the areas of risk contrasts with the high risk and low financial rewards available to the labour force of the permanently unemployed found in the poor working-class areas wheeling and dealing on the streets. Even in the alternative world of criminal employment the residents of the inner city and peripheral housing areas remain the objects of exploitation either as workhorses of the hidden economy or as its customers. Along with the changing opportunity structures of the post-Fordist city there are the illegal opportunity structures of the global drug economy. It is, however, the comparatively insignificant law and order consequences of the small players in the global criminal economy which stimulates concern about social order and which leads to the movement into what Young (1998) calls the 'exclusive society': a society in which surveillance and punishment become focused on those posing a so-called 'danger' to society and on how most effectively to 'exclude' them from respectable communities.

## Social control in the post-Fordist city

The clash between modernist and postmodernist impulses in the criminal justice systems of the world can be witnessed in the confusion surrounding how to police the post-Fordist city. For our purposes the central focus should be on what I will call the social control of public space in the post-Fordist city. Throughout the 20th century the key 'master shift' in penal policy (see Cohen, 1985) was towards the decentering of incarceration as the main punishment for criminals and the growth of non-custodial forms of disposal, whether that took the form of monetary fines, community corrections or suspended sentences coupled with therapeutic help. As Garland (1985) observed, the principles of welfare and rehabilitation became of primary importance in the age of Fordism. Punishment and social control became what Cohen (1985) calls 'inclusive': society in general became involved in policing and punishment because the deviants were no longer 'excluded' in purpose-built institutions, as they had been in the 19th century. As we have already noted, the optimism of the modernist architects of the welfare state throughout Europe (but not in the United States) fashioned a criminal justice system which would complement the integrative principles of the welfare state. This meant that those deviants propelled into anti-social behaviour by psychological or social pathology could expect an array of social services geared towards reintegrating them into respectable society. The rehabilitation principle was pivotal in the prison system as in other areas of welfare state theory. However, the rising crime rate and the crisis of containment within the prison system, especially since the 1960s, have led to the beginnings of yet another 'master shift', as we move away from a model of the 'inclusive' society and return to what Young (1998) wants to call the 'exclusive' society, in which public space is heavily monitored and controlled and the principles governing the treatment of deviants are focused on minimising the dangers they pose to society rather than on attempting to rehabilitate them.

In the 'exclusive' society public spaces are controlled by private interests, whether that be private security workers or private individuals. Urban promiscuity, the wrong people of the wrong age, gender or ethnicity being in the wrong place at the wrong time, is now a central preoccupation. Reference was made earlier to the *panoptic* control of closed circuit television throughout the post-Fordist city which has as its objective the reduction of urban promiscuity. Technology contributes to the creation of a *cordon sanitaire* around commercial and residential areas with the sole objective of 'excluding' those scapegoated as the 'underclass' because their behaviour is unpredictable when surrounded by the temptations of the consumerist society. This process has gone further in the United States than in Europe, and I refer again to the CIDs about which Kantor (1993) writes. The abandonment of the poor city areas by the middle classes and the hiring of private police forces to ensure that the residents of those poor areas remain contained within the boundaries of their 'abandoned enclave' is becoming more common in Europe. The intent is, as Young (1998) observes, neither to eliminate nor integrate those areas but to *exclude* them.

The uncertainties of the postmodern world, in which cultural and behavioural diversity increasingly demand tolerance from everyone in order for social harmony to be established, appear to lead instead to the search for ways of controlling, expelling or 'excluding'. Rehabilitation is dead and the actuarial measurement of risk is alive. Dangerousness to society is now the main concern in the fields of social work with families, juvenile justice and penal policy. It becomes a matter of 'getting your retaliation in first': rehabilitation worked with deviants after they had committed offences, but an actuarial approach seeks to identify and eliminate risk before a deviant act has been committed. It leads to the intrusive management of public spaces, the growth in the prison population and the emergence of 'net widening' in the form of electronic tagging and the growth of the private security industry. In the United States and Britain, if not throughout Europe, the anti-modernists are winning the intellectual battle with the modernists when it comes to the policing of the post-Fordist city.

In the light of tendencies in contemporary society to banish the poor from what Bauman has called 'the world of ethical duty' and what Young refers to as the 'exclusive society', questions are inevitably raised about the extent to which solidarity, social cohesion and caring remain features of welfare systems today. Can we explain the apparent loss of solidarity and benevolence expressed towards the poor and disadvantaged? The next chapter addresses this question.

# 7

# Postemotional society and amoral familism: emotions, caring and collective obligations

We have come to that part in the analysis when we must address a key issue about the changing form of the welfare state explicitly: do people genuinely *care* about the welfare of others? And are there sufficient reservoirs of emotionality in contemporary society which can be drawn on to motivate family and community members to do something about the poverty and hardship suffered by increasing numbers of fellow citizens marooned at the bottom of a polarising social hierarchy? At the centre of the ongoing process of argument about the future of welfare is the concern that, in Europe if not the United States, the alternatives to collective state provision being suggested will be incapable of providing a sustainable and humane foundation for social policy and social cohesion. This chapter will raise questions about whether the transfer of state welfare provision to civil society is practicable because welfare state theorists and social policy analysts, both in the universities and policy think tanks, have failed to confront that most difficult of issues when discussing the problem of who will do the caring, namely, the *emotional* side of social life. Welfare in the modern European tradition has been about community building and seeking to create a sense of solidarity among the citizenry of nation states. Indeed this has been the underlying assumption of the key welfare state theorists such as Titmuss (1970, 1974, 1987), Korpi (1978, 1980) and Marshall (1950): ultimately building a welfare state should be understood in terms of drawing on the reservoirs of compassion, empathy and sympathy within a society for the predicament of the poor and disadvantaged. Without a strong welfare tradition it has been assumed that there will not be the institutional channels available to release sufficient levels of emotional energy and involvement to build a collective sense of well-being. However a related

143

development in welfare policy may be undermining the prospects of building a socially cohesive welfare society, namely, the process known as the individualisation of the social (Ferge, 1997). The stress being placed on individuals as autonomous agents who should be entrusted with arranging their own provision weakens the principle of solidarity which the welfare state idea has rested on since 1945. What are the consequences for social integration resulting from the increasing stress being placed on individuals and their families to take responsibility for their own welfare, especially in a society where large sections of the population experience insecure employment? Who other than the state can provide for those who are unemployed?

Two key concepts drawn from quite different academic fields which, so far, have not been found in the social policy literature can illuminate what is beginning to happen to the welfare state in Western societies. The first concept to be described is 'postemotionality' which has been developed by Stjepan Meštrović (1997, 1998). It engages with the fast evolving sociological literature on postmodernism and makes visible the subtle and often neglected changes affecting the way emotions are experienced and expressed in contemporary society. The second concept to be explored will be that of amoral familism. Originally coined by Edward Banfield (1958), and referred to briefly at the end of Chapter 4, this notion is taken from the political analysis of backward, rather than underdeveloped, societies and describes a privatised attitude to civil society which always pursues selfish and family interests at the expense of engagement in concerted public activity (see Reis, 1998). To anticipate the argument a little: the transformation of late modern societies in the West by post-Fordist economic forces has led not only to a fundamental change in economic and social relationships but has also affected the emotional and caring side of human association. The consequences of these changes for social welfare urgently need to be explored.

## The emergence of a postemotional society

A key difference between modernity and postmodernity is that the trust which modernists place upon reason to bring about civilising change in modern societies is not shared by those of a postmodern disposition. At various points in the analysis I have pointed to the modernist impulse to apply systematic principles of knowledge to better understand and, crucially, control *all* fields of human endeavour. The welfare state idea has been part of that modern project to understand, control and eradicate social inequality and poverty by the application of empirically grounded knowledge to the shaping of social character and social behaviour. That is one version of modernity. Postmodern theory has injected a large dose of scepticism into this vision. Whatever advances science, and the scientific method, may claim for the general improvement in the human condition, we have a planet that is dirtier and more polluted now than it has ever been. And most people are accepting of the reality that whatever else the Western welfare states can claim as achievements, the eradication of poverty is not one of them. In recognition of these paradoxes, Rojek (1995) has pointed to the contradictory tendencies in modernity. Along with forces for order there are also forces for disorder and chaos. It is the acknowledgement of this fact that has led to the cynicism, nihilism and despair often associated with postmodernism.

One very significant casualty of modernity has been the displacement of what we might call *emotions* from our attempts to understand what makes society possible. Science, technology and modern social and economic theories have led to the eclipse of *emotionality*: emotions have been regarded as non-rational, non-purposive and distorting influences in the attempt to build systematic models of how things work. Indeed emotions may sometimes be regarded as a residual element remaining from the incomplete task of defeating traditionalism and religiosity which only find expression in those parts of the world and those areas of societies which the educative forces of rationalism have failed to reach. The Enlightenment project was conceived of by many social thinkers, such as Nietzsche (1967), as the triumph of rationality over emotions, or to put the matter in a different way, as the ending of *passion* and *passionate ideology*. In sociology, the focus has been on the impact, or should we say triumph, of the twin revolutions of capitalist industrialism and political democracy, which have been instrumental in a nation-building process leading to the 'end of ideology' (Bell, 1960) and, more recently, in the writing of Francis Fukuyama, to the 'end of history' in the aftermath of the collapse of East European communism (Fukuyama, 1992). This is a sociological history without emotions, culminating in a society without passionate ideology and beliefs. Sociological theory and method has accepted the view that modernity is driven by a positivism which inexorably excludes space for the expression of emotion. This now widely accepted mode of thinking about the relationship between modernity and emotions is rejected by Meštrović's interesting slant on postmodernism (1997 and 1998) and it is his substantive analysis of *postemotionality* that requires a fuller elaboration at this point.

## Caritas and postmodernism

Meštrović (1997) argues that emotions have not been eliminated in contemporary society, rather they are manipulated and have become what he calls new hybrids of an intellectualised, mechanical and mass produced set of responses orchestrated by the culture industry (the mass media and marketing infrastructures underpinning social, cultural and economic life in postmodern societies). He distances himself from postmodern thinkers such as Baudrillard who has argued that the world has become a giant simulation of reality (hyper-reality) in which cognitive categories, or our perception and ability to make sense of social reality, have been distorted and rendered inauthentic. For Městrović this type of analysis misses the point. Emotions are in fact very consciously evoked by economic and political interests of all kinds located at every position on the political spectrum. The false 'happiness' of Disney world, the super-efficient 'niceness' of McDonald's and the attempts by the heritage and leisure industries to repackage past experiences for tourists are just some of the examples on which Meštrović focuses our attention. Politically, all interests and groups seek to manipulate emotional realities: the imagined recovery of past values and social contentment sought by the anti-modern right; the false utopias of the radical and fundamentalist left; and the superficial 'feel good factors' pursued by an army of political spin doctors attached to governments and political parties are further examples where emotions are not absent but rather are made abstract, packaged and fed back to populations to serve the interests of powerful elites and minorities.

Baudrillard has argued that in contemporary postmodern conditions, within which simulation of reality rather than true reality is experienced through the insatiable appetite for computerised and cinematic images, there is no genuine compassion or pity (see Gane, 1991). The world of hyper-reality deadens the senses to anything approximating authentic feelings. We observe the suffering of our fellow human beings without emotion and without feeling through global communications media which penetrate everyday life. In contrast, Meštrović insists that we experience something closer to *compassion fatigue*. Emotion, compassion and pity literally pour out of the many institutions designed to deal with major humanitarian causes and problems in an orderly and systematic way. And that, of course, is the problem: our experience of the inhumane, the tragic and the truly horrific is filtered through a process of deconstruction and reconstruction by organisations and institutions whose sole purpose is to channel aid and appropriate assistance to those in need, but at arms' length from the people who fund it and legitimate it, the ordinary citizens. How we should feel about starvation in Africa and genocide in the Balkans and Eastern Europe is uncertain. And that uncertainty intensifies in the aftermath of major collectively experienced traumas such as the death of Diana, Princess of Wales. By way of clarifying the phenomenon being identified here Meštrović uses the notion of *caritas* as a general designation for the feelings and emotions expressed through sympathy, empathy and caring which hold the social order together. They make intimate social relationships possible and underpin our sense of interdependence and our sense of our own humanity. It is caritas rather than the imagined self-interest of economic theory which actually makes society possible. Durkheim would have understood this well. *Anomie* in modern societies arises partly because the pursuit of material self-interest is so relentless that collectively we lose sight of ourselves as social beings who are interdependent. An anomic society would be one in which the caring role would be allocated to specialist agencies rather than existing organically throughout the social structure in the everyday relationships between its members. Caritas would become residualised. In reference to the orchestrated and confused emotional responses to current major events, such as the war in the Balkans, which demand a humanitarian response from those not directly involved, Meštrović states:

> this distracted compassion is not the *caritas* of traditional times but a displaced, viscerated compassion churned out by the culture industry that is really more like pity. *Caritas* binds humanity together whereas pity isolates and divides people into those who have the luxury to look down on others versus those who are desperate. (Meštrović, 1997: 26)

The contrast between organised humanitarianism and individual compassion is a real one in a contemporary world in which synthetic rehearsed feelings are common. A recent theme in the sociology of late modernity being developed by Anthony Giddens is the critical reflexivity of people towards traditions: the meaning and symbolic significance of traditions are no longer accepted unquestioningly today because people require from them a discursive justification for their continued support. The idea is now circulating that society must recreate traditions and communities to fill the void left by modernity's destruction of old customs and unreflective ideas and replace those feelings of commonality destroyed by postindustrialism. The CIDs being founded all over the United States, and referred to in the last chapter (see Kantor, 1993), are an excellent example of what has been referred to as *synthetic communities*, and a facet of those artificially created communities is the attempt to reconstruct *synthetic traditions*, invariably consisting of elaborate laws and regulations of residence aimed at recreating a mythical past in contemporary urban life, along with 'dead emotions' believed to reflect a sense of the 'real America'.

## Society and social character

It is not only the inauthenticity of emotions which becomes problematic but also the inability to express emotions because of the social pressures to be 'nice' and, above all else, politically correct. At this point in the analysis Meštrović draws on David Riesman's classic study *The Lonely Crowd* (1969) and his typological distinction between character types in the context of changing social structures. Central to that analysis is the comparison of three characterological types (tradition directed, inner directed and other directed) which have been dominant at different times in the development of modern society. It is the other-directed type which is most significant for the analysis of postemotional society. However, an important emphasis in Riesman's position must be acknowledged at the outset. Riesman is very clear that:

> There is no such thing as a society or a person wholly dependent on tradition-direction, inner-direction, or other-direction: each of these modes of conformity is universal, and the question is always one of the degree to which an individual or a social group places reliance on one or another of the three available mechanisms. (Riesman, 1969: 30)

Tradition-directed types are those who are guided by the thoughts and meanings gifted to them by their ancestors. They will live in comparatively small circles of acquaintances and will order their lives in ways approved by that circle. It is a character type which Riesman associates primarily with traditional social orders and so historically it would have been *dominant* before the Renaissance and Reformation. Inner-directed types emerged with the Renaissance and Reformation and are associated with explorers, colonisation and imperialism. It is a character type suited to periods when great individuals were needed to take risks and push the frontiers of knowledge forward. More contemporaneously, inner-directed types work with a strong sense of self-belief and self-destiny and are little influenced by peer group pressures or social fashions. Indeed Riesman describes them as people who early in life would have 'incorporated a psychic gyroscope from parents and authority figures' setting them on a course which they and only they can navigate. Feelings of guilt accompany a sense of failure for those unable to fulfil their mission. Other-directed types are a product of the affluent post-1945 period. Other-direction emerges in urban and complex industrial societies where the anonymity of social life requires the cultivation of shallow pleasantries in order to lubricate the daily patterns of social interaction. It is the need to succeed as a corporate employee rather than as an innovator or entrepreneur which shapes this character orientation. Seymour Martin Lipset commenting on Riesman's analysis nicely encapsulates the differences between the inner-directed and other-directed entrepreneur:

> During the period of industrial expansion those involved in the market faced problems about things rather than people, whether as customers or colleagues. Scarcity of goods and relatively inefficient means of handling the technological problems of extraction, transportation, and manufacturing overshadowed the concern with marketing and personal relations. (Lipset, 1961: 137)

It was the problems of technological and intellectual processes involved in production rather than orchestrating human co-operation in the process which characterised the demands on the inner-directed entrepreneur. Lipset continues:

> According to Riesman, propitiating the customer was unnecessary because the customer had nowhere else to go, and the general scarcity of goods admitted no likelihood of overproduction. (Lipset, 1961: 138)

With the growth in the availability of goods and the difficulties of over production the entrepreneur changes:

> He becomes an 'other-directed' person who gives up the one-face policy of the inner-directed man for a multiface policy that he sets in secrecy and varies with each set of encounters. (Lipset, 1961: 138)

Riesman observed that the other-directed type working in a large organisation 'engages in competition for the scarce commodity of approval'. And what actually shapes behaviour is no longer *ambition* for the attainment of clear goals (which is the behaviour of the inner-directed person) but *antagonistic co-operation* where the important thing is one's relationship to others, their failures rather than one's own goals. As co-operation rather than rivalry is supposed to be the guiding principle in the work place, success is often accompanied by feelings of guilt. Can one be successful as an individual and remain a 'team player'? It is the sense of there being a competition or race but the uncertainty of what it is, where it is and what it is for that creates anxiety for the other-directed person.

Riesman also contrasts the different child-rearing practices of inner-directed and other-directed parents: the former seek to inculcate inner standards of behaviour and achievement which act, as already indicated, as a 'psychic gyroscope', the latter are more concerned about the child fitting in, being normal, popular and sociable. Contemporaries are the source of guidance and direction. And as Riesman observes: 'The goals toward which the other-directed person strives shift with that guidance: it is only the process of striving itself and the process of paying close attention to the signals from others that remain unaltered throughout life' (Riesman, 1969: 20). Whereas the traditional-directed type feels *shame* for being exposed as a deviant and the inner-directed type feels *guilt*, the other-directed type feels *anxiety*, especially about not being part of the crowd. The other-directed type is at home everywhere and nowhere and must develop ways of interacting which can accommodate the pluralities of modern urban life. Political correctness and shallow inauthentic expression of false 'niceness' are the preferred behaviours for avoiding controversial encounters. It is precisely this aspect of Riesman's analysis which Meštrović recasts as postemotionality.

While Riesman stressed in 1950 that no single character type will be found, either at an individual or group level, he also maintained that as modern societies developed, the expectation would be that the other-directed type would become hegemonic. The original analysis discusses 'the characterological struggle' between the three types of character. What is now being argued, as we enter the 21st century, is that the other-directed type has become the postemotional type. Whereas tradition-directed people hold to a small set of basic emotions which they embrace passionately and inner-directed people place great stress upon sincerity and integrity in their dealings and only express emotions which are genuinely felt, the other-directed type in a postemotional society holds to a vast array of superficial emotions which can be easily expressed depending on the appropriateness of the circumstances. Bigotry can be repressed when political correctness is called for; rehearsed emotions can be expressed about violence, genocide and political sleaze; and niceness can be cultivated to produce a 'synthetic, feigned and ultimately insincere form of friendliness'.

The interesting and difficult sociological subject which Riesman raised explicitly is the relationship between *social character* and *social structure*. In posing the question, Riesman sought answers in the mechanisms which are generated by a society and culture to ensure conformity. For example, he draws attention to Erich Fromm's suggestion that 'in order that any society may function well, its members must acquire the kind of character which makes them *want* to act in the way they *have* to act as members of the society... They have to *desire* what objectively is *necessary* for them to do. *Outer force* is replaced by *inner compulsion*, and by the particular kind of human energy which is channelled into character traits' (quoted in Riesman, 1969: 5). It is, therefore, the ways in which society ensures conformity through subtle ideological, moral and educative means which, for Riesman, constitute the making of social character.

However, the concept of 'social character' here should not be understood as a psychological category. Just as Durkheim's notions of egoism, *fatalism*, *altruism* and *anomie* in his study of suicide referred to pathological forms of social structure rather than psychological states, so Riesman's analysis of social character is an examination of how 'modes of conformity' have changed as societies move from earlier pre-industrial stages to the postmodern and postindustrial stage we are now beginning to witness. It is the economic and socio-cultural moulding of social attitudes and relationships which is being described. So as with Riesman's character types, postemotionalism should not be confused with a psychological state, despite its connotations of psychic disturbance. It is a concept which uncovers the ways in which a postmodern, postindustrial, post-Fordist and postwelfare state society in the West appears to be shaping social orientations to emotional phenomena.

To underline the essentially sociological character of these concepts Messinger and Clark (1961) detect an implicit theory in Riesman's work which they believe requires further development to rescue it from a reading of *The Lonely Crowd* as a theory of personality, or what they call the explicit focus on *personology*. For them the directed types are not so much historical, although there may be justification for seeing them in this way, as situational: 'We think that these types are best seen as descriptions of roles or systems of conduct organised in terms of situational exigencies, rather than as individuals' "drives and satisfactions"' (Lipset and Lowenthal, 1961: 82). There are connections between this view and some contemporary sociological analyses of emotions. As Burkitt (1997) maintains, emotions are not things which arise from within the person but instead are a product of relationships: they are historical and cultural products. We should not assume that how people feel about war, violence, welfare and caring is the same today as it was in the 19th century or earlier periods of the 20th century. How we feel about sad or frightening events is not a natural phenomenon. Burkitt argues:

> Sensation and thought can arise at one and the same moment within specific social contexts as a learned bodily response and disposition... I am following the notion of disposition as found in the work of Bourdieu... in that dispositions are not mechanical responses to a given situation, but are more like conditions which may or may not become manifested in certain contexts. One could say that a culture provides for people an *emotional habitus*, with a language and set of practices which outline ways of speaking about emotions and of acting out and upon bodily feelings within everyday life. (Burkitt, 1997: 43)

Emotional responses are shaped and conditioned by the social and cultural milieu within which they are expressed. This is the sociological foundation of the analysis of postemotionalism.

With respect to the mechanisms which influence the rise of postemotionalism, the close interplay between economic and cultural phenomena is important. First, the relentless global expansion of multinational leisure enterprises creates market vacuums in its wake which are filled by the icons of American culture such as McDonald's and Coca-Cola. Increasingly indigenous cultures must vie with all things American for their niche in the leisure and tourist market place giving rise to the phenomenon which has been referred to variously as the 'McDonaldisation of society' (Ritzer, 1992) or the 'Disneyisation of society' (Bryman, 1999). The sociological consequence of these processes is that the new post-industrial service industries force the standardisation of products, work practices and consumption patterns throughout the world. Inauthentic 'niceness' is the mode adopted for customer and commercial dealings lest commercial reputations be destroyed, customer loyalty damaged and, worst of all, lest resort may be taken to expensive litigation to repair damaged reputations and recoup wasteful capital outlays. Regarding this issue, Bryman (1999) discusses the training practices of the fast food and leisure industries in an interesting way: we now have something called emotional labour training in McDonald's and Disney where staff are trained in the 'act of expressing socially desired emotions during transactions'. In everyday life we are collectively forced to behave in postemotional ways. The preference for the other-directedness of a McDonald's type of fast food outlet (now acknowledged as the market standard) rather than the solitary and intimate experience of a restaurant, or Parisian café, is a fact that most parents on holiday with their children have come to accept. And, of course, the nature of the theme park is such that it is enjoyed as a collective rather than a solitary experience forcing all other tourist attractions to at least accommodate to this postemotional reality when trying to compete for customers. It is the everyday pressure towards other-directed experiences and away from inner-directed ones in the postindustrial society which is beginning to create the conditions within which postemotionalism predominates. As Messinger and Clark (1961) and Burkitt (1997) might observe, it is the situational constraints to be other-directed in modern society which are difficult to escape and which reinforce postemotionalism.

Second, the culture industry consisting of the global mass media has a crucial agenda-setting function which shapes consciousness and attitudes. Who can ignore the pivotal role played by the mass media in orchestrating and legitimising the postemotional hysteria surrounding the death of Diana, Princess of Wales, in 1997? We have a society succumbing to postemotionalism through the tremendous growth in broadcasting opportunities: with so many television and radio stations to fill, the content of programmes often reflects the insincerity, shallowness and insubstantiality of what Meštrović would identify as postemotionalism. Indeed, the number of television shows now being broadcast which revolve around the theme of personal disclosure in which members of the public confess all manner of deviant predilections for the entertainment of millions has increased rapidly in the last decade. A genre which could be called *post-therapeutic* television has become established throughout the world: it is Warhol's fifteen minutes of fame that appears to be the motivation behind participation in such shows rather than genuine unburdening. The witnessing of others' misery and discomfort from an uninvolved distance for the purposes of being entertained comes close to defining the postemotional condition.

Perhaps a note of clarification needs to be made at this point. The concept of postemotionalism risks being interpreted as an ideological weapon to criticise what some regard negatively as the Americanisation of contemporary culture. The notion is reduced to a description of the imperialist tendencies apparent in multinational leisure and fast food industries. The conclusion might be that as moral panics about trashy cultural developments emanating from the United States have been common for a century or more, what is revealed is not so much an interesting sociological concept but rather a display of *historical amnesia* (see Pearson, 1983). Such a conclusion would be based on a misreading of Meštrović's analysis: the concept of postemotionalism is illuminating about the *qualitatively* different nature of social relationships and emotional phenomena today compared with earlier periods. It is the disappearance of social as well as cultural space for inner-directed experiences and relationships which becomes problematic. Sociologically this is a situational and relational phenomenon rather than a matter of cultural politics.

The fascinating sociological question which arises from Riesman's work and Meštrović's analysis of postemotionalism is the implications for the way in which welfare is viewed. Certainly it suggests that the issue of public support for welfare is now a much more complex matter. For example, the inner-directed type of individual can clearly be identified in 19th-century philanthropic work. The members of the Charity Organisation Society were middle and upper middle-class individuals imbued with the same entrepreneurial spirit and Christian drive in the field of welfare that Weber had associated with the capitalist ethic. However, with the growth of state responsibility for welfare services and the decline of voluntarism and charitable provision throughout most of the 20th century, the disappearance of the inner-directed welfare worker led to the appearance of the pragmatic and detached health and welfare professional of the modern welfare state: postemotionalism became a necessary part of the practitioner's professional demeanour. As the idea of welfare pluralism becomes the new orthodoxy throughout the Western countries, can we expect a return to such inner-directed drives in a postmodern world in which the idea of the welfare state is now viewed as being counter to the individualism of the era?

There are, perhaps, two sides to this question. First, the scope for a strong inner-directed entrepreneurial drive among those seeking to provide welfare services on a commercial basis can already be observed and we should expect it to develop further as the 21st century progresses. Second, and more problematic in terms of what has become known as the informal sector of care by family, neighbours and communities, is the concern that people no longer possess the same levels of caritas, that is the same sense of empathy, sympathy and feelings of obligation, to make a devolved responsibility for welfare support from the state to civil society possible without doing harm to the humanitarian pretensions upon which the Western welfare state idea was built. There will always be inner-directed types in a market-based society whose main objective will be to gain a commercial foothold in the growing 'welfare industry', whether that be selling social insurance, private health care, sheltered housing or nursing care. However, the impact of such commercialism on the caritas which forms the 'glue' binding the social structure, and which makes informal care giving possible, is a neglected issue. Richard Titmuss (1958, 1987) raised similar concerns about the welfare ethic in the 1960s when he perceived the threat posed by the commercial nexus on social solidarity and the spirit of altruism which he maintained was fostered by the British welfare state. I think Titmuss, like Riesman in the United States, was providing an early analysis of the coming postemotionalism that we can now recognise at the beginning of the new century.

The links between the broad scope of the analyses offered by Riesman and Meštrović and their implications for the field of welfare require a further teasing out.

## Amoral familism and the individualisation of the social

The key to understanding the current stage of development of the Western welfare states is to recognise that the era of the modernist collective approach to social policy coincides with movements towards a postmodernist individualist approach. It is this uneasy conflict of principles which fuels the contemporary welfare state debate, and it is because of this factor that I have stressed throughout this book that we must retain a sense of the continuing political conflict between anti-modernists, modernists and postmodernists.

The rise of the postemotional type follows the logic of this dialectical tension: the individualism of the inner-directed type characteristic of 19th-century and early 20th-century society gave way to the sociable and socialised other-directed type of the mid- to late 20th century who was a product of the post-1945 Fordist welfare state idea in Europe. In the United States where the development of postemotionalism has gone further than in Europe, the introduction of collectivist welfare policies in the inter-war years and in the 'great society' project of the 1960s lies alongside the anti-welfare individualism promoted by all contemporary political parties. What is being suggested here is that the cultural and institutional residues of the Fordist welfare state remain evident in the state pension schemes, social security benefits, social housing and nationalised health care found throughout the OECD countries, even to some extent in the United States, and that this residual collectivist legacy in an era of individualism shapes consciousness and emotions about caring responsibilities. The contradictory consciousness created by the emotional attachment to the idea of a welfare state and the intellectual barrage of negative analyses of its impact on our economic well-being prepares the ground for a distinctly postmodern social consciousness as we enter the 21st century. By this I mean that the postemotional type of the early 21st century, certainly throughout Europe and the other English-speaking nations if not in America where there has been an absence of a European style of welfare state, combines an inward looking familist attitude to welfare with an intellectual recognition of the need to shape social policies which will make an effective difference to the full range of social problems such as poverty, social inequality and criminality confronting us at both national and global levels. The uncaring and often hostile attitudes expressed in public opinion surveys towards social security systems perceived to be featherbedding an 'indolent and undeserving underclass' are often contradicted by strong emotional support for free health care and sympathy for the plight of children exposed to violence and neglect by a welfare system insufficiently funded to provide protection. This is an uneasy mix of social conscience, with weakening institutional roots in a shrinking welfare state and individualist attitudes grounded in hostility to what is perceived to be a profligate tax spending state: the urge is to look after oneself and one's family by retaining more earned income. What appears to be different today when compared with the period between 1945 and 1980 is that the state is no longer universally accepted by growing numbers of people in the OECD countries as being the best or most appropriate instrument to bring about change in the human condition, but there is a sense of despair regarding what is the most effective way to establish welfare security.

There are two concepts which I suggest can assist us in making sense of the new conjuncture in welfare politics which together encapsulate the essence of welfare in the postemotional society. First I want to describe the fundamental changes affecting the way contemporary welfare provision and welfare services are being organised, leading to transformations which amount to a new *postmodern welfare paradigm*. The concept used by Hungarian sociologist Zsuzsa Ferge to describe this process is the individualisation of the social (Ferge, 1997). Second, I want to reintroduce the concept of amoral familism which I briefly described at the end of Chapter 4. The original concept was used by American political scientist Edward Banfield to explain the absence of civic involvement in a southern Italian region, and I used it in Chapter 4 to underline the nature and significance of social capital. I now want to extend my discussion of the concept by applying it to the contemporary welfare debate. I believe that as a descriptive concept amoral familism is not limited to the study of 'backward societies' but it can also provide insight into the ways in which attachment to welfare is changing and beginning to exhibit postemotional features.

## The individualisation of the social

Two key features of the evolving postmodern welfare paradigm are the abandonment of solidarity and the pursuit of equality as axial principles around which welfare services and benefits revolve. Both the anti-modernists and the postmodernists, in their different ways, have secured the place of 'pluralism' and the 'freedom of individual choice' in the welfare lexicon of the 21st century. In making the case for freedom of choice for the individual the anti-modern right has evoked the idea that the market is a purifying force through which the individual can gain liberation from the tyranny of state-sponsored collectivism, and the postmodern left has buttressed this notion of individualism, in some cases perhaps inadvertently, by attacking the bureaucratic and monolithic welfare state apparatuses created by the modernist social democratic left. The rhetoric of individualism, choice and responsibility has established a new centre of gravity in the welfare debate. The new welfare paradigm based on an expanding role for commercialism, voluntarism and familism contains the following features:

- A stress on individual and intergenerational security by means of private and freely chosen purchases of welfare products rather than security maintained by collective means.
- Encouragement to employers to reward their skilled personnel by building up an occupational system of welfare underwritten by big 'players' in the private social insurance business. Benefits may include, in addition to an occupational pension, private health insur-

ance and social care insurance for postretirement and the writing off of educational debts. These benefits may be subsidised.

- Families and family boundaries are increasingly acknowledged as setting the limits to which social responsibility need extend. The sense of the pooling of risk with other members of society is being lost.

- There is growing acceptance of unemployment, poverty and social polarisation as 'facts of life' *caused* by global economic forces beyond human control or the influence of nation states. The increasing stress on *individual autonomy* means that people are responsible for ensuring their future security and well-being rather than the state or the community.

- Social cohesion is no longer conceived of as a primary goal of social policy. The social integration of 'deviants' into society is being supplanted by the management of *excluded problem populations*. If necessary protection from criminals and anti-social behaviour can be purchased by individuals and private interests from the growing *private* security industry.

- Stress is placed on negative civil and political rights which guarantee 'freedoms' rather than positive rights which provide access to scarce resources and services underwritten by the welfare state.

A key idea at the heart of the new welfare paradigm is that of 'stake-holding' which was discussed in Chapter 5. A basic worry about this new direction in public welfare is that the emphasis placed on individual and family responsibility is premised on an unacknowledged problem: ideologically the *willingness* of populations to embrace a new welfare strategy in which social security and care is largely organised and funded through individual arrangements, whether that be private insurance or occupational benefits obtained from an employer, may be undermined by the absence of a *capacity* to participate in the new system because of the insecurities which accompany life in a postindustrial society dependent on a post-Fordist economy plugged into an uncertain global financial environment. The collapse of the 'tiger' economies of east Asia and the attendant economic anxieties generated throughout the world during 1998 and 1999 provide a warning for the future. In the past the way Western countries typically responded to such downturns in global events was to protect the indigenous population as far as possible with what we used to call the Keynesian welfare state. Now what appears to be happening, if we accept Will Hutton's general categorisation of Britain today as the 40:30:30 society (Hutton, 1995), is that only about 40 per cent of the population can be regarded as having either economic security and the capacity to purchase non-state welfare protection or access to non-state benefits through their occupational welfare perks. Public welfare will, inevitably, come to be regarded as providing only residual protection for the remaining bulk of the population. The divisions in society created by this individualisation of the social will exacerbate tendencies to isolate those at the bottom of the social hierarchy by the broadcasting of rhetorical labels which in turn will tend to legitimise punitive social control strategies. The concern must be that social control replaces social policy, an issue alluded to in Chapter 6.

## Amoral familism

The individualisation of the social most clearly manifests itself in the phenomenon of amoral familism. This concept has been associated only with the explanation of civic inaction in mainly rural and 'backward' societies, but I suggest that it can be applied with equally illuminating effect to the analysis of postemotional and postwelfare state societies. Banfield (1958) originally used the concept to describe the absence of a civic culture in southern Italy, and more recently Reis (1998) has applied the same notion to the analysis of Latin America. In the original formulation emphasis was given to the unwillingness of people to further the interests of the community or of society unless it was to their advantage to do so. The short-run strategy of maximising the material interests of individuals and their immediate family members was used to explain the undeveloped nature of political democracy and community activity in 'backward societies'. The particular features of the amoral familist highlighted by Banfield include:

- Someone with little interest in public affairs who considers that civic engagement is the responsibility solely of public servants.
- Someone with little concern about the integrity of public officials.
- Someone who believes that there is little point in being civically active unless there is a personal material gain.
- Someone who thinks official positions and privileged knowledge should be used for private advantage.
- Someone who thinks the law should be ignored unless there is a risk of detection and punishment.

- Someone who thinks bribery to achieve public goals and projects is commonplace and that everyone should give and receive bribes when opportunities free from risk arise.
- Someone who considers that the expression of social and political values claiming to reflect community rather than personal interests is inherently fraudulent.
- Someone who believes expediency rather than ideological commitment to a cause should guide behaviour.
- Someone who believes all forms of community leadership are about the pursuit of private advantage rather than the collective good.
- Someone who believes that the short-run material interests of one's family and oneself come before all other commitments.
- Someone who will oppose all public community projects which might benefit the wider society if it is not apparent how they will be of immediate or personal advantage.

The idea of amoral familism need not be restricted to the analysis of 'backward' societies. There are aspects of Banfield's description of the phenomenon in southern Italy which could be applied to many contemporary Western polities. In the cases of rural Italy and Latin America, a strong state replaces the absent civic culture. Community facilities and welfare services are provided in spite of the indifference of the people, but invariably of a very inferior kind and more often they are not provided at all. In contemporary Western societies it is ironically the divesting of responsibility by the state which is creating a social environment which generates an inward, selfish and postemotional posture towards welfare. To reaffirm the sociological interpretation of postemotionalism discussed earlier, the attitudes, lifestyle choices and, crucially, the economic relationships structured by the new welfare paradigm contribute to a society less concerned with solidarity and more concerned with self and family.

With respect to the current conjuncture of welfare politics in OECD countries, a case can be made that in a society dominated by postemotionality those who are reasonably secure will look on the plight of those who are not with detached 'concern'. An inward looking gaze in which the well-being of one's immediate family is the primary concern appears to have generated, at least to some extent, a general wish to reduce taxation in order to maximise the resources at the command of the individual. Caring and empathy for those who are unemployed will tend to be intellectualised rather than emotionally felt. This tends to be reinforced by the absence of institutional channels which traditionally have fostered solidaristic links between the 'haves' and the 'have nots'. Universal social benefits in which all members of society share are now regarded negatively in most OECD countries. This is not unconnected with the weakening of political movements, such as trade unions, which have fought to retain strong collectivist forms of welfare. While social class will tend to shape the nature of the amoral familism, for example whether the concerns are property based or not, it will not be limited only to those who have the resources to withdraw from civil society (recent policy thinking has identified the self-enforced exclusion of the rich and the very rich from society as a problem requiring governmental action. See Giddens, 1998). Working-class people can also be drawn into an amoral posture. As trade unions decline in strength and membership; as political parties of the old left rooted in areas of traditional manufacturing industries give way to new parties representing a more pragmatic social democratic left; and more and more unskilled and semi-skilled workers are employed in non-unionised conditions, the typical ideological insulation from right-wing market-based ideas about work, property and family responsibilities is evaporating.

Frank Parkin (1971) recognised many years ago that the deferential Conservative working-class voter was not deviant, because we should expect all workers in a market capitalist society to support and vote for right-wing parties given the inherent biases in the mass media, the education system and the political establishment operating behind the state's democratic facade. What really made a difference to the working-class voter, and ensured his support for the left, was the presence of strong trade unions with mass memberships in the key areas of industrial life, combined with working-class communities and a strong left-of-centre labour party which provided the ideological insulation for working-class people in the heyday of the Fordist welfare state, a point we alluded to in Chapter 3. Today those layers of insulation have been thinned by legal attrition, particularly the industrial relations legislation of the 1980s, and growing acceptance, not always justified, that politicians and trade unions can do nothing to protect working people. It was in the 1980s that we saw the consequences of that thinning layer of insulation as Thatcherism in Britain and Reaganism in the United States shifted the political centre of gravity to the right and the left found itself ill equipped to defend welfare principles which, historically, had been entrusted to it. The narrow concentration of trade unionists and workers on their wages and conditions rather than on the bigger political struggle against capitalism, often referred to as economism and welfarism, was derided by political activists and Marxists in the 1960s and 70s because of its limited social focus. However, economism and welfarism, which were at least based in collective struggles over the social wage, have given way to amoral familism and the pursuit of material well-being for self and family in a society where sympathy and empathy for those at the bottom of the social hierarchy appear to be residual and formalised emotions expressed increasingly through Red Nose Day, the BBC's Children in Need and sundry other public 'festivals' of 'caring': postemotionality and modern welfare consciousness are very close allies. What is very clear today is that the rhetoric of socialism is certainly not being matched by an emotional commitment to social praxis and class struggle. And, as the defence of the welfare state is no longer a priority for the 'new' social democratic parties gaining power throughout Western Europe, other means of dealing with poverty are being sought.

Stakeholding welfare is an idea which seems to be accepting of this general privatising focus of people in the OECD countries and may well exacerbate tendencies towards amoral familism in the future with very negative consequences if people pursue their own security with little regard for others, even distant and detached members of their wider family. On a more basic policy level, it is possible to witness the growth of amoral familism and the decline of civil society *in the community*. As the post-Fordist economy develops, the need for greater social and geographical mobility on the part of workers in order to match skills with jobs has become more evident. With the movement of families from one part of the country to another, the network of family and neighbourhood relationships, which together form the community care infrastructure, becomes less dense and so less able to cope with the increasing burden being devolved to the informal sector of care by the state. How families deal with this pressing problem has been the subject of a number of pieces of social policy research which we need not describe in detail here (see Finch and Mason, 1993; Qureshi and Walker, 1989; Challis *et al.*, 1995). It is the financial security of one's immediate family rather than the social and moral obligation to one's wider family, including aged parents, which inevitably becomes the primary concern. Amoral familism is not necessarily, or mainly, an attitude to caring and social obligations which arises because of a change in social values, but is to some extent a product of the changing structural requirements of a postmodern society demanding mobility and flexibility from its members. What needs to be acknowledged is the great variation in supportive networks and the capacity of families to provide caring assistance resulting from enforced population movements as people pursue a secure economic future (see Rodger, 1996; Wenger and Shahtahmasebi, 1990). Wenger and Shahtahmasebi (1990), for example, have identified at least six patterns of variation in social support networks. These variations are labelled:

1. family-dependent support network
2. local integrated support network
3. the local self-contained support network
4. the wider community-focused network
5. the private restricted support network
6. the independent household network.

The first two models probably equate with the underlying theory and assumptions informing community care policy. They both rely on there being close family, neighbours and friends nearby to assist with caring responsibilities. Variations 3 and 4, however, are characterised by an absence of close family contacts, although they are less problematic in terms of drawing on expensive professional backup in the short term because, as in 3, they are 'self-contained', and as in 4, they are focused on the wider community. However, in the longer term these patterns of support will also cause difficulties because there is an absence of close family relationships to contribute to the day-to-day caring if necessary. A similar picture emerges for variations 5 and 6 which are characterised by little or no community involvement and typically only one family relative assisting. In the case of 6, there is little contact with neighbours, no community involvement and few friends living locally. Community care as a policy appears to be failing because the assumptions being made about the willingness and capacity of people to care are undermined by the economic, financial and structural demands of a postmodern society.

The final issue which must be addressed is whether the movements and forces working globally will make resolution of these problematic social, cultural and policy issues more or less intractable. The potential role of the European Union, and the possibilities for a social Europe to balance the free market in a global economy, are issues to be addressed in the next chapter.

# 8

# Globalisation, social Europe and the future of social policy

Throughout this book we have examined a number of phenomena related to welfare state development and change in the postmodern era: changing conceptions of welfare obligations, changing conceptions of social citizenship, the decline of state welfare and the rise of welfare pluralism, concerns about the relationship between welfare and demoralisation, the search for communitarian solidarity, the destruction of urban communities and the rise of social exclusion and the rise of postemotionalism and amoral familism. Underlying the emergence of these social issues are the broad processes which collectively are being associated with the postmodern condition: the sense of rapid social change, cultural fragmentation, the loss of certainties about ideologies, social principles and the future. One phenomenon which frames all these social changes is globalisation. It is the disappearance of national boundaries in economic and cultural life which is driving forward a new consciousness that we may be living in a post-nation state epoch. The fear is that independent decision-making power, especially about matters relating to the welfare state and social policy, has been lost to all-powerful international economic forces and transnational corporations (TNCs).

In Chapter 3 we examined the debate about what determines welfare state growth and possible decline. The framework within which that debate has been organised is industrialism versus politics: the former position which is grounded in the 'logic of industrialism' suggests that all welfare states within the OECD group of nations are converging towards a standardised profile; the latter position suggests that we must recognise that there are varying welfare trajectories for nation states based on their distinctive political and cultural histories. Each position directs us to different features of welfare systems, a point that was made in Chapter 3. The focus on structural aspects of welfare systems such as demographic change and social expenditure ratios favoured by the 'logic of industrialism' school is not entirely incompatible with the 'politics counts' perspective which has revealed different types of welfare state regimes based on variations in political, cultural and ideological principles. In updating that debate by introducing the notion of globalisation to the analysis, we are again directed towards the relative influences of structural (global economic forces) and political (nation states) variables in determining welfare state development. I will argue that we should not lose sight of the extent to which global economic forces will be mediated by national and local points of resistance. Global capitalism must always negotiate the obstacles placed in its way by national politics and political institutions. While there is undoubtedly evidence that we are now living in a world characterised by greater interdependence due to the advances in information technology and a liberalisation of world trade, the extent to which these trends amount to the formation of a global society and culture may have been overstated: globalisation is a real phenomenon but so, too, is the nation state.

To adopt an eclectic position on globalisation may appear to be contradictory. Either nation states are being drawn into an interdependent economic world and being made to serve a secondary role to global capitalism or they are not. If they are, then talk of resistance and independent political control is sophistry. My response is that we are not at that stage in the development of nation states when their independent national interests are totally powerless in the face of relentless economic forces. We live in a world of contradictory movements at the level of both national and international economies and, in terms of the formation of political institutions, the emergence of nationalism, regionalism and devolved political power within nation states coincides with the international construction of power blocks such as the European Union. These movements towards political localism, which include Europe in relation to the rest of the world, constantly mediate the global forces which threaten to create a standardised world. In this context, the growth of the European Union can, perhaps, be interpreted not so much as an outgrowth of globalisation as a reaction to it and one which can provide resistance to it.

## Competing models of globalisation

The discussion in the last chapter centred on what Meštrović (1997) has called postemotionalism and one of the key factors nourishing that development is the 'Americanisation of society'. This development points to the globalisation of cultural forces which appear to be working to standardise the world, especially the rich OECD countries, so that all Western countries might be equally receptive to global consumer products and might respond to economic, political and, in the context of the subject matter discussed in Chapter 7, emotional phenomena in a predictable way. It is the relentless desire for global predictability and standardisation which lies at the heart of the global process. However, the concept of globalisation is seductively all embracing as an explanation of current social and economic changes and needs to be deconstructed in order to reveal its different dimensions. In this final chapter our main interest lies in the relationship between the nation state as the site where social policy needs are identified and the supranational political institutions which constrain the decision-making choices about those social needs in a global economic environment. The European Union is the most significant entity in this context.

Just as in the 'industrial logic' versus 'politics counts' debate, there are competing models of globalisation. There are three general themes to be discussed. First, there is a strong globalisation thesis which argues that we are now part of a world system in which national economies have fused with transnational economic forces so making the nation state redundant as an economic and political actor on the world stage. The strong globalisation thesis is premised on the emergence of a *borderless world*. Second, the contrary view which talks of the myth of globalisation, argues that the strong thesis has over-interpreted international agreements about liberalising trade and that the nation state remains the foundation of economic and political stability in the world system. And finally, a more pragmatic interpretation can be identified which concentrates on the diversity of methods of capital accumulation in the world economy, particularly the coexistence of Fordism with post-Fordism, and places explanatory emphasis on what has been described as *global commodity chains* (Gereffi, 1994). We need to examine these differences.

Developments in the global economy have strengthened the power of capital over organised labour and so weakened the traditional base of support for welfare state development, a point which has been made at several points in this book. However, beyond this there are concerns that the nation state is being undermined by the pressing problem of creating an investment environment for mobile capital. What has become clear from the emerging interest in globalisation, regardless of which perspective is adopted, is that the typical conception of the welfare state as an instrument for redistribution and social protection is no longer tenable. It is for this reason that we must situate our analysis of the future of social policy in an examination of global political economy.

## Globalisation in a borderless world

The notion of a borderless world comes from Kenichi Ohmae (1990, 1991) who has argued that the emergence of globalisation has meant that economic and market forces can break out of the constraints placed on them by nation states. He maintains that people want consumer products rather than attachment to outdated notions of nationalism and national identity: 'Sony not soil' is his slogan (see Ohmae, 1991). From his perspective the growth of what has become known as the TNC is a positively good thing for the world population: nation states have been inefficient at managing economic affairs especially in the past century and in an era of open global trading and movement of financial capital they have become positively dysfunctional. Within a global economy capital is free to invest in areas or zones of the world where it is scarce. In the contemporary situation this has meant the flow of capital to East Asia and to certain countries in South America. The globalisation thesis therefore views these developments positively as leading to industrial and economic development. A more pessimistic view of the same processes points to the potential for the super-exploitation of these newly industrialising countries, as mobile capital seeks out and takes advantage of cheaper labour in the Third World.

The rise of the TNCs with assets and annual sales far in excess of the GNP of many Third World countries has created fears about the political impact of their economic power. Indeed as Kiely (1998) observes: 'In the early 1990s, the combined sales of the world's largest 350 TNCs totalled nearly one-third of the combined GNPs of the advanced capitalist countries'(p. 96). The extent to which these massive TNCs have penetrated world markets is revealed by the fact that companies such as Colgate-Palmolive, Avon, IBM and Dow Chemicals earn half their revenue from foreign sales (see Sklair, 1995). The political consequences for nation states arising from this concentration of economic and market power flow from the inter-connected nature of the global economy. So too much taxation on the international entrepreneurial elites and on their capital projects will inevitably lead to the flight of capital out of a country to find alternative and more 'friendly' investment environments. Given this scenario, it is argued that the effective power of nation states has been weakened and their ability to make policy decisions which are perceived to be detrimental to the interests of international capital in a global economy has been undermined. The most that nation states can do is to take policy decisions which maintain their national competitiveness. This aspect of globalisation was alluded to in Chapter 6 in relation to the post-Fordist city and the marketing of place which seems to be a feature of many large cities around the world. A strong implication of the thesis is that governments and political movements will be forced to recognise that the relentless nature of globalisation means that ideas rooted in 19th- and early 20th-century political philosophy which view the state as an instrument through which capital can be controlled and the masses emancipated are now largely irrelevant.

However, there are logical flaws in the globalisation thesis. The nation state remains a strong player in the politics of the world system through the circuits of diplomacy. For instance, the thesis draws attention to the growing interconnectedness of the global economy. Market failure in one part of the world will have direct consequences for all countries within the global system. The global economic crisis of 1998 would be an example of this: economic collapse in the newly industrialising countries of South East Asia and the economic deflation in Japan had worldwide economic impact, especially through the explosion of international debt and the loss of economic confidence. The only solution to such world wide economic catastrophes is through co-ordinated action on the part of the main economic nation states. What truly global institutions that do exist, and it might be acknowledged that agencies such as the International Monetary Fund and the World Bank pass as such, they do not represent a higher level of global policy action above and independent of the major OECD nations. The supporters of the strong globalisation thesis should acknowledge, therefore, the continuing pivotal role for key First World nations in the world system. The thesis has been subjected to critical appraisal from a number of sources.

## The myth of globalisation

An alternative outlook on these same economic movements is provided by a number of sources of which Hirst and Thompson's book *Globalisation in Question* (1996) is the most sustained attempt to place the globalisation thesis in a more sceptical perspective.

Hirst and Thompson (1996) argue that while there is a growing liberalisation of trade between nations, this has tended to work through trading blocks rather than in a genuinely open free market world. Trading is regional in that free market blocs such as the European Union facilitate trade between member states rather than increasing trading activity between Europe and the rest of the world. Indeed, Hirst and Thompson have made the provocative argument that trading between economic blocs has returned the OECD countries to their 19th-century position. Globalisers, they maintain, have short memories. There is a tendency to think of globalisation as having started only in the 1970s when in reality many European economies were more open prior to 1914: focusing on the ratio of exports to GDP they point out that France's ratio in 1913 was 35.4 per cent and in 1973 it was 29 per cent; Germany's ratio in 1913 was 35.1 per cent and in 1973 it had only slightly increased at 35.2 per cent. Their argument also draws attention to the fact that capital was highly mobile, levels of foreign investment were high, especially 'for major international *rentier* states like Britain and France' (Hirst, 1997: 210) and adherence to the Gold Standard ensured that independent monetary decisions were beyond the nation state even then. The understanding that nation states should pool their sovereignty as part of a broader international project is not new.

Developing this theme, Kiely (1998), for example, has argued that there is indeed evidence of increasing globalisation: 'Among OECD countries, the ratio of exports to GDP increased from 9.5 per cent in 1960 to 20.5 per cent by 1990' (Kiely, 1998: 102). Further, direct foreign investment has also grown: three times faster than trade flows and four times faster than output in the 1980s. And tariffs have declined in the First World countries from 25 per cent in the 1950s to 5 per cent in the 1990s. However, he also agrees with Hirst and Thompson that for most TNCs foreign investment is less significant than domestic investment: 'Of the top 100 firms in the world in 1993, only 18 kept the majority of their assets abroad' (Kiely, 1998: 103). Most major TNCs in Germany, Japan and the USA sold between 70–75 per cent of their goods at home. And despite the changes mentioned, the share of Africa, Asia and Latin America in world trade has declined. The economic and trading position of the rapidly developing East Asian tiger economies has tended to obscure the reality that overall there has been a marked decline in the performance of Third World economies on the international trading markets. While Taiwan and South Korea were booming many of the African and Latin American countries were witnessing the deterioration of their trading position. Direct foreign investment in Third World countries tends to be concentrated in a few areas, with Singapore, Mexico, Hong Kong, Malaysia, Egypt, Argentina, Thailand and Taiwan being favoured. As Kiely (1998) summarises:

> The share of trade in the GDPs of the most successful First World economies remains comparatively small. Exports account for less than 12 per cent of the GDPs of the USA, Japan and Europe – lower than it was on the eve of the First World War... around 90 per cent of these economies are based on production for the domestic market (Kiely, 1998, 103).

While some theorists suggest that the Hirst and Thompson analysis is at the very least partial, there is an acknowledgement that their warnings against a precipitate acceptance of the globalisation thesis are timely. Giddens (1998) disputes the data or at least Hirst and Thompson's interpretation of them. He argues that a greater range of goods and services are tradable today than in the 19th century, and that whatever is being argued for international trade, the markets operating on a real time basis are truly global, dealing in 1 trillion dollars per 24 hour period on the financial exchange markets. This volume of business has risen by a factor of five in the past 15 years. For Giddens, the transformation of time and space is what globalisation is about, and the cultural influences stimulated by information technology and television have undoubtedly been significant. However, he too seems reluctant to accept the strong globalisation thesis offered by Ohmae and sees a role of continuing significance for the nation state.

In spite of the often used notion of globalisation this more sceptical perspective maintains that there are very few genuine TNCs or cohesive global economic and financial elites. Indeed it suits most of the large TNCs to continue to work from a national base and to support the federations of nation states which establish trading rules and regulations, authorise standards for property rights and work to sustain stability in exchange markets. The element of 'myth' in the globalisation debate arises because ideology is being confused for empirical description. Hirst (1997) argues that we are being offered a metanarrative, in both pessimistic and optimistic versions, about changes in the world economic system which does not fit the facts. Further, Robertson and Khondker (1998) are concerned about the lack of precision in the way in which the concept is being used around the world. They argue that globalisation is creating universal and particular features simultaneously: countries are developing similarities but are also celebrating their differences. Indeed, they suggest that an international form of 'political correctness' has emerged where there is talk everywhere of resistance to global forces. This tends to suggest that at the very least there is a sense of the global but it may be very different depending on which part of the globe the world is being viewed from. Discourses of globalisation abound. Regional discourses reflect strategic economic viewpoints: the French worry about Anglo-American cultural imperialism, East Europeans concern themselves about Westernisation and the homogenisation of their culture and many East Asian countries fear globalisation as a new colonialism. A self-fulfilling prophesy may be at work whereby talk of globalisation may be so heated and persistent that policy actors come to behave as if we do live in a standardised global world even though what is actually transacted, both economically and culturally, would undermine such a view. As Robertson and Khondker (1998) observe 'we are witnessing *both* trends in the direction of a borderless world and, at the same time, the shoring-up of the nation state' (p. 30). Indeed, globalisation has not obliterated the nation state but rather has secured its position 'as a formidable actor in the global arena'. Giddens (1998) has similarly talked about globalisation taking powers upwards while also pressing them downwards. The dual movements towards strengthening the European Union while also acknowledging the political significance of nationalism and devolved powers capture this idea.

There is undoubtedly a global dimension to economic, political and cultural life. However, the evidence in support of the 'strong thesis' is weak. Sklair (1995) believes we still have to develop a systematic understanding of what he would call the sociology of the global system. In establishing an agenda for such a project he eschews state-centrist approaches for a focus on 'transnational practices'. These are practices which originate with non-state actors in the economic sphere with the TNCs; in the political sphere with the transnational capitalist class; and in the cultural sphere with a consumerist elite operating in the international communication and media industries. Whether there is cohesion among and between these elites and institutional complexes is doubtful and, until it can be demonstrated otherwise, we should exercise some scepticism about the *strong globalisation thesis*.

## Global commodity chains

At various points in this book reference has been made to two distinct methods of capital accumulation: Fordism and post-Fordism. While a great deal of contemporary sociological and political analysis has concentrated on the signs of transition from one dominant method to another, from Fordism to post-Fordism, in reality that transition is incomplete. In Chapter 6 we described the changing landscape of our urban centres as they adjust to the decline of industrial and manufacturing employment and the growth of service and retail industries selling leisure and tourism. I also argued that notions of 'dual and quartered cities' testify to the incompleteness of the transition. Post-Fordism is about the introduction of flexible technologies, flexible trading and working relationships and the political adjustments which the state, organised labour and policy actors make to rapidly changing economic conditions. It is also about the proliferation of small businesses and production units as the large primary manufacturing industries decline. It does not fit well with a thesis which predicts the concentration of capital into TNCs largely free of national boundaries and loyalties. Instead the large core companies locate close to suppliers and final markets mainly in the First World. They do not represent what some have called 'footloose corporations' (Kiely, 1998).

Fordist methods of production and social policy principles and attitudes associated with the era of 'high Fordism' in the twenty years immediately after the Second World War remain in evidence. This is also the case throughout the global economic system. Indeed, in comparing Japanese with American car manufacturers, Kiely (1998) has pointed to the Fordist logic of American car production and the post-Fordism of the Japanese. The Fordist approach adopted by American manufacturers is one of evolving a 'world car strategy' where production of a single model for the whole world is spread across several countries in accordance with the logic of investing in low cost locations. By contrast the Japanese have 'not competed through global economies of scale' but instead have pioneered post-Fordist methods of organising car production. They have introduced multi-skilled shopfloor working practices which distinguish core from peripheral workers by sub-contracting some tasks to a secondary labour market. The logic of a 'retail model' has been imported into car production: under- and over-production are eradicated and location *near to* suppliers means that materials can be ordered on a daily basis and integrated into what is known as a 'just in time' system. This is a quite different way of minimising production costs when compared with the logic of Fordism. Investment has tended to be mainly at home but where it has been made abroad, as in Western Europe, it tends to be near to markets and founded on the recreation and reproduction of its home supplier structure in the host country. The proliferation of suppliers and small to medium sized companies around the post-Fordist production system is a feature.

Capital has tended to concentrate in the First World and where it has flowed to Second and Third World areas it has done so in selected concentrations. What is emerging is a *global hierarchy of production*. As Gereffi (1994) observes, 'the world economy today is a *global factory* in which production of a single good commonly spans several countries, with each performing tasks in which it has a cost advantage' (p. 219). There is a geographical spread of industries but only a limited number of favoured countries are in the commodity chain. It is often too risky, too costly and too time consuming for TNCs to invest in training and reputation building in untried locations, to say nothing of the start-up costs entailed in building production in Third World areas. This has meant that particular newly industrialising countries are favoured for investment, but the main stress of the TNCs is on investment in home and First World markets. Many Third World countries are left outside the global factory entirely but through time they will come to challenge those favoured newly industrialising countries currently hosting the mass production manufacturing enterprises lost by the First World. A system of international sub-contracting leads upwards from the Third World to a management and administrative centre in the First World. There are two general models of this. Producer-driven chains have arisen for aircraft, cars and computer systems where the site of production cannot easily be moved. The producers exert control over raw materials, component suppliers and retail outlets. Multi-layered production involving thousands of firms can be organised to serve a major production plant at the top of the hierarchy. Buyer-driven chains emerge where high value goods carrying brand names require cheap labour-intensive production methods. Invariably, the buyer in the First World will lack a production facility but sub-contracts work across a global chain. Control of the global hierarchy of production is exercised at the final consumption level. Core companies sub-contract the manufacture of sports clothing and equipment and other fashionable branded items to low cost Third World countries and exert backwards control over the producers through their control of design, product development, advertising and marketing. It is this feature in particular which has had an impact on First World manufacturing jobs: the decline of high cost textile manufacture in Britain, for example, has led to cheap labour-intensive production in Third World countries down the global hierarchy. A global chain can incorporate both Fordist and post-Fordist methods of production. That is why Gereffi (1994) has argued that we should not think of the flexible specialisation associated with post-Fordism as a superior form of manufacturing system which will inevitably displace the mass production characteristic of Fordism. The distinction between producer-driven and buyer-driven commodity chains in the global system indicates that they are not mutually exclusive and will co-exist.

The state is not an idle observer of these processes. Active competition between nation states, particularly in the First World economies, to maximise inward foreign investment and protect indigenous commercial and industrial development from attempts by Second and Third World countries to scale upwards on the global chain is a key feature of contemporary economic and political reality. The state is drawn into a system of 'marketing the country' in competition with other First World economies through lobbying for, and the subsidising of, plant location. As TNCs want to be near their final market, location within the European Union by American or East Asian companies leads to competition between member states for supplier and manufacturing plants or profitable high skilled designing and research and development units. The start-up costs which TNCs dislike about Second and Third World production projects are largely eliminated within the rich OECD countries because of their high levels of education and skills training which adapt them well for securing employment activity at the top of the global production hierarchy. The nation state also has to acknowledge and deal with what are genuinely global agencies in the international political economy of development. Organisations such as the World Bank, the International Monetary Fund, the International Labour Organisation, the OECD, as well as the General Agreements on Tariffs and Trade, International Business and International Investment, are lobbies and legal entities which pressurise governments into the pursuit of what are considered prudent economic and social policy strategies. Such agencies are also involved in stimulating and financing economic development throughout the global system (see Deacon, 1997). The scope for welfare within this complex international political and economic framework tends to be constrained.

Esping-Andersen (1996) conceptualises the central problem of globalisation from a welfare state perspective concisely: the market for unskilled labour has become international and the most expensive unskilled labour can be found in Europe and the English-speaking world. The loss of freedom to make independent decisions about fiscal and monetary policy has largely been accommodated by nation states pooling their sovereignty in an increasingly interdependent world economy. The process of monetary integration within the European Union is the best example of this. More problematic in social policy terms has been the social dislocation resulting from a growing pool of long-term unemployed workers at a time when society is ageing and family structures are changing. In addition, some First World countries, most notably southern European countries within the European Union, have had to address the problem of how their welfare systems can accommodate to the combination of deruralisation and deindustrialisation occurring simultaneously: mass unemployment among farm workers and the disappearance of labour-intensive assembly line jobs which might once have employed them are superimposed on welfare states yet to be fully developed by North European standards.

Rhodes (1996) observes that the pace of social and economic change is so rapid, and the risks associated with life in a global postindustrial environment so unpredictable, and multiplying, that the ability to control and reduce welfare systems is now a major problem for all countries within the European Union. The European tradition for 'fat' welfare states rather than 'lean' systems has meant that political legitimacy may be rapidly withdrawn from governments which attempt to emulate the American tradition of virtually no state welfare at all. In the USA the response to global competitive forces has been to pursue a low unemployment strategy by accepting income inequalities and the proliferation of low paying, comparatively insecure 'McJobs' (McDonald's again serving the purpose of providing graphic illustration of the typical post-Fordist American job profile for those discarded from the core workforce). As the dynamic behind the post-Fordist transformation of Western European economies leads to a shake out of unskilled manufacturing jobs there are three possible policy approaches which could be adopted. First, the costs of the transition to post-Fordism could be absorbed by expanding welfare budgets to compensate citizens for the loss of their employment. This has been the strategy in the 1980s and 90s because of the historical commitments to welfare in most North Western European countries. Esping-Andersen has referred to this approach as 'the exit strategy'. The welfare system assists people to leave the labour market and survive in decommodified status. Second, in the absence of an extensive social welfare programme, and in a political and ideological context antagonistic to state welfare support, those workers considered peripheral to the core areas of economic activity could be *coerced* into accepting employment in the relatively insecure, low pay service and retail sectors which expand in the post-Fordist economy. This could be said to be an Anglo-American strategy which mainland Europe has not adopted and Britain has flirted with because of a historical, and in the 1980s an intellectual, relationship with the USA (British policy actors have been more receptive to American economic and welfare theories than their counterparts in continental Europe). Wage deregulation and other measures to maximise the pressure on the unemployed to re-enter the labour market cheaply and without job security characterise this approach, especially in the USA. The third approach, and the one currently being adopted by a social democratic European Union as we enter the 21st century, is to invest heavily in education and training to redeploy and place discarded workers back into a high skilled and high wage labour market. There are elements of the Scandinavian strategy of active labour market policy involved in this but without the absorption of labour into welfare state jobs which has been a feature of the Swedish model. A residue of unskilled and semi-skilled workers who cannot be reabsorbed into the labour market would be supported by a very much reduced level of state welfare buttressed by commercial, voluntary and informal assistance.

The interesting policy dilemma among the members of the European Union is how can a co-ordinated strategy on welfare issues be constructed which is genuinely transnational and so capable of dealing with social protection in a context of open markets and an increasingly 'borderless world'. In the rich OECD countries movement towards what Jessop (1994) has called the *Schumpeterian workfare state* appears to be the objective of all European governments seeking to adjust to the global hierarchy of production. As referred to in Chapter 2, a concept of 'the active society' is being driven forward by the OECD and the European Union (see Walters, 1997). Its purpose is to shape conceptions of citizenship and attitudes to welfare: citizenship shifts from being regarded as a legal and social entitlement to income maintenance and instead should become a right of access to lifelong education and qualification for a continually transforming labour market (see Esping-Andersen, 1996). The difficulty is in manoeuvring the European welfare systems towards the realisation of this new welfare paradigm. Global economic pressures may have jolted them towards this objective. The expectation has been that increased economic competition will lead to the shrinking of welfare systems as member countries adjust to economic decline in their industrial manufacturing sectors by reducing social and public expenditure in order to stimulate enterprise and job creation in new clean manufacturing and service sectors of the economy. However, the reality is that welfare systems have not reduced in response to increasing global competitiveness but have actually expanded. The rise in unemployment in Western Europe resulting from the loss of manufacturing jobs to cheap labour areas down the global hierarchy has led to expanding social policy programmes and rising social security budgets as the state rather than industry has borne the brunt of economic adjustment. The problem lies in the complexity of the causes of rising welfare dependency: as has already been alluded to, rising unemployment is combining with the ageing of societies and changing family forms to create continuing pressure on welfare budgets for social care programmes. A fundamental contradiction has arisen within the European Union countries, therefore, between pressures to attract mobile capital by diverting public funds from welfare to subsidise plant location and reduce company and corporation tax and the need to fund the growth of welfare dependency in a climate of rising insecurity.

## A social Europe?

The analysis of this chapter so far has been situated in the political economy of globalisation. It is the world system which now shapes social policy thinking in all the advanced economies. In response to these broad economic and political forces the member states of the European Union are developing a consensus about what type of welfare state should be encouraged: it is the social investment model in which the state gives its citizens 'human capital guarantees' that education, training and active labour market policies will support their lifelong adaptability for a high skill, high wage but constantly changing economic environment. In seeking to achieve a level of protection for European workers from the threats posed to jobs by globalisation, particularly flexibilisation and the liberalising of trade, the European Union has evolved a large free market, now underpinned by monetary union. However, the attempts to complement the free market with an equivalent level of social protection, the social dimension, have proved to be less successful. Throughout the 1990s the concern has been about whether the framework of the European Union can accomplish this project or whether ultimately social policy must remain under the control of the nation state; whether, indeed, it is possible to conceive of a European level of social protection at all which is distinct from that of the individual member states forming the free market.

If social policy remains a responsibility of nation states, will the services and principles underlying national systems be compatible with the *active* strategy being sponsored by the European Union and the OECD? The key themes which have exercised the minds of European politicians and policy makers about social services are identical to those which have troubled them about the economy: the 'borderless' nature of social as well as economic activity. The themes of *social dumping, welfare tourism* and *harmonisation* together with the notion of the *exclusiveness of national welfare systems* have shaped the social policy agenda in Europe throughout the 1990s.

## *Social dumping and welfare tourism*

Increasingly global economic agencies such as the IMF and the World Bank are taking a broad world system perspective on the place of welfare support within a global free market. Trading blocks such as the North Atlantic Free Trade Area and the European Union differ in terms of the degree of regulation employed to guide policy in work and social protection, with the EU being more advanced in terms of both employment regulation and social policy. The concern often expressed by global finance and trading agencies is that trading blocks harbour social protection policies which might be regarded as restrictive or unfair in a global free market. The EU is constantly being forced to examine the development of its welfare strategy in this context (see Deacon, 1997). Internally, the problems surrounding the differences to be found between member states of the EU with large and comprehensive welfare systems, such as the Scandinavian countries, and member states with relatively undeveloped or laggardly systems, especially in southern Europe, highlight the issue of social dumping. The key issues can be set out without dispute:

- Welfare regimes vary enormously in terms of their generosity and in the proportion of GDP which is allocated to social programmes. The strong welfare systems of North Western Europe are the best in the world.
- The global economy creates conditions within which the strong welfare systems in North Western Europe are being undermined by

the need for their economies to adapt to harsher competition from the global economy. Particularly problematic is their assumption that a standard worker family model of welfare remains functional in a post-Fordist economic environment.

- In global terms, the strong welfare states of North Western Europe provide a poor model for other regions in the world system, including southern European members of the European Union. Northern welfare regimes are now too expensive to establish in backward welfare areas.

- While such strong welfare systems exist they will encourage either welfare tourism, as people from poor welfare countries gravitate towards the rich to maximise their welfare security, or social dumping as the poor welfare countries deprive their own workers of social security to undermine the competitiveness of strong welfare states. Capital will potentially flow to whichever countries afford it the best deal and, increasingly, it is signalling that 'lean' rather than 'fat' welfare systems are preferred.

Global economic competition may be impacting negatively on the provision of welfare: there is a great potential for the political battle within countries over social policy to result in a dumbing down of provision rather than the extension of the Northern European model to other parts of the globe. In the context of the European Union, there has been concern that the north/south divide in welfare provision may lead to conflicting interests between northern countries such as Britain, Sweden, Finland, Denmark, Germany, Austria and France and the southern states such as Spain, Portugal and Greece. Workers within a common and free market should enjoy similar advantages and benefits but the south may accuse the northern states of privileging their workers by providing extensive welfare support while it enjoys only the most rudimentary safety net cover. In countries such as Sweden, Denmark and Finland there is a fear and resentment of those who either work for international agencies or represent countries in the European Union other than their own, and who may be advocating the standardisation of welfare regimes downwards (see Andersen, 1993). Indeed the antipathy towards the EU from Norway has partly been explained by Geyer (1998) in terms of the strength of their 'entrenched' social democratic movement compared with Britain's weaker social democratic foundations: the EU is perceived by Norwegians as a threat to their social democratic welfare state, whereas the modernising British Labour Party, and some elements within the Labour movement, have historically been more receptive to Europe, seeing it as a source of defence against neo-liberal attacks on welfare in the 1980s and 90s. While the popular feeling is that welfare issues should respond to different rhythms from those of the market, in reality the two are inextricably bound together. It is for this reason that co-ordination of national welfare systems is likely to be an ongoing interest for those committed to an integrated Europe.

Hantrais (1995) has identified the central paradox of European social policy: social policy has traditionally been seen as a responsibility of nation states but without a European level of co-ordination of welfare, social dumping and welfare tourism may become a source of political instability in the future. The absence of a European level of social policy may also hinder the entry of Eastern European countries to the EU. Transitional societies such as Poland, Hungary and the Czech Republic seeking membership of the EU contain within their borders a potential for unleashing welfare tourism unless and until their economies and social infrastructures can be brought up to the standards of Western Europe. The prospect of large-scale unemployment leading to a westwards migration into more affluent European countries in search of work and social security is a major problem. The policing of the borders of the EU with external European countries will continue to be a problem until a broader based European solution to the economic imbalance between east and west can be found. De Swaan (1990) poses a series of questions highlighting the problematic nature of that relationship. Will it be a colonial one? Will a Western model of social policy be exported? And how can a welfare system driven largely by employmentship rather than citizenship access to welfare operate in societies where only a fraction of the population have been assimilated into a market economy? Such problems require a great deal of European level co-operation, and a stress on purely economic imperatives without also acknowledging the social dimension of the EU would undermine the broader strategy of integration.

### Exclusivity and harmonisation

How can a European level of social policy assert itself? De Swaan (1990) has suggested that there are mechanisms which might work to overcome the exclusive nature of social benefits. The free movement of capital, labour and people will tend to level down differences in wages, interest rates and profit margins. And the *exclusiveness* of welfare systems could be undermined by increasing economic and political interdependence.

These processes will undoubtedly create a context within which the vast differences between welfare systems inside the EU may through time become less exaggerated. However, such structural pressures must overcome the reluctance of political actors within nation states to relinquish control over an area of policy around which political controversy revolves and political legitimacy is gained or lost. The EU has evolved from a set of arrangements about economic co-operation to a more politically integrated concept of a united Europe. Historically it has been easier to establish agreements about employment related social measures than about broader non-work social programmes relating to social care which remain the sole responsibility of member states. The protection of workers rights has, therefore, been the only real field in which legislative guidelines have been made. Social legislation has largely been about establishing rules and procedures, regulatory activity dealing with setting standards and creating non-binding 'soft law' which has the force of political rather than legal obligation (see Cram, 1993). This is likely to remain the case at least until a higher level of convergence has been achieved between the varieties of welfare system. Gearing down welfare provision as part of a convergence process will inevitably cause political problems at a national level. This has meant that *harmonisation* of social policy has been limited to the recognition of the social security rights of workers from the member countries anywhere within the EU. Effectively this means that migrant workers are only entitled to the level of welfare support available in the host country. As the models of welfare prevailing within the EU vary enormously that might mean extremely generous benefits are available in the Nordic-Anglo-Saxon countries with nationalised and social insurance-based systems, but only rudimentary cover available in the southern European countries. Many of the first wave countries such as Germany retain a large measure of earnings-related inequality in their benefits which migrant workers must accept. Such variation is and is likely to remain politically difficult to eradicate in the foreseeable future.

The notion of a European social policy band similar to the European monetary system has been suggested as a means of making progress towards harmonisation (Hantrais, 1995). Such a system would encourage convergence by discouraging divergence: social expenditure ratios would be allowed to vary within a very limited band only. Convergence of social security systems would be its primary objective. In fact an implicit mechanism such as this will operate as part of the common currency arrangements. Together with the disciplines imposed by setting common interest rates and having a common currency, participants in the common monetary system must also impose self-controls on their propensity to increase social expenditure. It is precisely this issue which will concern the Scandinavian members of the EU with their historical commitment to state welfare. What becomes clear, however, is that it will ultimately be member states rather than a European-level welfare bureaucracy that will police and shape variations in welfare provision. Globalisation may be generating a common set of economic problems and dilemmas for Western countries but how they deal with those problems will vary, even within the EU. Aggregate sums of social expenditure may ultimately be imposed on all members of a common monetary system but the social principles, values and types of benefits which issue from such an arrangement may vary greatly, at least in the medium term.

The two key principles which will continue to vie with each other for policy supremacy are subsidiarity and solidarity. The EU has institutionalised the principle of subsidiarity or devolving powers to their lowest possible level: the principle seeks to ensure that the state will not take to itself powers which can best be devolved to lower levels. And this is the principle which is most likely to be evoked in the welfare debate. However, countries such as Britain, France, Sweden, Denmark, Finland and Austria have also historically adhered to a principle of solidarity to a greater or lesser extent. It remains to be seen whether a commitment to universalism and collectivist welfare can establish a space within an economic and political bloc geared more to facilitating capital than to assisting its human victims. How the tension between these rival principles will be relieved will ultimately depend on how competing visions of social Europe accommodate each other.

At a deeper level, the strains between European Union members over social policy may be a manifestation of historical and cultural differences regarding national identities. For example, Ian Buruma (1998) writes about *the rival spirits of Europe*. He points to the differences between those countries and regions forming the western seaboard of Europe and those countries forming the continental heartland of Europe:

An historic arc, from the Baltic states to the Hanseatic cities of northern Germany and all the way down to Lisbon via the British Isles and the Dutch coast; an arc of ports and great commercial cities, populated by people of many different creeds and races, suspicious of bureaucratic authority and aristocratic despotism. Beyond these cities, towards the east, lies the continental hinterland where the twin sirens of blood and soil have produced great romantic poetry and a history of ferocious violence. (Buruma, 1998)

The difference between these 'rival spirits' is that they give rise to different concepts of nationhood: to the east nationhood is defined by language, culture, history and romantic feelings about the land but to the west it is defined by political institutions. Buruma's amusing observation that 'a united Europe makes Germans feel less German and Britons less free' encapsulates the different perceptions nicely. The resistance to European integration and the loss of the welfare state may be greater in the Netherlands, Scandinavia and Britain, where large and strong welfare traditions have grown over the past century and where there may be a greater urge to consolidate social gains in institutional arrangements under national control. The Germans may be seeking to defend their national identity through control of the banking system rather than a concern for a welfare tradition which from its very inception in Bismarck's time was based mainly on political expediency: as a mechanism for undermining the collectivist urge for equality.

## Concluding remarks

It is unlikely that the EU will provide a defence of the principle of state welfare. It will remain the task of the member states to shape a welfare system which is compatible with a large integrated monetary system and free market. The social needs of their populations may be a secondary consideration compared with the day-to-day fine tuning required to maintain national economies within the disciplinary constraints which a common currency will inevitably impose on the very diverse economic conditions to be found throughout the EU. It will ultimately be the responsibility of nation states to negotiate their way to a conception of a postmodern welfare society which accommodates both the internal and external pressures of EU membership: the modernist's conception of a welfare state rooted in mid-20th-century thinking and social conditions will increasingly be seen as a product of a bygone era. The challenge is, of course, to ensure that on whatever basis a welfare society is established it retains a grounding in the humane foundations of the Western European welfare state tradition.

# Conclusion

The analysis began by suggesting that the context within which social policy must be constructed today has changed when compared with the immediate postwar years of the late 1940s. Contemporary European societies are far more pluralistic culturally, are politically more fragmented and are economically more uncertain because of the growing global interdependence of nation states. How social welfare should be organised and paid for in this internationally unpredictable environment remains a problem which students of social policy will be pondering in the coming years. We live in an era in which the cultural and economic barriers of the nation state are far more penetrable than they ever were in the 20th century resulting in the transformation of occupational, community and family life in the 21st century, especially compared with the 1950s and 60s when many of our received ideas about welfare were fashioned. In order to appreciate the complexities of the social welfare question today, students of social policy must incorporate ideas and concepts from sociological and cultural theory and recognise that the conceptual vocabulary and political insights of the 1980s are insufficient for the task of contemporary analysis.

An underlying argument running through the book has been that there is a contest, both intellectual and practical, between modernists, anti-modernists and postmodernists in politics, society and academia about the future character of a welfare society. The reason why the politics of welfare revolves around this notion of a welfare society is because there appears to be widespread recognition that since the early 1980s the role of the state in the provision of social care has been attenuated by the growth of the mixed economy of welfare. In addition there are changes likely to take place in the field of social security in the coming years as responsibility for pensions is transferred from the state to employers and individuals so further changing the basis upon which social solidarity and cohesion rest. This movement is already evident in a number of countries throughout the European Union. The anti-modernists can claim credit for counterposing the idea of a welfare society to the welfare state. By placing on to the social and political agenda the problematic of the relationship between state welfare and behaviour, important debates about social character, social capital and community have started where once there was only silence. However, the right's model of a welfare society is almost entirely based on the project of recovering the social principles and virtues of 19th-century British society as the basis for a reinvented and depoliticised civil society: the state and welfare are treated as being antithetical. The modernists by contrast remain wedded to a commitment to welfare state reform rather than the wholesale abandonment of a central political authority in the field of social policy. The new moral economy of welfare emanating from the social democratic parties in Europe seeks to transfer responsibility for welfare from the state to civil society but retain a residual role for the state to fund and organise what remains an extremely necessary aspect of life. It is the enduring reliance on the state to accomplish social change which characterises many on the centre left of politics as modernists: state and welfare are therefore deemed to be necessary and compatible ideas. The postmodernists are the sceptical realists of our time in that the plurality and fragmented nature of contemporary societies and cultures means that new and iconoclastic modes of thinking are required to restructure welfare in a globally uncertain environment. A postmodernist perspective on social policy highlights the reluctance of the modernists to acknowledge the extent to which the structural transformation of work in all societies by global capitalism means that the 19th- and 20th-century commitment to the work ethic as a basis for welfare will undermine all attempts to re-organise the way we think about social need in the 21st century. Perhaps the sketch of a welfare system based on the principles of associational democracy and a basic income policy, outlined in Chapter 5, can be taken as an exemplar of a postmodern vision of an alternative welfare society: based on self-governing associations, but supported by common political and legal institutions, its objective would be to maximise the accountability of the welfare system to its members while seeking to reconcile universalist and particularist needs. This would not be an easy task.

## Themes and arguments

A number of themes and arguments have been rehearsed in this book and it may be helpful to restate some of the key issues.

First, a welfare society must find principles of social cohesion similar to those institutionalised by the welfare state in the immediate postwar years through the creation of a nationalised health service, social housing, free public education and an extensive range of social benefits based on the social insurance principle. The 'strategy for equality' pursued by governments in the 1950s and 60s, irrespective of their political hue, was buttressed by a mass trade union movement intent on securing a 'social wage' for male workers and their families. The decline of the male breadwinner model of family combined with industrial restructuring has meant that the foundations of the Beveridge welfare state have shifted ground and a new basis for social citizenship will be required to re-establish the sense of cohesion which has been lost.

The industrial and economic transformations which have occurred in all Western societies since the early 1970s have meant that the forces and influences which led to welfare state expansion have weakened. The determinants of welfare growth may remain inextricably linked to economic growth and political mobilisation but the complexity of society today means that both the *industrialism* and *politics counts* models of explanation will have to adjust to a new configuration of economic and political power in the era of post-Fordism. Where is the constituency to fight for an expansion of the welfare state in the 21st century? New alliances will undoubtedly form but they may not necessarily be those which have been instrumental in building the welfare state in the 20th century and they may not be struggling over the same political stakes.

The search for a new stability in social and family life has encouraged a retreat into what Carol Smart (1997) has called 'wishful thinking and harmful tinkering' by some on the right who want to seek solutions for contemporary problems in pre-welfare times. The backward looking celebration of Victorian social virtues is perhaps rather selective. While undoubtedly there were features of 19th-century society which were commendable, particularly the solidarity of the poor and the excluded, the anti-modern analysis overlooks the degree to which that solidarity was less the product of a spontaneous generous spirit abroad in Victorian society than a necessary mode of survival in an extremely hierarchical and unjust social order. The concept of social capital discussed in Chapter 4 may be understood as a product of civic-minded behaviour but it can also be built or destroyed by structural forces beyond the control of the most community-minded citizen imaginable. The tendency to divorce social behaviour from the economic, industrial and cultural context with which it is framed is, perhaps, the major weakness of the anti-modern perspective.

The rediscovery of the idea of community towards the end of the 20th century has been one of the least convincing features of the new moral economy of welfare which I discussed in the introduction. While Chapter 4 examined an anti-modern perspective, Chapter 5 attempted to unpack the notion with reference to its philosophical and sociological roots before examining the theme in New Labour policies. The anti-modernist conception of civil society and a 'community without politics', and the postmodernist vision of a welfare system based on self-governing associations, appear extreme when compared with the pedestrian, prag-matic and practical efforts of current government reforms. Nevertheless, communitarianism and stakeholding remain underlying ideas guiding attempts to arrive at a new welfare settlement in Britain and the rest of the European Union.

The message of Chapters 6 and 7 was that the future of communitari-anism as a key idea in welfare restructuring is very uncertain to say the least. The impact of contemporary economic movements on urban forms has generated contrasting benefits for the modern city and those who live in the great urban connurbations: the wealthy, stylish and economically vibrant facade of the city centres conceals communities where poverty and criminality are pervasive and hope largely abandoned. Whose community is being discussed in the communitarian policy documents informing government and European Union policy? Social policy plan-ners must address the question of how the citizens of the inner cities and peripheral housing estates are to become members of a welfare society. The pursuit of the 'good economy' may lead to the complete abandon-ment of the project of seeking to build the 'good society'. The attachment to welfare and caring could be a casualty of the obsessive focus on the 'good economy', an underlying theme of Chapter 7. In place of solidarity and social cohesion we may be moving towards postemotionalism and amoral familism.

Globalisation and the evolution of supra-national political organis-ations and communities are facts of contemporary existence. However, in terms of the welfare debate we must guard against using the global market and the increasing interdependence of the world as excuses for relinquishing collective responsibility for those unable to support them-selves in an increasingly unforgiving global capitalist order.

## Social entrepreneurship and welfare

It may be the case that in the future the view held by both the anti-modernists and the postmodernists regarding the importance of self-organised welfare in a civil society in which state control is at 'arms' length' may come to pass through sheer necessity. The reformers of state welfare may discover that there is a natural limit to how far the Beveridge model, or indeed the Meidner-Rehn model, can be manipulated, altered, reoriented and adjusted to meet new social conditions. The poor and disadvantaged may be forced to rely on themselves because no one else will support them in societies which become increasingly individualistic. Taking state welfare in total, including tax expenditures, health and education services, the better off tend to win a disproportionate amount of resources. Perhaps a radical new look at the underlying principles of modern welfare provision is required. Journalist Melanie Phillips (1999) has called the welfare state as it currently operates an 'organised hypocrisy that pretends not to know that those who can afford it will make their own provision; those who cannot will remain trapped in a system that fails them while cynically pretending it cares'. She advocates the encouragement of what has been called *social entrepreneurship* which is based in the mutualism and self-help activities of the inner cities, ghettos and neighbourhoods where 'the real message of social inclusion must entail a mixed economy of welfare including public, private and not-for-profit provision. The welfare state must turn into the welfare society. Mutualism, rather than the state or the market, is the big idea'.

# Bibliography

Abbott, P. and Wallace, C. (1992) *The Family and the New Right* (London: Pluto Press)

Adorno, T. and Horkheimer, M. (1972) *The Dialectic of the Enlightenment* (London: New Left Books)

Alcaly, R. and Mermelstein, D. (1977) *The Fiscal Crisis of American Cities* (New York: Vintage)

Andersen, B. R. (1993) 'The Nordic Welfare State Under Pressure: The Danish Experience', *Policy and Politics*, **21**(2): 97–108

Archer, M. (1996) 'Social Integration and System Integration: Developing the Distinction', *Sociology*, **30**(4): 679–99

Ashley, D. (1997) *History Without a Subject: The Postmodern Condition* (Boulder: Westview Press)

Bagguley, P. (1994) 'Prisoners of the Beveridge Dream? The Political Mobilisation of the Poor Against Contemporary Welfare Regimes', in R. Burrows and B. Loader (eds) *Towards a Post-Fordist Welfare State* (London: Routledge)

Banfield, E. (1958) *The Moral Basis of a Backward Society* (New York: Free Press)

Banfield, E. (1970) *The Unheavenly City* (Boston: Little, Brown)

Banfield, E. (1974) *The Unheavenly City Revisited* (Boston: Little, Brown)

Bauman, Z. (1985) 'On the Origins of Civilisation: A Historical Note', *Theory, Culture and Society*, **2**: 7–14

Bauman, Z. (1990) 'Effacing the Face: On the Social Management of Moral Proximity', *Theory, Culture and Society*, **7**: 5–38

Bauman, Z. (1998) *Work, Consumerism and the New Poor* (Buckingham: Open University Press)

Bell, D. (1960) *The End of Ideology* (New York: Free Press)

Bell, D. (1973) *The Coming of Post-Industrial Society* (London: Heinemann)

Bell, D. (1979) *The Cultural Contradictions of Capitalism* (London: Heinemann)

Braithwaite, J. (1989) *Crime, Shame and Integration* (Cambridge: Cambridge University Press)

Bryman, A. (1999) 'The Disneyisation of Society', *Sociological Review*, **47**(1): 25–47

Burkitt, I. (1997) 'Social Relationships and Emotions', *Sociology*, **31**(1): 37–55

Burrows, R. and Loader, B. (eds) (1994) *Towards a Post-Fordist Welfare State* (London: Routledge)

Buruma, I. (1998) 'The Rival Spirits of Europe', *Sunday Times*, 29 November

Cahill, M. (1994) *The New Social Policy* (Oxford: Blackwell)

Carter, J. (ed.) (1998a) *Postmodernity and the Fragmentation of Welfare* (London: Routledge)

Carter, J. (1998b) 'Postmodernity and Welfare: When Worlds Collide', *Social Policy and Administration*, 32(2): 101–5

Castles, F. (1990) 'The Dynamics of Policy Change: What Happened to the English Speaking Nations in the 1980s', *European Journal of Political Research*, 18: 491–513

Castles, F. and Mitchell, D. (1992) 'Identifying Welfare State Regimes: The Links Between Politics, Instruments and Outcomes', *Governance*, 5(1): 1–26

Challis, D., Darton, R., Johnson, L., Stone, M. and Traske, K. (1995) *Care Management and Health Care of Older People* (Aldershot: Ashgate)

Cheal, D. (1991) *Family and the State of Theory* (London: Harvester Wheatsheaf)

Cloward, R. and Ohlin, L. (1960) *Delinquency and Opportunity: A Theory of Gang Delinquency* (London: Routledge)

Cohen, J. (1982) *Class and Civil Society* (Oxford: Martin Robertson)

Cohen, J. and Rogers, J. (1995) *Associations and Democracy* (London: Verso)

Cohen, S. (1985) *Visions of Social Control* (London: Macmillan)

Coleman, J. (1988a) 'Social Capital in the Creation of Human Capital', *American Journal of Sociology*, 94 Supplement: S95–S120

Coleman, J. (1988b) 'The Creation of Destruction of Social Capital: Implications for the Law', *Journal of Law, Ethics and Public Policy*, 3: 375–404

Cousins, C. (1998) 'Social Exclusion in Europe: Paradigms of Social Disadvantage in Germany, Spain, Sweden and the United Kingdom', *Policy and Politics*, 26(2): 127–46

Cox, R. (1993) *The Development of the Dutch Welfare State* (Pittsburgh: University of Pittsburgh Press)

Cram, L. (1993) 'Calling the Tune Without Paying the Piper?: The Role of the Commission in European Social Policy', *Policy and Politics*, 21(2): 135–46

Culpitt, I. (1992) *Welfare and Citizenship: Beyond the Crisis of the Welfare State?* (London: Sage)

Danson, M. and Mooney, G. (1998) 'Glasgow: A Tale of Two Cities? Disadvantage and Exclusion on the European Periphery', in P. Lawless, R. Martin and S. Hardy (eds) *Unemployment and Social Exclusion* (London: Jessica Kingsley)

Davies, S. (1987) 'Towards the Remoralisation of Society', in M. Loney with R. Bocock, J. Clarke, A. Cockrane and P. Graham (eds) *The State or the Market* (London: Sage)

Davis, M. (1992) *City of Quartz: Excavating the Future in Los Angeles* (New York: Vintage)

De Swaan, A. (1988) *In Care of the State* (Cambridge: Polity)

De Swaan, A. (1990) 'Perspectives for Transnational Social Policy Preliminary Notes', *Cross-National Research Papers*, 2(2): 7–72

Deacon, B. with Hulse, M. and Stubbs, P. (1997) *Global Social Policy: International Organisations and the Future of Welfare* (London: Sage)

Dean, H. (1989) 'Disciplinary Partitioning and the Privatisation of Social Security', *Critical Social Policy*, **24**

Denzin, N. (1986) 'Postmodern Social Theory', *Sociological Theory*, **4**(Fall): 194–204

Donzelot, J. (1980) *The Policing of Families* (London: Hutchinson)

Doyal, L. and Gough, I. (1991) *A Theory of Human Need* (London: Macmillan)

Durkheim, E. (1964) *The Division of Labour in Society* (New York: Free Press) (orig. 1895)

Ellison, N. (1997) 'Towards a New Social Politics: Citizenship and Reflexivity in Late Modernity', *Sociology*, **31**(4): 697–717

Engbersen, G., Schuyt, K., Timmer, J. and van Waarden, F. (1993) *Cultures of Unemployment: A Comparative Look at Long-term Unemployment and Urban Poverty* (Oxford: Westview Press)

Esping-Andersen, G. (1990) *The Three Worlds of Welfare Capitalism* (Cambridge: Polity)

Esping-Andersen, G. (1996) 'Positive-Sum Solutions in a World of Trade-Offs?', in G. Esping-Andersen (ed.) *Welfare States in Transition* (London: Sage)

Etzioni, A. (1993) *The Spirit of Community* (New York: Simon & Schuster)

Falk, R. (1994) 'The Making of Global Citizenship', in B. van Steenbergen (ed.) *The Condition of Citizenship* (London: Sage)

Featherstone, M. (1988) 'In Pursuit of the Postmodern: An Introduction', *Theory, Culture and Society*, **5**(2–3): 195–215

Felson, M. (1994) *Crime and Everyday Life* (London: Pine Forge Press)

Femia, J. (1981) *Gramsci's Political Thought* (Oxford: Clarendon Press)

Ferge, Z. (1997) 'The Changed Welfare Paradigm: The Individualisation of the Social', *Social Policy and Administration*, **31**(1): 20–44

Field, F. (1996) *Stakeholder Welfare* (London: Institute for Economic Affairs)

Finch, J. (1989) *Family Obligations and Social Change* (Cambridge: Polity)

Finch, J. and Mason, J. (1993) *Negotiating Family Responsibilities* (London: Routledge)

Flora, P. and Heidenheimer, A. (eds) (1981) *The Development of Welfare States in Europe and America* (London: Transaction Books)

Fraser, N. and Gordon, L. (1994) 'Civil Citizenship against Social Citizenship?' in B. Van Steenbergen (ed.) *The Condition of Citizenship* (London: Sage)

Frazer, E. and Lacey, N. (1993) *The Politics of Community: A Feminist Critique of the Liberal-Communitarian Debate* (Hemel Hempstead: Harvester Wheatsheaf)

Fukuyama, F. (1992) *The End of History and the Last Man* (Harmondsworth: Penguin)

Fukuyama, F. (1995) *Trust: The Social Virtues and the Creation of Prosperity* (New York: Free Press)

Fukuyama, F. (1997) *The End of Order* (London: Social Market Foundation in association with Profile Books)

Galbraith, J. K. (1992) *The Culture of Contentment* (London: Sinclair-Stevenson)

Gane, M. (1991) *Baudrillard: Critical and Fatal Theory* (London: Routledge)

Garland, D. (1985) *Punishment and Welfare* (Aldershot: Gower)

Gass, J. (1988) 'Towards the Active Society', *The OECD Observer*, No. 152 (June–July)

Gatrell, V. (1980) 'The Decline of Theft and Violence in Victorian and Edwardian England' in V. Gatrell, B. Lenman, and G. Parker (eds) *Crime and the Law: The Social History of Crime in Europe since 1500* (London: Europa)

Gatrell, V. and Hadden, T. (1972) 'Nineteenth Century Criminal Statistics and Their Interpretation', in E. Wrigley (ed.) *Nineteenth Century Society* (Cambridge: Cambridge University Press)

George, V. (1996) 'The Future of the Welfare State', in V. George and P. Taylor-Gooby (eds) *European Welfare Policy: Squaring the Circle* (London: Macmillan)

George, V. (1998) 'Political Ideology, Globalisation and Welfare Futures in Europe', *Journal of Social Policy*, **27**(1): 17–36

Gereffi, G. (1994) 'Capitalism, Development and Global Commodity Chains', in L. Sklair (ed.) *Capitalism and Development* (London: Routledge)

Geyer, R. (1998) 'Globalisation and the (Non-)Defence of the Welfare State', *West European Politics*, **21**(3): 77–102

Giddens, A. (1994) *Beyond the Left and Right: The Future of Radical Politics* (Cambridge: Polity)

Giddens, A. (1998) *The Third Way: The Renewal of Social Democracy* (Cambridge: Polity Press)

Gilder, G. (1973) *Sexual Suicide* (New York: Quadrangle)

Gilder, G. (1974) *Naked Nomads: Unmarried Men in America* (New York: Quadrangle)

Gilroy, R. and Speak, S. (1998) 'Barriers, Boxes and Catapults: Social Exclusion and Everyday Life', in A. Madanipour, G. Cars and J. Allen (eds) *Social Exclusion in European Cities* (London: Jessica Kingsley)

Ginsburg, N. (1999) 'Review: Bringing Britain Together', *Critical Social Policy*, **19**(2): 281–5

Goldthorpe, J., Lockwood, D., Bechofer, F. and Platt, J. (1968–69) *The Affluent Worker in the Class Structure* (Cambridge: Cambridge University Press)

Gordon, P. (1983) 'Medicine, Racism and Immigration Control, *Critical Social Policy*, **7**: 7–20

Gordon, P. (1986) 'Racism and Social Security', *Critical Social Policy*, **17**: 23–40

Gough, I. (1975) *The Political Economy of the Welfare State* (London: Macmillan)

Gould, A. (1996) 'Sweden: The Last Bastion of Social Democracy', in V. George and P. Taylor-Gooby (eds) *European Welfare Policy: Squaring the Welfare Circle* (London: Macmillan)

Gray, J. (1988) 'The Politics of Cultural Diversity', *The Salisbury Review*, **38**

Gray, J. (1993) *Beyond the New Right* (London: Routledge)

Green, D. (1993) *Reinventing Civil Society: The Rediscovery of Welfare Without Politics* (London: Institute of Economic Affairs)

Green, D. (1996) *Community Without Politics: A Market Approach to Welfare Reform* (London: Institute of Economic Affairs)

Habermas, J. (1976) *Legitimation Crisis* (London: Heinemann)

Habermas, J. (1981) 'Modernity versus Postmodernity', *New German Critique*, **22**(Winter): 49–55

Habermas, J. (1986) *The Theory of Communicative Action*, Volume I (Cambridge: Polity)

Habermas, J. (1987) *The Theory of Communicative Action*, Volume II (Cambridge: Polity)

Habermas, J. (1989) *The Structural Transformation of the Public Sphere* (Cambridge: Polity)

Halsey, A. H. (1996) 'Short-term Relationships: Reaping the Liberal Whirlwind', in N. Baker (ed.) *Building a Relational Society* (Aldershot: Ashgate)

Halsey, A. and Dennis, D. (1988) *English Ethical Socialism: From Thomas More to R. H. Tawney* (Oxford: Oxford University Press)

Hantrais, L. (1995) *Social Policy in the European Union* (London: Macmillan)

Hantrais, L. and Letablier, M. (1996) *Families and Family Policies in Europe* (London: Longman)

Harris, J. (1989) 'The Webbs, the Charity Organisation Society and the Ratan Tata Foundation: Social Policy from the Perspective of 1912', in M. Bulmer, J. Lewis and D. Piachaud (eds) *The Goals of Social Policy* (London: Unwin Hyman)

Heath, A., Jowell, R. and Curtice, J. (eds) (1994) *Labour's Last Chance?* (Aldershot: Dartmouth)

Herbertson, D. (1950) *The Life of Frederic Le Play* (Ledbury: Le Play House Press)

Heron, E. and Dwyer, P. (1999) 'Doing the Right Thing: Labour's Attempt to Forge a New Welfare Deal Between the Individual and the State', *Social Policy and Administration*, **33**(1): 91–104

Higgins, J. (1981) *States of Welfare: Comparative Analysis in Social Policy* (Oxford: Blackwell/Martin Robertson)

Hill, D. (1992) 'The American Philosophy of Welfare', *Social Policy and Administration*, **26**(2): 117–28

Hill, M. (1996) *Social Policy: A Comparative Perspective* (Hemel Hempstead: Harvester Wheatsheaf)

Hills, J. (1995) *Joseph Rowntree Foundation Inquiry into Income and Wealth*, Volume 2 (York: Joseph Rowntree Foundation)

Himmelfarb, G. (1995) *The De-Moralisation of Society: From Victorian Times to Modern Values* (London: Institute of Economic Affairs)

Hirst, P. (1994) *Associative Democracy: New Forms of Economic and Social Governance* (Cambridge: Polity)

Hirst, P. (1997) *From Statism to Pluralism: Democracy, Civil Society and Global Politics* (London: UCL Press)

Hirst, P. and Thompson, G. (1996) *Globalisation in Question* (Cambridge: Polity)

Hoggett, P. and Thompson, S. (1998) 'The Delivery of Welfare: The Associationist Vision' in J. Carter (ed.) *Postmodernity and the Fragmentation of the Welfare State* (London: Routledge)

Hughes, G. (1996) 'Communitarianism and Law and Order', *Critical Social Policy*, **16**(4): 17–42

Hutton, W. (1995) *The State We're In* (London: Cape)

Hutton, W. (1997) *Stakeholding and Its Critics* (London: Institute of Economic Affairs)

Ignatieff, M. (1989) 'Citizenship and Moral Narcissism', *Political Quarterly*, **60**: 63–74

Jacobs, S. (1985) 'Race, Empire and the Welfare State: Council Housing and Racism', *Critical Social Policy*, **13**: 6–28

Jessop, B. (1994) 'The Transition to post-Fordism and the Schumpeterian Workfare State', in R. Burrows and B. Loader (eds) *Towards a Post-Fordist Welfare State?* (London: Routledge)

Jones, C. (1985) *Patterns of Social Policy: An Introduction to Comparative Analysis* (London: Tavistock)

Jones Finer, C. (1997) 'The New Social Policy in Britain', *Social Policy and Administration*, **31**(5): 154–70

Jordan, B. (1987) *Rethinking Welfare* (Oxford: Blackwell)

Jordan, B. (1996) *A Theory of Poverty and Social Exclusion* (Cambridge: Polity)

Kangas, O. (1991) 'The Bigger the Better? On the Dimensions of Welfare State Development: Social Expenditures Versus Social Rights', *Acta Sociologica*, **34**: 33–44

Kantor, P. (1993) 'The Dual City as Political Choice', *Journal of Urban Affairs*, **15**(3): 231–44

Katz, M. (1989) *The Undeserving Poor: From the War on Poverty to the War on Welfare* (New York: Pantheon)

Keane, J. (1988) *Democracy and Civil Society* (London: Verso)

Kiely, R. (1998) 'Globalisation, Post-Fordism and the Contemporary Context of Development', *International Sociology*, **13**(1): 95–115

Kinsey, R., Lea, J. and Young, J. (1986) *Losing the Fight Against Crime* (Oxford: Blackwell)

Knight, B. and Stokes, P. (1996) *The Deficit in Civil Society in the United Kingdom* (Birmingham: Foundation for Civil Society, Working Paper No. 1)

Kraemer, P. (1966) *The Societal State: The Modern Osmosis of State and Society as Presenting Itself in the Netherlands in Particular* (J. A. Boom en Zoon: Uitgevers Te Meppel)

Korpi, W. (1978) *The Working Class in Welfare Capitalism: Work, Unions and Politics in Sweden* (London: Routledge)

Korpi, W. (1980) 'Social policy and Distributional Conflict in the Capitalist Democracies: A Preliminary Comparative Framework', *West European Politics*, **3**: 296–316

Layder, D. (1994) *Understanding Social Theory* (London: Sage)

Lea, J. (1997) 'Post-Fordism and Criminality', in N. Jewson and S. MacGregor (eds) *Transforming Cities* (London: Routledge)

Leonard, P. (1997) *Postmodern Welfare: Reconstructing an Emancipatory Project* (London: Sage)

Lewis, G. (ed.) (1998) *Forming Nation, Framing Welfare* (London: Routledge in association with the Open University)

Lewis, J. (1993) 'Developing the Mixed Economy of Care: Emerging Issues for Voluntary Organisations', *Journal of Social Policy*, **22**(2): 173–92

Lewis, J. (1995) *The Voluntary Sector, The State and Social Work in Britain: The Charity Organisation Society/Family Welfare Association since 1869* (Aldershot: Edward Elgar)

Lipset, S. (1960) *Political Man* (London: Heinemann)

Lipset, S. (1961) 'A Changing American Character?', in S. Lipset and L. Lowenthal (eds) *Culture and Social Character: The Work of David Riesman* (New York: Free Press)

Lipset, S. and Lowenthal, L. (eds) (1961) *Culture and Social Character* (New York: Free Press)

Lockhart, C. (1984) 'Explaining Social Policy Differences Among Advanced Industrial Societies', *Comparative Politics*, **16**: 335–50

Lockwood, D. (1976) 'Social Integration and System Integration', in G. Zollschan and W. Hirsch (eds) *Social Change: Explorations, Diagnoses and Conjectures* (London: Wiley)

Lockwood, D. (1996) 'Civic Integration and Class Formation', *British Journal of Sociology*, **47**(3): 531–50

Marcuse, H. (1964) *One Dimensional Man* (New York: Beacon Press)

Marcuse, H. (1969) *Eros and Civilisation* (London: Sphere)

Marcuse, P. (1989) 'Dual City: A Muddy Metaphor for a Quartered City', *International Journal of Urban and Regional Research*, **13**(4): 697–708

Marcuse, P. (1993) 'What's So New About Divided Cities', *International Journal of Urban and Regional Research*, **17**(3): 355–65

Marcuse, P. (1996) 'Space and Race in the Post-Fordist City: The Outcast Ghetto and Advanced Homelessness in the United States today', in E. Mingione (ed.) *Urban Poverty and the Underclass* (Oxford: Blackwell)

Marshall, T. H. (1950) *Citizenship and Social Class* (Cambridge: Cambridge University Press)

Marsland, D. (1996) *Welfare or Welfare State?* (London: Macmillan)

Mayo, M. (1994) *Communities and Caring: The Mixed Economy of Welfare* (London: Macmillan)

Meidner, R. (1980) 'Our Concept of the Third Way: Some Remarks on the Socio-Political Tenets of the Swedish Labour Movement', *Economic and Industrial Democracy*, **1**: 343–69

Mellor, R. (1997) 'Cool Times for a Changing City', in N. Jewson and S. MacGregor (eds) *Transforming Cities* (London: Routledge)

Messinger, S. and Clark, B. (1961) 'Individual Character and Social Constraint: A Critique of David Riesman's Theory of Social Conduct', in S. Lipset and L. Lowenthal (eds) *Culture and Social Structure* (New York: Free Press)

Meštrović, S. (1997) *Postemotional Society* (London: Sage)

Meštrović, S. (1998) *Anthony Giddens: The Last Modernist* (London: Routledge)

Midwinter, E. (1994) *The Development of Social Welfare in Britain* (Buckingham: Open University Press)

Millar, J. and Warman, A. (1996) *Family Obligations in Europe* (London: Family Policy Studies Centre)

Miller, W. B. (1958) 'Lower Class Culture as a Generating Milieu of Gang Delinquency', *Journal of Social Issues*, **14**(5): 5–19

Mishra, R. (1984) *The Welfare State in Crisis* (Brighton: Wheatsheaf)

Mishra, R. (1990) *The Welfare State in Capitalist Society* (London: Harvester Wheatsheaf)

Mollenkopf, J. and Castells, M. (eds) (1991) *Dual City: Restructuring New York* (New York: Russell Sage Foundation)

Mooney, G. and Danson, M. (1997) 'Beyond Culture City: Glasgow as a "Dual City"', in N. Jewson and S. MacGregor (eds) *Transforming Cities* (London: Routledge)

Morris, L. (1994) *Dangerous Classes: The Underclass and Social Citizenship* (London: Routledge)

Mulhall, S. and Swift, A. (1996) *Liberals and Communitarians*, 2nd Edition (Oxford: Blackwell)

Murray, C. (1996) *Charles Murray and the Underclass: The Developing Debate* (London: Institute of Economic Affairs in association with the *Sunday Times*)

Nietzsche, F. (1967) *The Will to Power* (New York: Random House)

Nisbet, R. (1970) *The Sociological Tradition* (London: Heinemann)

Novak, M. (1995) *Awakening From Nihilism: Why Truth Matters* (London: Institute of Economic Affairs)

Nozick, R. (1974) *Anarchy, State and Utopia* (Oxford: Blackwell)

Nussbaum, M. (1992) 'Virtue Revived' in *Times Literary Supplement*, 3 July: 9–11

Oakeshott, M. (1962) *Rationalism in Politics and Other Essays* (London: Methuen)

O'Brien, M. and Penna, S. (1998) *Theorising Welfare: Enlightenment and Modern Society* (London: Sage)

O'Brien, M., Penna, S. and Hay, C. (1999) *Theorising Modernity* (London: Longman)

O'Connor, J. (1973) *The Fiscal Crisis of the State* (New York: St Martin's Press)

O'Connor, J. and Brym, R. (1988) 'Public Welfare Expenditure in OECD Countries: Towards a Reconciliation of Inconsistent Findings', *British Journal of Sociology*, **39**(1): 47–68

OECD (1999a) *A Caring World: The New Social Policy Agenda* (Paris: OECD)

OECD (1999b) *The Battle Against Exclusion Volume 2: Social Assistance in Belgium, the Czech Republic, the Netherlands and Norway* (Paris: OECD)

Offe, C. (1984) *Contradictions of the Welfare State* (London: Hutchinson)

Offe, C. (1996) *Modernity and the State* (Cambridge: Polity)

Ohmae, K. (1990) *The Borderless World* (London: Collins)

Ohmae, K. (1991) 'Global Consumers Want Sony, Not Soil', *New Perspectives Quarterly*, Fall

O'Sullivan, N. (1993) 'Political Integration, the Limited State, and the Philosophy of Postmodernism', *Political Studies*, **41,** Special Issue edited by A. Shtromas: 21–42

Page, R. (1999) 'The Prospects for British Social Welfare' in R. Page and R. Silburn (eds) *British Social Welfare in the Twentieth Century* (London: Macmillan)

Pampel, F. and Williamson, J. (1988) 'Welfare Spending in Advanced Industrial Democracies, 1950–1980', *American Journal of Sociology*, **93**(6): 1424–56

Papadakis, E. (1992) 'Public Opinion, Public Policy and the Welfare State', *Political Studies*, **40**(1): 21–37

Parker, H. (1995) *Taxes, Benefits and Family Life: The Seven Deadly Traps* (London: Institute of Economic Affairs)

Parkin, F. (1971) *Class Inequality and Political Order* (London: MacGibbon & Kee)

Pearson, G. (1983) *Hooligan: A History of Respectable Fears* (London: Macmillan)

Peden, G. C. (1991) *British Economic and Social Policy: Lloyd George to Margaret Thatcher*, 2nd Edition (London: Philip Allan)

Penna, S. and O'Brien, M. (1996) 'Postmodernism and Social Policy: A Small Step Forwards?', *Journal of Social Policy*, **25**(1): 39–62

Perez-Diaz, V. (1998) 'The Public Sphere and European Civil Society', in J. Alexander (ed.) *Real Civil Societies: Dilemmas of Institutionalisation* (London: Sage)

Phillips, M. (1999) 'Lilley is Half Right and the Tories are all Wrong', *Sunday Times*, 2 May

Pierson, C. (1991) *Beyond the Welfare State?* (Cambridge: Polity)

Pinch, S. (1997) *Worlds of Welfare: Understanding the Changing Geographies of Social Welfare Provision* (London: Routledge)

Piven, F. and Cloward, R. (1972) *Regulating the Poor: The Functions of Public Welfare* (London: Tavistock)

Popenoe, D. (1988) *Disturbing the Nest* (New York: Aldine de Gruyter)

Power, A. and Mumford, K. (1999) *The Slow Death of Great Cities? Urban Abandonment or Urban Renaissance* (York: Joseph Rowntree Foundation)

Putnam, R. (1995) 'Bowling Alone: America's Declining Social Capital', *Journal of Democracy*, **6**(1): 65–78

Qureshi, H. and Walker, A. (1989) *The Caring Relationship: Elderly People and their Families* (London: Macmillan)

Radice, G. (1996) *What Needs to Change: New Visions for Britain* (London: HarperCollins)

Rawls, J. (1971) *A Theory of Social Justice* (Cambridge, MA: Harvard University Press)

Rawls, J. (1993) *Political Liberalism* (New York: Columbia University Press)

Rehn, G. (1984) *Cooperation between the Government and Workers and Employers on Labour Market Policy in Sweden* (Stockholm: Swedish Institute)

Reis, E. (1998) 'Banfield's Amoral Familism Revisited: Implications of High Inequality Structures for Civil Society', in J. Alexander (ed.) *Real Civil Societies: Dilemmas of Institutionalisation* (London: Sage)

Rhodes, M. (1996) 'Globalisation and West European Welfare States: A Critical Review of Recent Debates', *Journal of European Social Policy*, **6**(4): 305–32

Riesman, D. (1969) *The Lonely Crowd* (London: Yale University Press) (Abridged Edition)

Ritzer, G. (1992) *The McDonaldisation of Society* (London: Sage)

Robertson, A. (1988) 'Welfare State and Welfare Society', *Social Policy and Administration*, **22**(3): 222–34

Robertson, R. and Khondker, H. H. (1998) 'Discourses of Globalisation: Preliminary Considerations', *International Sociology*, **13**(1): 25–40

Robson, W. (1976) *Welfare State and Welfare Society* (London: Allen & Unwin)

Rodger, J. (1996) *Family Life and Social Control: A Sociological Perspective* (London: Macmillan)

Rojek, C. (1995) *Decentering Leisure* (London: Sage)

Rojek, C., Peacock, G. and Collins, S. (1988) *Social Work and Received Ideas* (London: Routledge)

Rose, G. (1978) *The Melancholy Science: An Introduction to the Thought of Theodor Adorno* (London: Macmillan)

Rosenberry, S. (1982) 'Social Insurance, Distributive Criteria and the Welfare Backlash: A Comparative Analysis', *British Journal of Political Science*, **12**(4): 421–48

Ruggiero, V. and South, N. (1997) 'The Late-Modern City as a Bazaar', *British Journal of Sociology*, **48**(1): 54–70

Sandel, M. (1982) *Liberalism and the Limits of Justice* (Cambridge: Cambridge University Press)

Saunders, P. (1993) 'Citizenship in a Liberal Society', in B. Turner (ed.) *Citizenship and Social Theory* (London: Sage)

Schottland, C. (1967) *The Welfare State* (New York: Harper)

Scruton, R. (1980) *The Meaning of Conservatism* (London: Macmillan)

Scruton, R. (1986) *Sexual Desire* (London: Weidenfeld & Nicolson)

Silver, H. (1996) 'Culture, Politics and National Discourses of the New Urban Poverty', in E. Mingione (ed.) *Urban Poverty and the Underclass* (Oxford: Blackwell)

Simpson, R. and Walker, R. (1993) *Europe: For Richer or Poorer* (London: Child Poverty Action)

Sinfield, A. (1986) 'Poverty, Privilege and Welfare' in P. Bean and D. Whynes (eds) *Barbara Wooton: Essays in Her Honour* (London: Tavistock)

Sklair, L. (1995) *Sociology of the Global System*, 2nd Edition (London: Prentice Hall/Harvester Wheatsheaf)

Smart, C. (1997) 'Wishful Thinking and Harmful Tinkering? Sociological Reflections on Family Policy', *Journal of Social Policy*, **26**(3): 301–22

Sorensen, A. (1998) 'On Kings, Pietism and Rent-Seeking in Scandinavian Welfare States', *Acta Sociologica*, **41**: 363–75

Spicker, P. (1994) 'Understanding Particularism', *Critical Social Policy*, **13**(3): 5–20

Squires, P. (1990) *Anti-Social Policy* (London: Harvester Wheatsheaf)

Stephens, J. (1979) *The Transition from Capitalism to Socialism* (London: Macmillan)

Stokes, P. and Knight, B. (1996) *Organising a Civil Society* (Birmingham: Foundation for Civil Society, Working Paper No. 2)

Strong, T. (1995) 'Civil Society, Hard Cases and the End of the Cold War', in M. Walzer (ed.) *Toward a Global Civil Society* (Oxford: Berghahn)

Sutherland, E. and Cressey, D. (1966) *Principles of Criminology* (Philadelphia: J. P. Lippincott)

Sykes, G. and Matza, D. (1957) 'Techniques of Neutralisation: A Theory of Delinquency', *American Sociological Review*, **22**: 664–70

Tawney, R. (1931) *Equality* (London: Allen & Unwin)

Taylor, I., Walton, P. and Young, J. (1973) *The New Criminology* (London: Routledge)

Taylor-Gooby, P. (1985a) *Public Opinion, Ideology and State Welfare* (London: Routledge)

Taylor-Gooby, P. (1985b) 'Attitudes to Welfare', *Journal of Social Policy*, **14**(1): 73–81

Taylor-Gooby, P. (1994) 'Postmodernism and Social Policy: A Great Leap Backwards?', *Journal of Social Policy*, **23**(3): 385–404

Taylor-Gooby, P. (1997) 'In Defence of Second-best Theory: State, Class and Capital in Social Policy', *Journal of Social Policy*, **26**(2): 171–92

Tester, K. (1997) 'Making Moral Citizens: on Himmelfarb's Demoralisation Thesis', *Citizenship Studies*, **1**(1): 57–72

Tester, S. (1996) *Community Care for Older People: A Comparative Perspective* (London: Macmillan)

Therborn, G. (1990) 'Social Steering and Household Strategies: the Macropolitics and the Microsociology of Welfare States', *Journal of Public Policy*, **9**(3): 371–97

Therborn, G. (1995a) *European Modernity and Beyond: The Trajectory of European Societies 1945–2000* (London: Sage)

Therborn, G. (1995b) 'Routes To/Through Modernity', in M. Featherstone, S. Lash, and R. Robertson (eds) *Global Modernities* (London: Sage)

Thompson, S. and Hoggett, P. (1996) 'Universalism, Selectivism and Particularism: Towards a Postmodern Social Policy', *Critical Social Policy*, **16**(1): 21–44

Titmuss, R. (1958) *Essays on the Welfare State* (London: Allen & Unwin)

Titmuss, R. (1970) *The Gift Relationship* (London: Allen & Unwin)

Titmuss, R. (1974) *Social Policy* (London: Allen & Unwin)

Titmuss, R. (1987) *The Philosophy of Welfare*, B. Abel Smith and K. Titmuss (eds) (London: Allen & Unwin)

Toennies, F. (1963) *Community and Society* (New York: Harper Torchbook)

Turner, B. (1993) 'Contemporary Problems in the Theory of Citzenship', in B. Turner (ed.) *Citizenship and Social Theory* (London: Sage)

Turner, B. (1994) 'Postmodern Culture/Modern Citizens', in B. van Steenbergen (ed.) *The Condition of Citizenship* (London: Sage)

Turok, I. and Edge, N. (1999) *The Jobs Gap in Britain's Cities: Employment Loss and Labour Market Consequences* (Bristol: Policy Press)

Twine, F. (1992) 'Citizenship: Opportunities, Rights and Routes to Welfare in Old Age', *Journal of Social Policy*, **21**(2): 165–76

Twine, F. (1994) *Citizenship and Social Rights: The Interdependence of Self and Society* (London: Sage)

Uusitalo, H. (1984) 'Comparative Research on the Determinants of the Welfare State: The State of the Art', *European Journal of Political Research*, **12**: 403–22

van Doorn, J. (1978) 'Welfare State and Welfare Society: The Dutch Experience', *The Netherlands Journal of Sociology*, **14**: 1–18

van Kersbergen, K. and Becker, U. (1988) 'The Netherlands: A Passive Social Democratic Welfare State in a Christian Democratic Ruled Society', *Journal of Social Policy*, **17**(4): 477–99 van Krieken, R. (1992) *Children and the State: Social Control and the Formation of Australian Child Welfare* (Sydney: Allen & Unwin)

van Mierlo, H. (1986) 'Depillarisation and the Decline of Consociationalism in the Netherlands: 1970–85', *West European Politics*, **9**(1): 97–119

van Steenbergen, B. (ed.) (1994) *The Condition of Citizenship* (London: Sage)

Vincent, D. (1991) *Poor Citizens: the State and the Poor in Twentieth Century Britain* (London: Longman)

Walklate, S. (1998) *Understanding Criminology: Current Theoretical Debates* (Buckingham: Open University Press)

Walters, W. (1997) 'The Active Society: New Designs for Social Policy', *Policy and Politics*, **25**(3): 221–34

Watt, I. (1997) 'Old Politics and "New" Issues: Resisting the End of History?' Paper presented at the British Sociological Association annual conference, University of York

Weber, M. (1958) *The City* (Glencoe: Free Press)

Wenger, C. and Shahtahmasebi, S. (1990) 'Variations in Support Networks: Implications for Social Policy', in J. Mogey (ed.) *Aiding and Aging: the Coming Crisis* (New York: Greenwood Press)

Whelan, R. (1996) *The Corrosion of Charity: From Moral Renewal to Contract Culture* (London: Institute of Economic Affairs)

Williams, F. (1989) *Social Policy: A Critical Introduction* (Cambridge: Polity)

Williams, F. (1994) 'Social Relations, Welfare and the Post-Fordism Debate', in R. Burrows and B. Loader (eds) *Towards a Post-Fordist Welfare State* (London: Routledge)

Woolcock, M. (1998) 'Social Capital and Economic Development: Toward a Theoretical Synthesis and Policy Framework', *Theory and Society*, **27**: 151–208

Wright Mills, C. (1940) 'Situated Actions and Vocabularies of Motive', *American Sociological Review*, **5**(6)

Wright Mills, C. (1959) *The Sociological Imagination* (Oxford: Oxford University Press)

Young, J. (1998) 'From Inclusive to Exclusive Society: Nightmares in the European Dream', in V. Ruggiero, N. South and I. Taylor (eds) *The New European Criminology: Crime and Social Order in Europe* (London: Routledge)

Young, M. and Halsey, A. (1995) *Family and Community Socialism* (London: Institute for Public Policy Research)

Young, J. and Jones, T. (1986) *The Islington Crime Survey: Victimisation and Policing in Inner-City London* (Aldershot: Gower)

Young, J. and Matthews, R. (1992) *Rethinking Criminology: The Realist Debate* (London: Sage)

Zijderveld, A. (1986) 'The Ethos of the Welfare State', *International Sociology*, **1**(4): 443–57

# Index

References in **bold** indicate extensive treatment of a topic